SQUATTI
BRITAIN
1945-1955

SQUATTING IN BRITAIN
Housing, Politics, and Direct Action
1945-1955

DON WATSON

MERLIN PRESS

First published in 2016 by
The Merlin Press ltd
Central Books Building
Freshwater Road
London
RM8 1RX
www.merlinpress.co.uk

© Don Watson, 2016

ISBN 978-0-85036-728-7

Catalogue in publication data is available from the British Library

Printed in the UK by Imprint Digital, Exeter

CONTENTS

LIST OF ILLUSTRATIONS

Cover

Squatters entering empty prison officers' quarters at Barlinnie, Glasgow, 1946 (*Trinity Mirror Publishing – Mirrorpix/Daily Record*)

Between pages 128 and 129

Squatters entering huts at Chester le Street, County Durham, 1946 (*Beamish Museum Photographic Archive*)

Interior of a hut at Chester le Street, County Durham (*Beamish Museum Photographic Archive*)

Squatters outside a hut at Alexandra Park, Manchester, 1946 (*Manchester Library, Information and Archives, Manchester City Council*)

Interior of a hut, Alexandra Park, Manchester (*Manchester Library, Information and Archives, Manchester City Council*)

ABBREVIATIONS USED

CA	Cumbria Archives
CEA	City of Edinburgh Archives
DCRO	Durham County Record Office
GLS	Gateshead Local Studies Library
GA	Gloucestershire Archives
HALS	Hampshire Archives and Local Studies
LHASC	Labour History Archive and Study Centre
ML	Mitchell Library
NA	National Archives
NCRO	Northumberland County Record Office
NLS	National Library of Scotland
NRS	National Records of Scotland
OHC	Oxfordshire History Centre
SHC	Somerset Heritage Centre
SA	Sussex Archives
TWAS	Tyne and Wear Archives Service
WSHC	Wiltshire and Swindon History Centre

ACKNOWLEDGEMENTS

The images of the squatters at Chester le Street, County Durham are reproduced by kind permission of the Beamish Museum Photographic Archive. Quotations from the radio documentary *Squatters' Delight* appear by kind permission of BBC Radio Oxford. I am grateful to John Suggett for permission to quote from his recorded interview with Jim Tatters, and to J & J Publishing and Mrs Violet Fraser for permission to quote from her book, *Huts for Houses – A Forres Squatter's Childhood*. Quotations from material held by the Somerset Heritage Centre appear by kind permission of the South West Heritage Trust. The quotations taken from Hansard Commons Debates contain Parliamentary information licensed under the Open Parliament license v3.0.

The photograph of the Barlinnie squatters appears by arrangement with Trinity Mirror Publishing – Mirrorpix/Daily Record, and those of the Alexandra Park squatters by arrangement with Manchester Library, Information and Archives, Manchester City Council.

While this work was in progress I had the benefit of discussions with coll-eagues in the North East Labour History Society and the WEA Durham branch. I am also grateful for the discussion after my paper on squatting at the Radical Histories/Histories of Radicalism conference at Queen Mary University of London in 2016. Thanks are due also to Liz O'Donnell, DJ Johnson-Smith and Bill Lawrence for help with references, contacts and sources; and particularly to Kevin Davies for his help in locating newspaper material in the North East of England. John Suggett introduced me to an ex-squatter, the late Jim Tatters in Calverton; even in old age Jim showed what a determined force some of the squatters of 1946 must have been. The staff and volunteers at all the archives, record offices and libraries listed in the text were unfailingly helpful throughout my research. I particularly remember the attention and support of the staff at the City of Edinburgh Archives.

Finally I am grateful to Professor James Hinton and Professor Willie Thompson for reading a draft of the text and offering their corrections, comments and suggestions. Any errors of fact or interpretation that may remain are of course entirely my responsibility.

Chapter One

INTRODUCTION

Britain in the summer and autumn of 1946 witnessed some extraordinary episodes of direct action. Tens of thousands of families walked into empty army camps and took them over as places to live. This movement – referred to at the time as 'the squatters' movement' – was nationwide, with disused camps and other sites occupied across the country from Shetland to Southampton. By the end of October that year a conservative estimate was that nearly 40,000 people in England and Wales and up to 7,000 people in Scotland were taking part, while in Northern Ireland around 1,000 people were squatting in camps outside the city of Derry.[1]

Under English civil law at that time their action was potentially wrongful and under Scottish law they could be charged with committing a criminal offence; indeed some of them were so charged. Nevertheless they were prepared to risk confrontation with the government, local councils and the military authorities. At stake was their unauthorised solution to desperate problems of unavailable, unaffordable or overcrowded housing. Many participants were ex-servicemen and their families; whereas after the First World War it had been unemployment that had mobilised this group, after the Second World War it was a crisis of housing. Nevertheless this should not be understood solely as a movement of ex-servicemen because as will be seen women too were active in it throughout.

This was the first challenge to the 1945 Labour government to come from 'below', from a popular movement. There had been a brief and unofficial dock strike in some ports a little earlier, and some Conservative-inspired protest about bread rationing, but this was the first extensive working-class action the government had to face. 'Luxury squatting', as it was called, prompted by these examples, took place in empty mansions, hotels, and upmarket blocks of flats in London and Glasgow. Many of these were organised by the Communist Party or other activists and this drew retaliatory action from the government. After 1946 responsibility for the squatted camps was shifted to local authorities – within financial parameters set by central government – and this frequently generated contention that was to last into the 1950s.

Local authorities were often keen to ensure that families were not seen to be gaining advantage from 'unconstitutional' action; several sought to control a narrative about 'queue jumping' and some sought control and powers of exclusion through being providers of services to squatters and by their housing policies. This could include actual discrimination. In response those who occupied the ex-army camps campaigned to secure inclusion in the mainstream of council housing and the waiting list for tenancies: they used communal organisation and highlighted their own narrative of respectability and wartime service.

David Fiddimore's novel *The Forgotten War* follows the progress of a young airman following his demobilisation in 1945. The story includes Communist-organised squatting in an unoccupied London mansion; the author's endnote quotes a throwaway remark attributed to Prime Minister Clement Attlee that the squatting movement was the only event that came close to bringing his government down. Although housing remained a key domestic issue throughout the 1940s there is no evidence that Attlee believed or said any such thing. Nevertheless the fact that the author passes on the anecdote illustrates a point that has been made by one observer of the subject: the squatters of 1946 have featured far more prominently in popular culture than they have in historical studies. For example Andrew Marr's *A History of Modern Britain* television series and accompanying book mentions the squatters, as did an earlier programme and book by Paul Addison. One of the volumes of David Kynaston's series on post-war Britain refers to the events, as does Allan Allport's book on the soldiers' experience after the war and the popular account by Lynsey Hanley about the evolution of public housing in Britain. Similarly there has been at least one English local radio documentary on the subject. Several local history societies in England and Scotland have drawn together interesting material about the squatted army camps in their areas, although not always with the national context required for a full explanation.[2]

In contrast there are historical studies where the events are referred to but always briefly. These are some of the histories of the Attlee governments, or of the British welfare state, where they are cited as evidence of the housing crisis of the post-war years. Some examples are the works by Kenneth O. Morgan, Nicholas Timmins and Alison Ravetz. Minister for Health Aneurin Bevan had responsibility for housing at the time and his principal political biographers mention the squatters, and Michael Foot's volume includes a defence of the action Bevan took to contain and curtail the squatting movement in private property.[3]

Probably the first historical discussions of these events were published in the early 1970s by the housing activist Ron Bailey, and by Colin Ward, a prolific writer on housing and urban issues from an anarchist perspective. Ward had written about squatting in the anarchist press at the time and reprised his material without much revision thirty years later. These accounts are again brief and contain some factual errors and misinterpretations which will be discussed in due course. Another housing activist gave an account of the London 'luxury squatting' of 1946 with some debatable observations about the Communist leadership that organised it.[4]

Political activists who were involved at the time have also contributed to the history. In the 1980s Noreen Branson organised and recorded a conference of the Communist Party veterans who had organised the great London squats of 1946 and the subsequent campaign against eviction. The squatters, but especially the London events, also provide a short chapter in her *History of the Communist Party of Great Britain 1941-1951* published in 1997.[5]

The conference proceedings edited by Branson aside, the first thing that these different accounts – popular, academic, or activist – have in common is their brevity. They provide short descriptions of the events of 1946 and there they largely end. Thus the impression is created that the squatting phenomenon at this time was a short-lived issue and therefore worth only limited attention in general histories of the decade.

The main exception to this routine brevity is the principal study of the squatters so far, an article by James Hinton in 1986. He examines the squatters in the disused army camps, particularly in Birmingham and Bristol, although not after 1946, and then the Communist-inspired squats in private hotels and blocks of flats in London which as he says shifted the political dynamic. He identifies the squatting movement as a popular rejection of the 'bureaucratic paternalism' characterising Labour's social policy, but one that the political right were able to use to 're-endorse individualist values'. Paul Burnham has provided another detailed study of the large squats at Amersham and Wycombe, considered in the context of national political events and with some attention paid to local developments in the following years.[6]

Thus a study of the squatting phenomenon necessarily contributes to the debates over the record of the 1945-51 Labour governments. The Attlee administrations recorded some significant achievements in post-war social reconstruction such as comprehensive national insurance, some limited nationalisation of key industries, full employment and a national health service free at the point of use. Nevertheless an argument runs that despite the public appetite for change Labour missed its opportunity to reconfigure British society in a more progressive direction. Others point to the ideological constraints of Labour's sense of its objectives at the time as well as the practical constraints imposed by the powers ranged against it. They also query just how strong the popular will for radical change really was once national insurance, healthcare, full employment and some nationalisation had been achieved.[7] In this context a study of squatting in the early post-war years is also an examination of what has been identified as 'labourism'. This is the principle of the orthodox labour movement that social change can only be achieved through existing institutional frameworks and activities, a principle that derives from the absorption by the mainstream Labour Party of the basic values of the state. The squatting movement introduces a probing discussion of what labourism meant in a specific historical context and a debate about policy and practice at that time. This examination necessarily involves an appreciation of the feasible alternatives that may have been available, including some put forward by those whose imaginative horizons were less restricted than those of the government.

The second thing that all of these accounts have in common is that they do not deal with the squatting movement in Scotland. This is an important lapse because for different legal and other reasons there were some notable differences in the response of local authorities to the occupation of service camps in Scotland compared to England; in several cases it was more aggressive and punitive. Direct action north of the border also included occupying condemned tenement buildings, and episodes of squatting in service camps continued for several more years after 1946 than was the case in England and Wales. Squatting in Glasgow in 1946 has been covered, albeit briefly, by Charlie Johnstone as a background to his studies of Glasgow council tenants' struggles in the 1950s and later. There is also a very brief participant's account of organising squatting in the city in 1946.[8] The Scottish experience deserves to be explored in more depth.

Howard Webber queries whether the squatters can be said to have constituted a 'movement' in the political sense, and concludes that their lack of political aims meant that they objectively colluded with the government in denying their action political significance. He suspects that this explains the lack of attention paid to them by historians.[9] This is certainly plausible, but so too is another view: that historians have assumed that the squatting movement was short-lived and largely contained, if not resolved, within about two months of its emergence and therefore is not in need of detailed examination. In fact as this book argues after those two months the issues moved to the local level and it was at that level that government policies and their parameters were negotiated.

Nevertheless this does raise the issue of the characteristics of these squatting episodes as social movements, as agencies of popular protest. These need to be understood, and the extent to which they exerted an influence on policy making and implementation needs to be evaluated. In this context there is a need to examine some real contrasts in local reaction and experience and to try to identify the reasons. These include the roles of the left and the responses of different local Labour Parties and local authorities; the inter-plays between local and central government; and whether any lack of clear direction in Whitehall and the Scottish Office became a problem or an opportunity at the local level. Further, the role of political activists in relation to these examples of popular movements needs to be explored. What did 'leadership' mean, and how did that role differ from providing advocacy, say, or simply offering support or championing the cause.

This book makes a claim that there is more to this squatting movement than has been covered so far; it deserves examination in more detail and its significance deserves greater recognition. Therefore it offers the first comprehensive account of squatting in Britain in the first decade after the Second World War, placing it in the context of housing issues in the inter-war years and during the war itself; it examines what happened after 1946 when the struggles of the squatters shifted from the national to the local level. Squatting as a response to housing crisis appeared again in the late 1960s and 1970s of course but the events that began at the end of the war deserve detailed attention in their own right.

This account begins with an examination of the politics of housing in the inter-war years. This is to demonstrate how the belief in the need for the state to intervene against the failure of the market to meet general housing needs came about, and thus the background to Labour's intentions in 1945. It shows that there was a background of housing struggles before the war, and that housing issues were of persistent concern to local activists.

As an historical episode post-war squatting should be understood in the light of the sporadic episodes of direct action over housing that had already taken place during the war itself. For example one of the key demands of the left and others during the squatting episodes was for extensive requisitioning.

The call was for local authorities and central government to take over empty private properties for the use of families in inadequate accommodation. This was to include property taken over by government departments for the duration of the war and now due to be returned to their owners, or large properties with absentee landlords and owners, including empty hotels. The legislation to enable this had in fact been enacted in 1941 after pressure from Clydeside shipyard workers and their parliamentary representatives and extended in 1945. In this last case it was a direct response to squatting initiatives that broke out before the war had ended. Requisitioning was a response to and a stimulus to the housing campaigns of the political left and this is part of the context of the 1946 squatting phenomenon. How organised private property owners reacted to requisitioning and the constraints governments imposed on it provide some important context which needs to be understood.

Similarly consideration needs to be given to what happened after, as well as before, the events of 1946. It is worth repeating that although the news media soon moved on to other issues and the priorities of the movement's political supporters changed too, the squatters remained and so did the campaigns that had driven their original action.

The digitalisation of local newspapers is only at an early stage through the British Library but the existing material permits a wider geographical spread of evidence than has been used so far. There is also a need to incorporate evidence from some of those who took part in the events, or the children of those who did, through memoir, broadcast and interview. This is because some of these narratives suggest a less positive experience of camp squatting than was reported in the newspapers at the time and which have not been considered by most of the accounts.

This is also a book about agency. It is concerned with historical examples of how those most affected by inadequate housing conditions and shortages have responded to them; how by their own actions they have themselves shaped policies and events instead of passively receiving them. It also, in the same spirit, examines and places on record something summed up in the recollection of one of the organisers of the London 'luxury squats' of 1946:

... The thing I'll never forget is that if I'd ever had doubts about the problems of working people taking on and managing their own affairs, I lost them forever during this squatting thing. Because without any hassle, fuss, argument, they found what they could do, and collectively decided that it should be done, and then went off and did it.[10]

NOTES

1   Hansard House of Commons Debates 10 October 1946 vol.427 cc. 330-382; *The Derry Journal*, 26 August 1946.

2   David Fiddimore, *The Forgotten War* (London, Pan Macmillan, 2008, p. 247); The point about popular and academic studies is made in Howard Webber, 'A Domestic Rebellion: The Squatters' Movement of 1946,' *Ex Historia*, King's College London (August 2012, pp. 125-47); Andrew Marr, *A History of Modern Britain* (London, Fontana, 2007, pp. 71-3); Paul Addison, *Now the War is Over: A Social History of Britain 1945-1951* (London, BBC/Jonathan Cape, 1985, pp. 56-60); David Kynaston, *Austerity Britain 1945-1951* (London, Bloomsbury, 2007, pp. 122-3); Allan Allport, *Demobbed: Coming Home after the Second World War* (New York, Yale University Press, 2010, pp. 76-7); Lynsey Hanley, *Estates: An Intimate History* (London, Granta Books, 2012, p. 74); OXOHA: LT900: BBC Radio Oxford, *Squatters' Delight* (1994). Two good examples of squatted camps thoroughly examined by local history societies are the Vale of Leven Project (www.valeofleven.org.uk) and Amersham Local History Society (www.amersham.org.uk). Both viewed 2014.

3   Some examples are Nicholas Timmins, *The Five Giants: A Biography of the Welfare State* (London, Harper Collins 2001, p. 144); Kenneth O. Morgan, *Labour in Power 1945-51* (Oxford, Oxford University Press, 1989, p. 166) and *The People's Peace: British History 1945-1990* (Oxford, Oxford University Press, 1990, p. 40); Alison Ravetz: 'Housing the People' in Jim Fyrth (Ed): *Labour's Promised Land? – Culture and Society in Labour Britain 1945-51* (London, Lawrence and Wishart, 1995, pp. 159-160). Michael Foot, *Aneurin Bevan: A Biography Vol. 2: 1945-1960* (London, Davis-Poynter, 1973, pp. 82-3); John Campbell, *Nye Bevan: A Biography* (London, Hodder and Stoughton, 1994, p. 160). There is also some coverage in Kevin Marsh and Robert Griffiths, *Granite and Honey: the Story of Phil Piratin, Communist MP* (London, Manifesto Press, 2012, pp. 98-100).

4   Ron Bailey, *The Squatters* (Harmondsworth, Penguin Books, 1973, pp. 22-4); Colin Ward, *Anarchism in Action* (London, Freedom Press, 1973, pp. 20-27) and *Housing: An Anarchist Approach* (London, Freedom Press, 1976, pp. 5-6); Andrew Friend, 'The Post-War Squatters' in Nick Wates and Christian Wolmar (Eds) *Squatting: The Real Story* (London, Bay Leaf Publications, 1980, pp. 110-19).

5   Noreen Branson (Ed.), 'London Squatters 1946', *Our History* no. 80 (August 1989); also her *History of the Communist Party of Great Britain 1941-1951* (London, Lawrence and Wishart, 1997, pp. 118-29).

6   James Hinton, 'Self-Help and Socialism: The Squatters' Movement of 1946', *History Workshop* Issue 25 (spring 1988, pp. 100-126); Paul Burnham, 'The Squatters of 1946: A Local Study in National Context', *Socialist History*, no. 25 (2004, pp. 20-46).

7   Ralph Miliband, *Parliamentary Socialism: A Study in the Politics of Labour* (London, Merlin Press, 2009); Willie Thompson, *The Long Death of British Labourism: Interpreting a Political Culture* (London, Pluto Press, 1993);

Ross McKibbin, *Classes and Cultures: England 1919-1951* (Oxford, Oxford University Press, 1998); Nick Tiratsoo (Ed.), *The Attlee Years* (London, Pinter, 1991); Steven Fielding, Peter Thompson and Nick Tiratsoo, *England Arise! : The Labour Party and popular politics in 1940s Britain* (Manchester, Manchester University Press, 1995); James Hinton, '1945 and the Apathy School,' *History Workshop Journal* Issue 43 (Spring 1997, pp. 266-73).

8   Charlie Johnstone, *The Tenants' Movement and Housing Struggles in Glasgow 1945–1990* (PhD University of Glasgow, 1992); also his 'Early Post-War Housing Struggles in Glasgow', *Journal of the Scottish Labour History Society* no. 28 (1993, pp. 7-29); and his 'Housing and Class Struggles in Post-War Glasgow' in Michael Lavalette and Gerry Mooney (Eds), *Class Struggle and Social Welfare* (2000, pp. 139-55). Bob Saunders, 'The Glasgow Squatters, 1946', *Scottish Marxist* no.7 (October 1974, pp. 25-28).

9   Howard Webber, 'A Domestic Rebellion: The Squatters' Movement of 1946', p. 145.

10   Tess Gorringe in Branson (Ed.), *London Squatters 1946*, p. 22.

Chapter Two
HOUSING THE WORKING CLASS: POLITICS AND RESOURCES

Any list of British achievements in the nineteenth century would not include the housing of the working population. This chapter summarises why that was the case, and how the attempts to deal with the issues between the wars were the background to the Labour Party's housing priorities after 1945. It also notes the background of tenant organisation and local political activity over housing that was also a feature of the inter-war years.

A fundamental change in the distribution of the population took place within a hundred years when Britain moved from an agricultural economy and rural society to an industrial economy and urban society. In 1750 London and Edinburgh were the only British cities with more than 50,000 residents; a century later there were 29 cities of that size including nine with over 100,000. In the first half of the nineteenth century water supplies, street cleansing and sanitation in the cities could not cope with the mass migration of people to them. The quality of life for many was observed by the future collaborator of Karl Marx, who made a personal study of Manchester in the early 1840s. He observed that:

> ... we must admit that 350,000 working people of Manchester and its environs live, almost all of them, in wretched, damp, filthy cottages, that the streets that surround them are in the most miserable and filthy condition, laid out without the slightest reference to ventilation ...

Engels's work was of course a polemic but his observations were shared by a number of contemporary authorities, several of whom he quoted. In fact such reports about the conditions of the urban poor were common currency among philanthropists, the clergy and social reformers in Victorian Britain. It was the pattern throughout the industrial cities of the country during the early nineteenth century.[1]

Charles Booth's monumental survey *Life and Labour of the People of London* was published in a series of seventeen volumes, the first appearing later in the century in 1889. His work mapped the concentrations of overcrowding, families living in one room in conditions 'which would hardly be endured unless poverty compelled'. Also, the overcrowding experienced by 'those who must give whatever is necessary to enable them to live near their work': the dock workers, general labourers, coal porters and street sellers generated by the economy of the capital and who were a vital component of its success. Around the same time that the first volume of Booth's research was appearing an indictment of the effects of poverty and overcrowding in the Second City of Empire had been published. Although Glasgow did not have a Booth it did have an active Medical Officer of Health, who published what had originally been a lecture, *Life in One Room* in 1886. This used data from the 1881 Census to show that Glasgow had a higher density of population per acre than any other city in Britain apart from Liverpool; 25 per cent of the population lived in one room and 45 per cent in two rooms. Once again there was a concentration of people near their workplaces in the shipyards and related engineering industries. This overcrowding was the cause of the high death rates in Glasgow, particularly 'the enormous proportions of deaths in children.'[2]

According to Jim Dyos, the housing conditions of the working class in Victorian Britain were not just an unfortunate by-product of the growth of industrial capitalism; they were essential to it. Better housing would have required higher wages to pay the rents required but instead of profit being distributed through earnings it was ploughed back into the commercial machine. This was because higher wages would have increased the cost of products for export and thus risked reducing the growth of the export trade. Insecure and poorly-paid employment, always possible when labour was cheap and abundant, for example on the docks, was thus a frequent phenomenon. There were equally frequent consequences for the type of housing those workers could afford. The end of slum housing would require regular employment and higher incomes for the poorest together with a wider sharing of resources in general. This agenda, argues Dyos, was only likely to be met when labour became organised and represented in local and central government.[3]

Until such a time though either fear or philanthropy were the motors of change. Fear arose from the cholera epidemics and greater awareness of public health and hygiene issues, accompanied by the fear of crime and moral degeneracy in slum areas. The Public Health Act 1875 gave local authorities the power – but not the duty – to control building standards; the power to demolish and replace unfit housing came with the 1875 Artisans' and Labourers' Dwellings Act. This legislation had its counterparts in Scotland. Eventually the 1890 Housing of the Working Classes Act consolidated earlier slum clearance legislation and gave councils the power to build and rent houses for general needs. However no central government finance was made available; therefore, predictably, there was considerable local variation in municipal responses to housing problems. These arrangements were not exactly an incentive and so it is unsurprising that between 1880 and 1914 the houses built by councils came to less than one per cent of the total housing construction. There was an ideological rejection of public subsidy for working-class housing through the nineteenth century other than for slum clearance; even in this event there was no guarantee that the inhabitants would be rehoused. Such attempts as were made were always subject to political challenge. For example the London County Council, Liverpool Corporation and Glasgow Corporation were attempting municipal housing programmes by the early 1900s but were prevented by their oppositions from subsidising housing through the rates. The recurring issue was that the levels of rent charged by councils to recover their commitment excluded the poorest sections of their communities, those occupying the most overcrowded and insanitary accommodation.[4]

Apart from the inconvenience, severe discomfort and cramped conditions for domestic work there was clear evidence that much working-class housing was a health hazard. Poor, especially overcrowded housing and bad health went together. For example, noting the persistently higher than average infant mortality rate in County Durham, and the significantly higher rate of overcrowded accommodation identified there by the 1901 Census, the County Medical Officer observed in 1907 that 'I am fully convinced that the gross overcrowding in many of the mining districts of the county, especially when associated with insanitary dwellings, is one of the chief factors of our continued high infant death rate'. This had barely changed twenty years later. In 1927 the infant mortality rate for County Durham was reported to be 96 per 1,000 births compared to the rate for England and Wales of 70 per 1,000 births. Among adults the rates of tuberculosis and other diseases associated with overcrowding remained persistently higher than the national average in areas of colliery housing even at the end of the 1930s. In some areas they actually widened during that decade.[5]

Although towards the end of the nineteenth century skilled workers in regular employment were able to afford the higher rents of better accommodation, progress in most towns and cities was limited. In the absence of central government finance a housing programme for the rest of the working population would depend on funding from the rates, but councils were dominated by business interests who were reluctant to increase their own rates and the rates of those who had elected them. As regards housing improvements they relied on what Gareth Stedman Jones calls the 'levelling-up assumption': providing better accommodation for the middle classes would free up property for poorer people to occupy. In practice Daunton's conclusion about municipal housing in Cardiff immediately before the First World War can in fact be applied to the whole of Britain:

> ... it was impossible to provide decent working-class housing at a market rent for the simple reason that a market rent was bound to be too high for the working class to afford, given current wage levels.[6]

In the 1870s the notable Birmingham politician and urban improver Joseph Chamberlain argued that if something was not done quickly to address the problem of working-class housing, 'the people might well succumb to wild socialist theories'. Dr. Russell in Glasgow also believed that 'those one and two-roomed houses are filled with restless, uncomfortable souls, wakening up to the contrast between their misery and the luxury of their neighbours, and ready to grasp at any theory or project, however wild, which promises material relief'.[7] Fears about the spread of socialism therefore accompanied fears about the spread of cholera in the pressure for reform from above. Working-class organisation shortly before, during and after the First World War was to create the pressure from below.

Labour unrest and the growth of municipal housing

It was only when those most affected by poor housing opportunities became effectively organised and secured electoral representation that change on a significant scale appeared to look possible. In the north of England the Independent Labour Party gained some local electoral successes based on its social policies including municipal housing. In addition, trades councils were beginning to campaign for municipal housing at affordable rents. In Glasgow too socialists campaigned for the surpluses generated by the city's municipal enterprises to be used to build municipal cottages to let at affordable rates. However the number of socialist councillors and their supporters in Britain were too few to achieve real change and by 1914 only a limited progress had been made in solving the serious problems of housing.[8]

However in the years immediately before the First World War trade union organisation and militancy were marked; during this 'Great Labour Unrest' union membership doubled from two to four million between 1910 and 1913, and during 1912 there were significant industrial disputes in many key industries. There was a parallel growth in tenant organisation which in several cases was associated with the growth of trade union influence. In the Midlands the Amalgamated Society of Engineers was active in supporting plans for tenant organisations and in 1913 Wolverhampton Trades Council organised a rent strike against increases; in the same year and in 1914 trades councils and Labour Parties were organising rent strikes in Birmingham, Leeds and Bradford.

The outbreak of war in 1914 curtailed house building and then generated another problem. During the war years workers moved to areas where munitions and war-industry work was providing full employment; private landlords took full advantage of this by steadily increasing their rents. In response to this a series of mass rent strikes took place in London, Birmingham and Sheffield for example; but the most significant and celebrated was of course in Glasgow where the extent of working-class mobilisation and the participation of women over the issue were huge. The scale of these protests led directly to the Rent and Mortgage Restriction Act, passed by the government in 1915, although this legislation did not prevent tenants, as distinct from property owners, profiteering by sub-letting rooms in the properties they rented themselves.[9]

1918 brought a recognition that the state had a role in housing provision, albeit a recognition driven by the political necessity to respond to the popular unrest generated by the war. The government established Commissions of Enquiry into Industrial Unrest to investigate this in eight areas of the country and they had reported in 1917 that 'an acute but not universal cause of unrest' was the 'want of sufficient accommodation in congested areas'. For example in Wales inadequate housing was a 'factor of great importance in the causation of unrest' and the recommendation was for state assistance to local authorities on favourable terms for house building. Similarly as regards Scotland the Commissioners noted that the housing situation was 'undoubtedly a serious cause of unrest as well as a danger to public health'. Further, this 'can only be allayed by the Government taking steps to grapple with a problem which appears to have grown too great for private enterprise now to meet'.[10]

Politicians on all sides were explicit about the need for social reforms to respond to the war-time industrial unrest and the statement by Prime Minister Lloyd George about the need for 'homes fit for heroes' has passed into the language. It appeared for the first time that the British state was to have a greater role in housing than simply over health issues: it was to facilitate public sector housing provision to meet local needs. The Housing Act of 1919, known as the Addison Act after the Minister of Health who introduced it, was the first of a series in the inter-war years which accepted the need for central government subsidy and for councils to have statutory housing plans. It permitted a subsidy to local authorities to build houses and limited their need to contribute to the costs through the rates; in addition, the continuation of the wartime Rent Restrictions Act until the early 1920s meant that there was the possibility that houses could be let at rents affordable by poorer tenants. At the same time the political complexion of key local authorities began to shift towards those most likely to take advantage of these opportunities: Durham County Council and Rhondda Urban District Council for example returned their first Labour majorities in 1919. Nevertheless building was retarded by scarcities of labour and materials, the Treasury was reluctant to provide sufficient funds, and councils with pressing needs, such as in South Wales, were unable to raise or borrow enough capital themselves. Local authorities in other coalfield regions such as Chester le Street in County Durham also tried in vain to secure Treasury support for loans for their housing proposals.[11]

The government responded to the economic recession of 1921 with an austerity programme that included reducing such housing subsidies as were available. This continued until the first Labour administration in 1924. Therefore the council building programmes could not hope to meet demand, and this led to instances of direct action by those most affected. Two episodes in County Durham are particularly interesting because they are uncannily prescient of what was to happen there again, and as we shall see all over Britain, twenty-five years later.

During the First World War a large number of Belgian refugees had been settled at Birtley to work in munitions factories. When they left in 1918 the local authority approached the Ministry of Munitions about taking over the vacant hut dwellings for emergency accommodation due to the housing problems in the area, exacerbated by the large numbers of 'young people getting married and living with their parents by the score'. The council received no response from the Ministry but by 1920 local people had occupied the huts of their own accord. Eventually it was agreed that they pay a rent to the Ministry of Munitions through the council. In line with the political mood of the region at the time their action had been supported by Birtley Parish Council, which in 1919 achieved a Labour majority and included several activists from the Demobilised and Demobbed Sailors' and Soldiers' Federation; over the next few years they supported the hut occupiers' efforts to have the huts improved and the rents re-negotiated. In Sunderland the following year a number of young families principally consisting of ex-servicemen occupied abandoned buildings at an aerodrome in North Hylton. They had, as the local paper described it, 'previously lived where they could' and this could include six adults and two children in a two-roomed house. The first families occupied the best hutments they could find and then as the news spread by word of mouth others followed them and 'a mad search for the best apartments was conducted without any tangible ill-feeling'. The squatters made their claims by writing their names on the door of their chosen hut and leaving a chair or item there until they could move their possessions in by cart, and this system was 'widely respected' by the other hut seekers.

These huts were 'well-built and in a fair state of repair', the occupants of the former cookhouse hut were the only ones with an oven but they shared this with the others as the need arose. Those without fireplaces 'cleverly constructed small brick fireplaces with flues'. This was a self-regulating community of 89 adults and 58 children, determined to see that no damage was done and that 'there would be no disturbances'; for example after an episode of domestic violence the culprit obeyed the collective response to stop or he would have to leave. At a meeting with Sunderland Rural District Council squatters' representatives explained that they were 'law-abiding citizens' who 'had no intention of getting something for nothing'. As one explained:

> Ninety per cent of us fought for King and country and we were told by the politicians that they were going to make the country fit for heroes to live in. They have done nothing yet. We went into this place through stress of circumstances.

The local authority was sympathetic: it arranged for water to be supplied, and in view of the fact that the occupiers were undertaking conversion work themselves rather than incurring council expenditure on it the residents of 'Liberty Villas', as they called their community, were officially recognised by the council. These were both examples of families in housing need who had grown impatient with and sceptical about official efforts to address their problems and so had simply found their own solution. The local authorities saw little alternative but to accept these solutions after the event.[12]

The Labour government of 1924, a short and minority administration, was able to achieve very little but it did temporarily strengthen the council house movement. John Wheatley, the Minister of Health who also had responsibility for housing, had a background in the Independent Labour Party in Glasgow and the wartime rent struggles there. He steered legislation (the 'Wheatley Act') which not only restored but increased central government subsidies for council house building. Once more these were curtailed in 1926 by their Conservative successors who favoured the private sector building houses for sale. In the municipal sector rents had to be set at a level that would repay the building costs to the local authorities. In addition the Ministry of Health refused to sanction the building of additional homes in areas where there were high levels of rent arrears. The local authorities therefore tried to ensure that prospective tenants were only those who would be a good risk when it came to rent payments; in this way they could safeguard the Ministerial contributions to their clearance programmes.[13] However one consequence of the national mining lockouts of 1921 and 1926 were an accumulation of rent arrears in the British coalfields. In the aftermath of these disputes, particularly that of 1926, many miners had periods out of work. Others faced reduced hours and wages, and in many cases were obliged to pay back the Poor Law relief payments loaned to them during the lockouts. A predictable result was rent arrears and as a result the effective exclusion of those seeking council housing.[14]

Housing in the 1930s

The second Labour government of 1929 was almost immediately enmeshed in another economic crisis and instead of a major mainstream housing programme the emphasis was narrowed to re-housing following slum clearance. This was the legislation of 1930 known as the Greenwood Act – again after the Minister who designed it – which provided some central government funding to local authorities specifically to replace condemned houses or rehouse those in overcrowded accommodation.

Overcrowding was a persistent problem in several parts of the country. The 1931 Census showed that eleven and a half million families in Britain were living in ten and a half million dwellings, and so therefore many families were sharing a home. Further, in England and Wales 12 per cent of the population was living two persons or more to a room and in Scotland the overcrowding was such that 35 per cent were living with more than two persons per room.[15] A Census on Overcrowding in 1935 was published by the government, research which was criticised at the time and since for adopting a definition of 'overcrowding' that was calculated to reduce the appearance of the problem rather than to accurately measure it. It found 4 per cent of working-class housing in England and Wales to be overcrowded, although as always the national figure concealed local variations: in Hebburn-on-Tyne for example the figure was 25 per cent. In Scotland 23 per cent of working-class housing was stated to be overcrowded with the town of Clydebank as high as 45 per cent. Thus, even according to definitions considered by housing historians to be a sleight of hand, there were parts of the country where overcrowded housing was still a serious problem in the mid-1930s.[16]

There remained too the persistent problem regarding lower-paid workers: how to adequately house people who were unable to afford to pay economic rents. As one hard-pressed Medical Officer of Health expressed it, writing of his own mining district but in fact with relevance to large parts of the country:

> There seems to be only one way in which this difficulty can be met, and that is by an intensive campaign of building houses at rents which tenants can afford to pay … Current unfit housing legislation could enable the worst properties to be replaced but will not meet the needs of the district in respect of shortages. An unjustifiable burden in a depressed area like this, it should be shouldered by the National Exchequer.[17]

However in 1931 the Labour Prime Minister Ramsey MacDonald and some of his colleagues had responded to the economic crisis by forming a 'National Government' with the Conservatives. In the subsequent General Election the Labour Party suffered a calamitous defeat, and Conservative-dominated governments held office until the outbreak of war eight years later. In the subsequent austerity programme of the early 1930s an early casualty was council housing. Despite the slow progress in improving working-class housing the subsidies for council house building were removed in England and Wales and drastically reduced in Scotland. The only Treasury assistance for council housing that remained was for slum clearance, and those subsidies were themselves reduced later in the decade.

Nevertheless the later 1930s witnessed the biggest private sector housing boom that Britain had ever experienced and it was a major feature of national economic activity. However almost two-thirds of the houses built were for sale, not rent, and the greater part of it took place in London and the South East of England or the prosperous areas of the Midlands.[18] These were among those parts of Britain that experienced economic growth and development during the inter-war years, but even where regularly employed skilled workers could afford the new estates other problems could emerge, as Ross McKibbin has shown. He argues that there was a frequent lack of co-ordination between the building of homes and the building of factories, because central government would not interfere with private sector business decisions or make serious efforts at planning. For example the Becontree and Dagenham housing estates were built on the far east of the Greater London area whereas most of the new factories were built on the far west. The new plants opening in Dagenham in the late 1930s did so purely by chance and did not at first actually employ any residents of the local estates. As Ross McKibbin describes it:

> The result was that many men had to travel the width of London to the Great West Road for their work – a daily round trip of about three hours. This experience was to some degree repeated throughout the country.

In short a lack of comprehensive urban planning could mean that new housing even for comparatively affluent working people might still bring problems and additional living costs. It is worth noting too that those buying their own homes on new estates in the later 1930s sometimes faced problems arising from poor building quality. In some cases this led to celebrated 'mortgage strikes' in which political activists were to be found.[19] Although there were genuine local achievements with slum clearance and its replacement by new council housing this same lack of comprehensive urban planning brought problems there too. Contemporary observers noted that these housing schemes were often being built away from town centres – to take advantage of the cheaper land – with no local shops or other amenities, and thus requiring public transport to reach them.[20] This in turn added to the cost of living in the new schemes and this could cause problems as we shall see.

The politics of rationing

One effect of demand far outstripping supply was that it introduced the politics of rationing, as local authorities attempted to manage the competition for their tenancies. The most obvious example was the level of council house rent relative to the income level of the housing applicant. Although this was understandable one consequence could be that those who might need a council house the most, the poorest, were also those least likely to be able to afford the rents on a regular basis. As such they were not a favourable prospect as far as the landlord, the local authority, was concerned. In the mining district of Chester le Street in County Durham the Medical Officer of Health commented on this in his annual report for 1933:

A serious difficulty confronting this Council is the fact that the first thing they have to consider is the making of the Council's property a paying concern. In other words the first consideration must be, is this applicant able to pay the rent. The result of this state of affairs is that the most necessitous cases, e.g. man, wife, and five or six children, with only one worker in the household, are not likely to get into a Council house. However much the Council may sympathise with an applicant of this kind, there is no doubt that even with the best of intentions he is not unlikely to get into arrears with the rent. There was a similar situation with a very poor family where a member has TB – the Council are compelled to refuse the applicant's request for a house in the majority of cases.[21]

As we have seen, areas with high levels of council house rent arrears would not receive Ministerial support for new schemes and this affected those on irregular incomes or affected by the national position of their industries. This was long recognised by the National Unemployed Workers' Movement, the political and advocacy organisation of the unemployed led by the Communist Party during the inter-war years. The NUWM is associated with welfare rights advice and representation, and demonstrations against unemployment, but it was also a persistent lobbying group on rent and housing issues. In Chester le Street again the local branch pointed out to the Urban District Council that 'very few people who are miners will be able to show a clean rent book these last few years', due to the employment conditions in the collieries, and in effect they and the unemployed were being excluded from new council housing. Nevertheless the council were bound by the financial penalties over rent arrears that central government had imposed.[22]

Instead unemployed workers, those on reduced hours and low incomes and their families could be found in the worst housing, as a Ministry of Labour report noted in 1934. When a colliery closed permanently, for example, its owners could sell 'large blocks of colliery houses at scrap prices' to landlords who could let them 'at the very lowest rents, no matter how unsatisfactory their condition, to the undoubted attraction of the most impoverished, and still make a profit'.[23] In some areas it was acknowledged that even where families were more fortunately placed a large number of council tenants were only able to pay their rent because they had taken in lodgers. Others sub-let one or two rooms in their houses to another family, which obviously exacerbated overcrowding, although it was not unknown for councils to turn a blind eye to this if it avoided rent arrears. In the depressed areas of Scotland too it was recognised that poverty was generating overcrowding; for example 'sub-letting by unemployed persons as a means of assisting in rent payments' was identified as a source of overcrowding, particularly where rent arrears were common. In Glasgow during the 1930s overcrowding was often a consequence of taking in paying lodgers to ensure that rent commitments could be met. Working-class people throughout Britain had to endure the consequences of overcrowding as a better alternative to the consequences of eviction or even of having rent arrears.[24]

Another rationing issue taken up by the NUWM in the inter-war years was the system local authorities used to allocate housing tenancies. For example in County Durham, Communist councillors and local NUWM leaders took up issues of council procedures over housing tenancies; they seem to have been a source of popular resentment, with allegations that people less deserving than others on the waiting list were being rehoused earlier because they knew or had influenced the appropriate people. In some authorities the practice was for the Chairmen both of the Council and the Housing Committee, and the Town Clerks, to select the new tenants when council houses became vacant. These three individuals alone were involved and the argument was that this was 'undesirable and unfair to all concerned'. Instead Communists and the left proposed an open system on a 'points' basis that would prioritise slum clearance families, those suffering from overcrowding and those in substandard accommodation.[25] These popular assumptions that the way to get a scarce council house was to be a friend of, a relative of, or be able to return a favour for a local councillor were by no means confined to North East England. It has been recorded that in the 1930s stories about nepotism and corruption in the Labour councils of South Wales achieved the status of folk legend. In Glasgow too it was widely assumed that the council house allocation system was ridden with favouritism, and there were so many allegations that in 1932 a Corporation sub-committee was established to investigate them.[26]

How far such beliefs were justified – and in some cases there is little doubt that they were – is not really the point. The important fact is that they were widely believed in several areas of Britain and were the direct result of attempting to manage a scarce resource without the kind of open system advocated by some Communist councillors and others. In fact such a transparent allocation procedure, based on published eligibility and priority criteria, was not widely adopted by councils around Britain until just after the Second World War. As we shall see in a later chapter, this was in response largely to the post-war housing crisis and the role of major landlord that was given to local authorities. Even so popular claims of favouritism and even corruption in council housing allocation were to surface regularly even well after the Second World War.

Rent strikes and housing action

It has been noted that in the 1920s all housing authorities in the British coalfields had problems with rent and rates arrears as a direct consequence of the lockouts and conditions in the coal industry. As the levels of arrears influenced the attitude of the Ministry of Health towards further council house building authorities sometimes felt compelled to address the problem robustly. In 1931 for example Rhondda Urban District Council in South Wales sent in bailiffs to evict some tenants in arrears at Mardy, where a hostile crowd gathered to oppose them. Local Communist and National Unemployed Workers' Movement leader Arthur Horner persuaded the UDC to withdraw the bailiffs and negotiate an arrangement, but he and many others were later gaoled for incitement and riot on police evidence.[27]

As was stated earlier rents on new council estates tended to be set at a level that would recoup the long-term costs of building and could often therefore be higher than the new tenants were used to, or indeed could afford. In 1938 it was estimated that council house rents in Bristol were too high for almost a third of the city's working-class population. In the main they were within the budgets of skilled workers, who were in stable employment, but people on the lower incomes could often struggle with high rents, and the defaults in payments that resulted could in turn mean that they had to move out or be evicted:

> Before 1940, when full employment made default less common, there was in consequence a continuous population turnover. In Sheffield, by 1931, nearly one-fifth of the original inhabitants of 1920s estates had left; most other estates had removal rates of at least ten per cent a year.[28]

Sheffield Council later attempted to keep rents at a reasonable level but could only do so by reducing expenditure on facilities on the council estates.[29] Therefore people on low incomes who were rehoused into modern accommodation – this was particularly true of the unemployed and those in slum clearance programmes – could find that they had exchanged one set of problems for another. In Stockton-on-Tees during the 1930s the Medical Officer of Health (Dr M'Gonigle) studied the family incomes, diets and health status of unemployed people living in a new slum clearance estate. He compared them with those of unemployed families who were still living in slum housing. The findings, a source of considerable debate and controversy at the time, were that unemployed people on the new estates were suffering from even more ill-health than before they were re-housed. The higher rents that went with the new council houses meant that they struggled to be able to afford the diet they needed to maintain their health. He concluded that some external financial assistance was needed if rehousing was going to achieve the social objectives it was assumed to bring.[30]

A rent strike in Sunderland in 1939 provides a good example of exactly the point M'Gonigle was making, along with the dilemmas created for local authorities by the lack of central subsidy, and the responses to the problems that could be organised by the tenants themselves.

The Housing Act of 1930 had introduced government subsidy for slum clearance but progress had been slow for financial reasons; as we have seen the National Government had, by 1933, scrapped any Treasury subsidy for mainstream council house building. This issue was taken up by the Commissioner for the Special Areas. These administrative regions had been established under the Special Areas Act 1934, in what was probably the only response by the National Government to the long-term structural unemployment afflicting parts of Britain. They had a national Special Areas Fund budget of £2 million and a remit to promote the economic development of designated areas such as County Durham and Tyneside, South Wales and central Scotland. The Commissioners were not allowed to fund public works and the government was ideologically reluctant to direct inward investment to the areas of persistently high unemployment. Therefore the Special Areas legislation had only a marginal effect on employment rates and has been judged as representing only a hesitant and ineffective intervention.

As regards housing the Commissioner stated in his first Report in 1935 that 'The overcrowding problem in the Special Areas in the North East is acute and there is a pressing need for more houses to be let at low rents.' The obstacle was that whereas the legislation allowed some central government subsidies for slum clearance or alleviating overcrowding local authorities were required to contribute through the rates. This, in impoverished Durham and Tyneside, they could not afford to do and the law did not permit the Commissioners to subsidise house building by councils. The solution was to establish a not for profit 'public utility society', the North East Housing Association, expressly for 'providing accommodation for members of the working classes in the North East Special Areas'. This partnership was legally able to combine the central government subsidy to councils with contributions from the Special Areas Fund and by this means houses could be built and let at rents the tenants could afford.[31]

By 1937 6,000 new dwellings had been built and 27,000 people re-housed in Durham and Tyneside under these arrangements. However a year later central government subsidies for re-housing projects were again reduced, increasing the cost of houses for the NEHA; the Association passed these increased costs on to its tenants in the form of rent increases.[32]

In Sunderland the response was a rent strike by at least 1,600 people on the affected estates, organised by local tenants who were also active in the National Unemployed Workers' Movement. A leading role in the demonstrations, deputations and dialogues with the local press was taken by the women on the estates. They used M'Gonigle's work as campaign material against the rent increases, highlighting the effect they would have on the household budgets of people already surviving on low benefit scales. They quoted examples of how tenants were struggling to afford vital outgoings as things were, and said that 'the provision of new houses and fresh air doesn't make up for the loss of food'. The local NUWM were also able to put this in the context of the diet, income and health debates of the time, using the survey evidence from the British Medical Association and others to argue that the average tenant's income was already below that needed for an adequate diet. Unemployment was widespread on the estate, which was also affected by the same problems that were becoming associated with new schemes elsewhere: distances from shops, schools and other amenities, infrequent and expensive bus services; these too added to the real costs of re-housing for the tenants. At the same time an estate in Jarrow was threatening a rent strike for the same reasons.[33]

The case against rent increases on the estates was put to the Ministry of Health by Sunderland Council and the NEHA Board, and it is unlikely that this would have happened without the tenants' action. The episode demonstrates that a consortium of agencies could produce solutions to the problem of providing housing for low-income tenants. However, even in the improved financial conditions of the later 1930s the reluctance of central government to provide financial support meant that the additional costs were likely to be shifted to the low-paid and unemployed people for whom the schemes were designed.

Birmingham and rent strike politics

The months before the outbreak of the Second World War were marked by rent strikes and radical campaigns on housing issues all over Britain. The events in Sunderland were part of a national movement: between June and the end of August 1939, for example, the *Daily Worker* carried reports of at least 27 different tenants' disputes around the country, frequently leading to a rent strike. Several councils or private companies did resort to legal action, using bailiffs to try to serve summonses for non-payment of rent or eviction orders. There are several reports of tenants, local women, the NUWM, standing sentry on estate entrances ready to blow warning whistles at the approach of the bailiffs. This would produce an instant picket of tenants to bar their way. There were occasional arrests and outbreaks of violence, for example in Stepney and Enfield in London and Barrhead near Glasgow when police baton charges were used to clear a path for the bailiffs. In Scotland the NUWM was often to the fore in these actions and its leader Harry McShane was to continue as a housing campaigner in Glasgow after the war.[34]

The most celebrated and probably the most successful rent strike of the inter-war years was organised in Prime Minister Neville Chamberlain's own constituency, Birmingham. The city had experienced industrial prosperity during the 1930s and as such it was in position that was almost the opposite of Sunderland's. Nevertheless if unemployment was not a pressing issue housing certainly was; work opportunities were attracting an expanding population and like most the municipal housing programme lagged well behind the known need. For example by 1938 there were thirty thousand on the council waiting list in the city with more than twenty new ones added each day. In 1939 the response of the Conservative-controlled City Council was to introduce a rent pool system. It attempted to introduce rent increases for fifty thousand council tenants with a means test for those claiming that they could not afford them, so that the better-off tenants would be subsidising those who were poorer. The reasoning was that the better-off tenants would be encouraged to move into the private sector and then housing would become available for those on the waiting list. This, of course, was little more than the 'levelling-up' assumption that had been common in the previous century. Such policies of rent-pooling were recommended by central government and had proved controversial elsewhere on account of the means testing that was involved. In 1935 Labour had lost control of Leeds Council because it had introduced this for council rents.[35]

In Birmingham the Municipal Tenants' Association – whose leaders included several local Communists – was to organise a mass petition through its 36 branches, hold several demonstrations involving thousands of tenants, mainly women, and finally a rent strike of some 49,000 tenants. The council issued summons for rent arrears to selected activists but bailiffs were thwarted by mass pickets of other tenants. After ten weeks of the strike the council capitulated, withdrawing the increases, the summonses, and recognising the Birmingham Municipal Tenants' Association.[36]

This was a popular protest which had significance for the Communist Party's agenda at the time. The Party Congress of 1938 had been told that local agitations were a vehicle to put pressure on and help to remove the National Government. Local Communists then should be raising every issue affecting 'the mass of the people ... the interests of all workers and the discontented middle class ...' in such a way as to develop a strong movement that 'can sharpen the whole fight against the National Government'. The strategy for this should be joint activity through 'winning the co-operation of Labour and Progressive councillors for those demands on which we are all agreed'. This was intended to be part of the campaign to build unity in action against the Chamberlain government's policies of appeasement towards European fascism as well as over domestic issues, principally the effects of austerity economics.[37] The Birmingham Municipal Tenants' Association included the prominent local Communist Jessie Eden as its General Secretary and among those summonsed for non-payment of rent were three Labour councillors, including Councillor Bradbeer JP. This apparent co-operation in action between Labour and Communist seemed to vindicate the latter Party's strategy of seeking unity in action and eventually affiliation to Labour. As we shall see in a later chapter these same individuals were to meet again in housing struggles immediately after the war, but as opponents and not allies.

The Birmingham episode began to have a national impact before the outbreak of war that September. In July two thousand delegates representing a hundred thousand tenants attended a conference of the new National Federation of Tenants and Residents, held in Birmingham and chaired by Communist and housing activist Jim Borders. Their charter of demands with which to lobby parliament and influence Labour policy was of course overtaken by international events. Nevertheless among the raft of emergency legislation introduced when war was declared was the 1939 Rent Restriction Act. This pegged rents at August 1939 levels in the private sector in England. The National Federation of Tenants and Residents believed that the Act was 'a tribute to the strength of the tenants' movement' which had shown the government that it could 'expect the same unrest' as had broken out between 1914 and 1918 if rents rose as they had during that war.[38]

As far as the activists were concerned there was always a local or a national political agenda to accompany work on housing issues. In Birmingham, as we have seen, it was unity in action between the Labour and Communist Parties in the constituency of the leader of the National Government, Prime Minister Neville Chamberlain. In the East End of London the campaigns were for private landlords to carry out essential repairs, but the Communists who were active with tenants' groups made a point of campaigning and organising rent strikes on estates where the British Union of Fascists had support. In the words of the tenants' organiser, Communist councillor and post-war MP Phil Piratin it was about helping tenants to '… understand, through their own experience, the nature of capitalism itself'. Consequently, also, they would be brought into the struggle against the capitalist system and into socialist politics. How far they were able to reach this objective is of course another matter. Certainly during the 1930s those Communists who were elected to local authorities in Britain were, almost invariably, well-known local activists in the NUWM who had campaigned relentlessly with tenants and the unemployed. It was this work that had earned them their electoral success; however, it was the respected local individual who had earned that rather than the Party itself. The Communists never succeeded in resolving this failure to translate their local campaigning successes into permanent advances in membership and influence. Nevertheless the Party and its satellite organisations such as the NUWM had established themselves as activists around housing as well as unemployment and trades union issues.[39]

Summary

From the Victorian era to 1939 the housing problems of Britain and their consequences in terms of public health and limited life chances had been well known. The responses had lacked a consistent, nationally driven and funded movement to address them in planned and practical terms.

Some historians – seeking to counteract the received image of the 1930s as a decade of economic depression and social stagnation – have emphasised the substantial progress made during the 1930s on slum clearance and improving the housing standards of many working people. By 1939 local authorities had rehoused over a million people and overcrowding – albeit according to the notoriously inadequate definition of the 1935 survey – had been reduced by a quarter. A million council houses had been built and this represented more progress than during any other decade so far.[40] Nevertheless, as they admit, the national picture conceals significant regional inequalities in economic activity and security, coupled with inequalities in housing quality. A decade of government support for private housing development had favoured the middle classes by 1938-39: surveys then indicated that 18 per cent of manual workers were owner-occupiers compared to 65 per cent of workers in secure white-collar occupations.[41] This support had been accompanied by an antipathy to public spending and hence cuts to local authority housing funds after 1926. The national picture of housing improvement for working people also ignores the problems relating to rent and income that had emerged as a consequence of this austerity policy. These problems come into focus, as we have seen, when the account includes how those most affected by this policy organised to press for change.

The market had failed to provide private housing for general need and in the absence of consistent government subsidy, and secure regular employment across Britain, council housing at affordable rent was restricted. This was the housing position with which Britain entered war in 1939 and encountered the social changes it produced.

NOTES

1   Eric Hobsbawm, *Industry and Empire: An Economic History of Britain since 1750* (London, Weidenfeld and Nicolson, 1969, p. 67); Frederich Engels, *The Condition of the Working Class in England* (Oxford, Oxford University Press, 1999, p. 75). See also John R. Short, *Housing in Britain: The Post War Experience* (1982, p. 24); Sean Damar, *Glasgow: Going for a Song* (London, Lawrence and Wishart, 1990).

2   Harold Pfautz (Ed.), *Charles Booth on the City: Physical Pattern and Social Structure* (Chicago, University of Chicago Press, 1967, pp. 254-58). Dr James Burn Russell, *Life in one room: or, some serious considerations for the citizens of Glasgow* (Glasgow, James Maclehose and Sons, 1888, pp. 11-14).

3   H.J. Dyos: *Exploring the Past: Essays in Urban History* (Cambridge, Cambridge University Press, 1982, pp. 142-53). Also relevant is Hobsbawm: *Industry and Empire*.

4   Hamish Fraser, 'Municipal Socialism', in R.J. Morris and Richard Roger (Eds), *The Victorian City: A Reader in British Urban History 1820-1914* (London, Longman, 1993, pp. 258-81).

5   GLS: *High Infant Mortality in the Administrative County of Durham: Report of the County Medical Officer* (Durham, Durham County Council, 1907, p. 7); GLS, *Annual Report of the Medical Officer of Health for County Durham 1927* (Durham, Durham County Council, 1928, p. 8); John Stevenson and Chris Cook, *Britain in the Depression: Society and Politics 1929-39* (London, Longman, 1994, p. 55).

6   Gareth Stedman Jones, *Outcast London: A Study in the Relations Between Classes in Victorian Society* (London, Peregrine Books, 1984); M.J. Daunton, *Coal Metropolis: Cardiff 1870-1914* (Leicester, Leicester University Press, 1977, p. 105).

7   Chamberlain quoted in Tristram Hunt, *Building Jerusalem: The Rise and fall of the Victorian City* (New York, Metropolitan Books, 2005, p. 350); Russell *Life in one room*, p. 30.

8   Keith Laybourn, 'Recent Writing on the History of the ILP', in David Jones, Tony Jowitt and Keith Laybourn (Eds), *The Centennial History of the Independent Labour Party* (Halifax, Ryburn Academic Publishing, 1992, pp. 317-37); Joan Smith, 'Taking the leadership of the labour movement: the ILP in Glasgow, 1906-1914', in Alan McKinlay and R.J. Morris (Eds), *The*

ILP on Clydeside, 1893-1932: from foundation to disintegration (Manchester, Manchester University Press, 1991, pp. 56-83); John R. Short, *Housing in Britain: The Post War Experience* (1982, p. 28).

9   John Grayson and Maggie Walker, *Opening the Window: Revealing the Hidden History of Tenants' Organisations* ((London, Tenant Participation Advisory Service and Northern College, 1996, pp. 18-23); Joseph Melling, 'Clydeside rent struggles and the making of Labour politics in Scotland 1900-39', in Richard Roger (Ed.), *Scottish Housing in the Twentieth Century* (Leicester, Leicester University Press, 1989, pp. 54-89).

10   NA: MUN 5/49/300/34, *Commission of Enquiry into Industrial Unrest Summary of Reports 1917*, p. 5; MUN 5/49/300/31, *Commission of Enquiry into Industrial Unrest for Division 7 Wales and Monmouthshire 1917*, pp. 33-4; MUN 5/49/300/32, *Commission of Enquiry into Industrial Unrest for Division 8 Scotland 1917*, p. 4. On the political consensus about the need for social reform in response to unrest see, for example, P.B. Johnson, *Land Fit for Heroes: The Planning of British Reconstruction 1916-39* (Chicago, University of Chicago Press, 1968).

11   *Chester le Street Chronicle*, 1 August 1919.

12   *Chester le Street Chronicle*, 9 May, 13 and 20 June 1919; 22 January 1922. *Sunderland Echo*, 8 and 12 April 1921.

13   Robert Ryder, *Council house building in County Durham 1900-1939: the local implementation of national policy* (University of Durham M.Phil., 1979, p. 251).

14   Robert Ryder, *Council house building in County Durham 1900-1939*, p. 261; John McIlroy, Alan Campbell and Keith Gildart (Eds), *Industrial Politics and the 1926 Mining Lockout: The Struggle for Dignity* (Cardiff, University of Wales Press, 2009).

15   Noreen Branson and Margot Heinemann, *Britain in the Nineteen Thirties* (London, Granada Publishing, 1973, p. 200).

16   For a discussion of the definitions used and the effect see Stephen Merrett, *State Housing in Britain* (London, Routledge, 1979, pp. 59-60).

17   GLS: Chester le Street Rural District Council: *Annual Report of the Medical Officer of Health for the Chester le Street Rural District Council for 1933* (Chester le Street, Chester le Street Rural District Council, 1934, pp. 67-8).

18   Andrew Thorpe: *Britain in the 1930s: The Deceptive Decade* (Oxford, Blackwell 1992 p.97-99).

19   Ross McKibbin, *Classes and Cultures: England 1919-1951* (Oxford, Oxford University Press, 1998, pp. 196-7); on home buyers and 'mortgage strikes' see Noreen Branson and Margot Heinemann, *Britain in the Nineteen Thirties*, pp. 206-10.

20   For example George Orwell, *The Road to Wigan Pier* (London, Gollancz Left Book Club, 1937); G.D.H. Cole and M.I. Cole, *The Condition of Britain* (London, Gollancz Left Book Club, 1937).

21   GLS: Chester le Street Rural District Council: *Annual Report of the Medical Officer of Health for the Chester le Street Rural District Council for 1933* (Chester le Street, Chester le Street Rural District Council, 1934, p. 60).

22   Correspondence between Chester le Street Rural District Council and the Chester le Street Unemployed Association quoted in Don Watson, *No Justice Without A Struggle: The National Unemployed Workers' Movement in the North East of England 1920-1940* (London, Merlin Press, 2014, p. 46). On the NUWM in general see Richard Croucher, *We Refuse to Starve in Silence: A History of the National Unemployed Workers' Movement 1920-1946* (London, Lawrence and Wishart, 1987).

23   Ministry of Labour, *Reports of Industrial Conditions in Certain Depressed Areas: Durham and Tyneside* (London, Ministry of Labour, 1934, p. 75).

24   Ryder, *Council house building in County Durham 1900-1939*, pp. 265-66. Ministry of Labour, *Reports of Industrial Conditions in Certain Depressed Areas: Scotland* (London, Ministry of Labour, 1934, p. 219); John Butt, 'Working-Class Housing in Glasgow 1900-1939', in Ian MacDougall (Ed.), *Essays in Scottish Labour History: A Tribute to W.H. Marwick* (Edinburgh, John Donald, 1978, pp. 143-70).

25   Watson, *No Justice Without a Struggle*, pp. 201-5.

26   Chris Williams, *Democratic Rhondda: Politics and Society 1885-1951* (Cardiff, Cardiff University Press, 1996, p. 175); Sean Damer, *Glasgow: Going for a Song* (London, Lawrence and Wishart, 1990, pp.170-71).

27   A detailed account is in Nina Fishman, *Arthur Horner: A Political Biography, Vol. I, 1894-1944* (London, Lawrence and Wishart, 2010, pp. 232-8).

28   Andrew Thorpe, *Britain in the 1930s: The Deceptive Decade*, p. 100; Ross McKibbin, *Classes and Cultures: England 1919-1951*, pp. 195-6.

29   Matthew Worley, *Labour Inside the Gate: A History of the British Labour Party between the Wars* (London, IB Tauris, 2005, p. 202).

30   G.C.M. M'Gonigle and J. Kirkby, *Poverty and Public Health* (London, Gollancz Left Book Club, 1936). On M'Gonigle generally see Susan McLaurin, *The Housewives' Champion: Dr G.C.M. M'Gonigle, Medical Officer of Health for Stockton-on-Tees 1924-1939* (Stockton, Printability Publishing, 1997). An account of the pressure that the government tried to exert to silence doctors like M'Gonigle is included in Charles Webster, 'Healthy or Hungry Thirties?', *History Workshop*, Issue 13 (Spring, 1982, pp. 110-30).

31   *First Report of the Commissioner for the Special Areas* (London, HMSO, 1935, p. 32); *Second Report of the Commissioner for the Special Areas* (London, HMSO, February 1936, pp. 45-6); *Third Report of the Commissioner for the Special Areas* (London, HMSO, October 1936, pp. 92-3).

32   *Fourth Report of the Commissioner for the Special Areas* (London, HMSO, September 1937, p. 135); *Sunderland Echo*, 5, 8 and 9 June 1939.

33   *Sunderland Echo* 27 July, 2 and 3 August 1939. A detailed account of the Sunderland Rent Strike is given in Don Watson, '*We Don't Intend Paying It*: The Sunderland Rent Strike 1939', *North East History*, no. 38 (2007, pp. 103-19).

34   Harry McShane and Joan Smith, *No Mean Fighter* (London, Pluto Press, 1978).

35   Worley, *Labour Inside the Gate*, p. 202.

36 The Birmingham rent strike is covered by Kevin Morgan, 'Mass struggles in Birmingham 1939-1941', in his *Against Fascism and War: Ruptures and Continuities in British Communist Politics 1935-41* (Manchester, Manchester University Press, 1989, pp. 278-86); Noreen Branson, *History of the Communist Party of Great Britain 1927-1941* (London, Lawrence and Wishart, 1985, pp.201-3); contemporary coverage is in the *Daily Worker*, 3 June–5 July 1939.

37 NLS: *Report of the Central Committee to the Fifteenth Party Congress* (London, Communist Party of Great Britain, 1938, pp. 12-13; *Party Organiser* 2 (August 1938, pp. 1-3).

38 *Daily Worker*, 17 July, 4 and 7 September 1939.

39 Quoted in Kevin Marsh and Robert Griffiths, *Granite and Honey: the Story of Phil Piratin, Communist MP* (London, Manifesto Press, 2012, p. 41) which has an account of his work with Stepney tenants. Piratin's own account is in his autobiography, *Our Flag Stays Red* (London, Lawrence and Wishart, 1980, pp. 33-50); on the NUWM, the Communists and local election successes see Watson, *No Justice Without A Struggle*, pp. 212-14.

40 For example John Stevenson and Chris Cook, *Britain in the Depression: Society and Politics 1929-39*, pp. 10-11, 28-30; Andrew Thorpe, *Britain in the 1930s: The Deceptive Decade*, pp. 97-99, 119-23.

41 Stephen Merrett and Fred Gray, *Owner Occupation in Britain* (London, Routledge and Kegan Paul, 1982, p. 15).

Chapter Three
WAR, PEACE AND REQUISITIONING:
HOUSING AND POLITICS 1939-1945

The Second World War introduced several new elements into the housing problems of the British working class. Two-thirds of the skilled building workforce went into the armed forces and the remainder worked solely on government contracts, so that new house building work was severely curtailed. This included slum clearance and measures to deal with over-crowding. Aerial bombardment destroyed over 200,000 houses in Britain or damaged them beyond repair, and a further two houses out of seven were damaged to the extent of needing important repairs done to them. Although the effects of the London blitz are well-known other places too suffered serious destruction: over two nights in 1940 for example Coventry had lost a third of its houses and Clydebank a year later was reduced to only seven homes without damage. This meant that workers in the essential war industries and their families had to be billeted in requisitioned hostels, often some distance from the area and requiring long journeys to work. Conditions in the temporary Rest Centres for the bombed-out or otherwise homeless could be grim, particularly in London. One example was a classroom in an empty school, crudely divided into four with a family in each corner with bunks; rent and fuel costs were nevertheless charged.[1]

The movement of labour necessitated by the war effort introduced another range of issues. Factories around Oxford, the Midlands and the South-East of England for example, converted to war production, were paying above average wages and thus attracting an influx of workers. They, and often their families, had to be billeted in any rooms that were available. Another problem was profiteering. The Rent and Mortgage Interest Restriction Act introduced on the eve of war offered no protection to the tenants or sub-tenants of furnished accommodation. People with rooms to spare took full advantage of this and the massive level of demand compared to the level of supply. This was in addition to the problem identified throughout the

1930s: people struggling on low incomes unofficially renting out rooms. Both they and their 'tenants' were exacerbating overcrowding as a means of financial survival.

Rents as such may have been restricted in some cases but there was no such provision for reduced incomes, and the effect that could have on the family housing situation. When members of a household, who contributed to the family income, entered the forces and their wages were replaced by government allowances the result could often be a reduced family budget. The result of this in turn was an inability to maintain rent payments and the consequent threat of eviction. Jarrow MP Ellen Wilkinson, before she entered the wartime government, raised this problem in the House of Commons. She argued too that whereas people in this position could appeal eviction proceedings through the county court this was not a course of action likely to be pursued by working-class women. Her intervention led to assurances by some local authorities that no evictions for rent arrears would take place where the husband was in the armed forces. In addition Communist Party branches organised tenants and housewives to campaign against the threat of eviction for servicemen's families, for example in Slough, Kirkcaldy and Brighton. Elsewhere shop stewards at an aircraft factory in north London protested to the Home Office about threatened evictions at a nearby housing estate where a rent strike was in progress.[2]

These campaigns by local Communist Parties over housing, rents and incomes at this stage of the war were always part of a wider political agenda, one that changed significantly in 1939 and again in 1941. On the outbreak of war the Party had supported it as a continuation of the anti-fascist struggle of the 1930s. It argued that given his record of appeasing Hitler and Mussolini there could be no confidence in the anti-fascist credentials of a government led by Neville Chamberlain, and so the Party campaigned for it to be replaced by a 'people's government' that would take the war seriously. A month later this position was reversed to conform to the needs of the Soviet Union, which had earlier reached a pact with Nazi Germany: the conflict was now an 'imperialist war' fought at the expense of the working classes of all the nations involved. The Communist Party called for a negotiated truce but, as these housing campaigns show, and as Kevin Morgan argues, local activists could still maintain a momentum of action over the legitimate grievances generated by the war. The Party initiated the 'People's Convention' movement as a broad coalition of groups with different perspectives on the war but willing to collaborate on other aims to achieve political change and better conditions. It was the attention the People's Convention attracted that led to the banning of the *Daily Worker* in the summer of 1940; the government believed that is propaganda could prove dangerous to morale if the war went badly. As regards local campaigning the Communists had a distinct advantage over Labour; with war came the suspension of local and national elections, and thus the primary focus of local Labour Parties was removed.[3]

The pre-war problems still remained of course. Bob Saunders, who was later to be involved in the squatting movement, has left a vivid account of the conditions in Glasgow during and at the end of the war:

> Hundreds were the victims of the sub-let racketeers who had acquired old tenement buildings, large houses etc., and after installing the barest minimum of furniture, let them out, a family to each room at very enhanced rents. A classic example of this type of sub-let building was one which Comrade Margaret Hunter and I visited in Balmano Street, where on each floor seven or eight families were housed, a family in each room.
>
> There was no gas or electric light and illumination was by paraffin lamp. The sanitary facilities consisted of one toilet on each landing and one iron sink and tap for the communal use of all on that floor. Rats were no strangers either.[4]

Unsurprisingly then squatting and other direct action by homeless people took place.

Squatting, direct action and lobbying

Militant, or more accurately desperate, action by the homeless during the war seems to have been more common in Scotland, a predictable consequence of the greater levels of overcrowding and generally poor housing conditions there. In Aberdeen for example there were individual instances of squatting; in one episode an organised group of up to thirty families, many those of servicemen, occupied a condemned property. A Tenants' Protection Association led a deputation to the City Council where they argued the case that they should be allowed to stay and pay rent. They also argued that where possible an effort could be made to rehabilitate property that might normally be condemned, so that it could be occupied for longer. In Lanarkshire a local authority allowed the wives of servicemen squatting in condemned houses to stay on this basis and carried out some renovation work. It was the action of the squatters that had prompted the authorities to adopt this course.

The Trespass (Scotland) Act had been passed in 1865 in an attempt to combat land occupations by rural crofters. Under this Public Prosecutors could bring actions against squatters in the criminal court, unlike in England and Wales where it was a matter for the civil court; securing an eviction order, though, would as in England or Wales be a matter for the civil court. As we shall see this difference in the legislation was to explain different reactions to the squatting movements between the two countries. In some cases when the squatters were brought to court during the war local Communist Party activists such as International Brigade veteran Bob Cooney spoke for them as unofficial advocates, or as the National Unemployed Workers' Movement had put it before the war, as 'working-class lawyers'.[5] In practice this meant working-class people who needed assistance with their dealings with authority would approach a well-known local activist who had experience of negotiation, advocacy and dealing with the system concerned.

A squat in the Clydeside shipbuilding town of Greenock at the end of 1943 involved more than twenty families occupying a condemned tenement that had lain empty for three years. The local authority had it in mind to requisition and renovate the property for re-letting and could not do so while the building was occupied. Unfortunately and as their representatives continually stressed the squatters had nowhere else to go to. A deputation to Greenock Corporation described their circumstances, which included, in some cases, being obliged to leave a rented room because a member of the owner's family had returned from the forces and needed it back. However the Corporation issued a notice to quit; the squatters refused to leave until alternative accommodation had been found for them but, of course, nothing was forthcoming. Therefore the Corporation took action through the courts for eviction proceedings after the notice to quit had expired; it also cut off their water supply so that they had to carry in water from some distance away.[6] The case prompted a campaign in Greenock to support the squatters. A Tenants' Association organised a petition to the Corporation which attracted 8,000 signatures; a shop stewards' committee protested to the Corporation; Greenock Trades Council urged the Secretary of State for Scotland, Tom Johnson, to intervene to prevent 'the shameful scandal' of the families being put on to the street. Nevertheless the Sheriff's Court heard a test case against one squatter, a local shipyard worker who explained to the court that his was essential war work and he required to live near the yard. He and others had made rooms habitable by installing windows, floorboards, doors and fire grates themselves. All this had been done under the eyes of Greenock Corporation workmen who had taken no action. This willingness of some squatters to carry out their own renovations in the properties they occupied was to feature later in the

1940s too, as we shall see. The Court found against the squatters and issued eviction notices, although the Secretary of State urged the council not to evict unless alternative accommodation was available. The evictions appear to have been carried out by the end of 1944 when the squatters had been in occupation for almost a year.[7]

One of the most successful popular campaigns of the war years was not concerned with housing as such but nonetheless it was to have an indirect influence on the post-war squatting events in London. In the early stages of the wartime bombing raids on the capital some Communist veterans of the pre-war housing campaigns continued their direct action, albeit in different circumstances. As early as 1938 Communists and the Labour Left had been arguing for public works schemes to build deep air-raid shelters throughout the country. In London, once war began, Communists such as future MP Phil Piratin, tenants' leader Tubby Rosen and the Party's London District Secretary Ted Bramley campaigned for deep public shelters to protect the civilian population against air raids. When the London raids began the government attempted to prevent the use of tube stations as shelters – locking the gates – but these campaigners organised Londoners to occupy them. During September 1940 the most dramatic example of direct action over shelters occurred when during a raid Piratin led a large party to occupy the deep, safe and luxurious shelter reserved for guests at the Savoy Hotel. This also made the political point of contrasting the provision that was available for wealthy people with that available for the working class. In the same month a Communist broke open the gates of a tube station with a crowbar when a raid began and used a megaphone to invite people in. By the next month the Home Secretary had agreed to the use of underground platforms as shelters. This episode had shown how effective direct action could be in emergency circumstances and some of the organisers, themselves veterans of tenants' campaigns, would attempt to use similar tactics of direct action over housing in London at the end of the war.[8]

Westminster too was left in no doubt about the seriousness of the housing problem. Dumbarton Burghs MP and former Independent Labour Party stalwart David Kirkwood for example, made several impassioned speeches in the House of Commons about the housing conditions in his constituency. He drew attention to the temporary accommodation that was being quickly erected for war workers in some parts of the country; why was this not done for the Clydeside shipyard workers? He certainly had a point. In 1941 Minister for Labour Ernest Bevin had established The National Service Hostels Corporation, which had the task of building accommodation for essential war workers who were away from home. Some 30,000 places had been built by 1945, which suggests that there was a potential there to improve at least the worst of the mainstream housing conditions. Even so, even when they had been built other problems were emerging. At Workington in Cumbria an estate had been built –hastily and badly – for war workers by the North East Housing Association. As the war was winding down the overtime opportunities for the tenants declined and redundancies began to increase. Thus they struggled with the economic rents they were being charged and evictions were applied for; however, after a petition campaign a sympathetic judge arranged for rent arrears to be repaid by instalments instead.[9]

Another initiative also had the potential to relieve the pressure on housing both during and after the war, but in a significant clash between the government and vested interests this potential was not reached. This was the Housing (Temporary Accommodation) Act 1944 which provided funds for pre-fabricated –'pre-fab' – housing aimed to meet the needs of bombed-out families. In 1944 Stafford Cripps, the Minister for Aircraft Production put the case for the aircraft companies to manufacture prefabricated aluminium houses after the war. This was something they would clearly have the capacity to do once the war-time need for aircraft ceased. The Ministry proposed the production of at least half a million houses both for Britain and export to Europe. However the contract proved to be just for 14,000 houses, the aircraft companies judging that other fields of production could generate greater returns. In the words of historian Richard Croucher the project foundered due to the manufacturers, already looking ahead to the post-war market, 'being more concerned with profits than providing houses'.[10]

David Kirkwood, describing the effects of the war on the already appalling housing conditions in his constituency, also indicated that there was a potential for industrial action over the issue. He stated in the House of Commons that people had left Clydebank because of air raids and had sub-let their houses to war workers. These home owners were now returning because the threat of air raids had diminished and they were evicting war workers who had no other accommodation. He said that he had dissuaded Clydebank shipyard workers from a token strike in protest against their housing conditions. They had however passed a resolution that:

> We view with alarm and great concern the present living conditions of the people in the Burgh of Clydebank. We draw attention to the mass of citizens who are still without a home, living in unsatisfactory conditions

and having to travel long distances to and from work. We condemn the Government for the inadequacy of its housing policy and its decision to allocate only 200 houses to the Burgh of Clydebank. We view with alarm the ultimate effects of prevailing conditions and the possible loss of additional lives through the ravages of consumption and other diseases. Believing that the housing of bombed-out people is an essential part of the war effort, affecting not only the problem of production but the morale of the citizens, we call upon the Government to declare Clydebank an emergency area and to utilise all the resources at its command in material and labour, so far as present conditions will permit, in a great national effort to rehouse the homeless people.[11]

This lobbying by a range of concerned organisations and politicians eventually produced a result, and one that was to prove directly relevant to post-war struggles over housing.

Requisitioning private property

The raft of emergency Defence Regulations introduced at the beginning of the war included one to permit the temporary requisitioning of property. Empty private houses could be requisitioned for the duration of the war by the armed forces; later the local authorities were given the power to requisition property to house evacuees, essential war workers, or those made homeless by enemy action. As the war progressed campaigns began to extend these powers to benefit the wider population. Deputations from the London County Council, the Association of Local Authorities and Edinburgh City Council for example pressed the government for requisitioning powers to help them to deal with serious housing shortages that were being exacerbated by the war.

It was in response to this widespread campaigning that the government, 'to mitigate the increasing housing difficulties' agreed in 1943 to make 'powers of requisitioning more widely available'. Under this new Circular 2845 local authorities in England and Wales were given the power – but not the duty; there was no statutory obligation – to 'requisition, repair and adapt empty properties for the purpose of providing housing accommodation for persons at present inadequately housed' provided that the cost did not exceed a stated limit per house. The local authorities were expected to have regard to 'insanitary conditions' and 'overcrowding' when selecting people to be housed in requisitioned properties. The authorities were responsible for selecting the tenants of these properties and should charge rents that the tenants would normally expect to pay for such a property, and the Ministry of Health would reimburse the councils where it was necessary for them to subsidise the rent. North of the border this power was initially given to the authorities in Glasgow, Clydebank and Greenock (the most affected by war damage and the needs of essential workers) but then extended throughout Scotland. Local authorities could make recommendations for requisitioning to the regional Principal Housing Officers of the Ministry of Health, or the office of the Secretary of State in Scotland; the owners of the affected properties could appeal the recommendation by stating their intention to occupy, let or sell the premises. This initiative must have seemed a godsend to many at the time; when the intention to introduce this policy was announced on the BBC on 22 July 1943 it apparently led to 'a wave of people asking for houses' at their local council offices.[12]

Nevertheless there were immediate problems and the government was literally inundated with enquiries and requests for clarification from local authority Town Clerks. One from the County Borough of Croydon, for example, pointed out that the most urgent need in their borough was for accommodation at low rents. At the same time the empty properties that were available to them were in districts where the rents would normally be high. The rents should, if requisition were to have any effect on the problem, be fixed with regard to the income of the family to be rehoused. Further – and this must have been a widespread concern – the war had left the council without the numbers of staff needed for the administrative work needed for requisitioning. The council asked for confirmation that if it subsidised the rents in requisitioned properties and took on the additional staff required would the Ministry reimburse them? In a borough like Croydon, which was experiencing a significant influx of people from the blitzed working-class areas of London, additional resources would have been a major issue. However in this as in many other instances the Ministry seems unwilling to become involved in specific local matters.[13]

   Many local authorities were aware of the practical difficulties surrounding the new policy. In Hull for example the circular was greeted with caution. The city had been severely damaged by aerial bombardment throughout the war and had a lot of experience in using the original emergency powers to requisition accommodation for bombed-out families. The local authority was aware that the supply of empty houses was far less than what would be required to meet the needs of people inadequately housed, and the properties likely to be identified would need a great deal of work before they could be occupied. It doubted that the labour and materials would be available. The fact that requisitioned properties would eventually revert back to their original owners would deter some councils from investing such scarce resources in adapting them. There was also the issue of preferences. Again in Hull it was reported that even people in desperate circumstances would not return to certain areas, and there was an almost ingrained resistance to the prospect of living in a flat rather than a house.[14]

The Communist Party identified that if requisitioning was going to have an impact on the housing crisis then the key issue was going to be rent. Just as authorities like the Borough of Croydon were in fact pointing out, if economic rents were to be charged when working-class families were offered a move to middle-class areas it was likely that they would not be affordable. During the following month the Executive Committee of the Party pressed the Ministry of Health on four issues: that requisitioning empty property to meet housing needs should be a duty for local authorities, not simply a power; that the time limit for owners to let houses to avoid requisitioning be limited to three weeks. Also, that the rents charged for requisitioned properties 'to be defined on working-class standards' and that Regional Officers of the Ministry of Health should have the duty to transfer families from one borough to another within their span of control where this was desirable. It is easy to see why the Party took up the issue of requisitioning with such enthusiasm. It was a good example of a political campaign appropriate to its changed attitude to the war.

In 1941 the Nazis had attacked the Soviet Union and thus brought that country into the war on the Allied side. The primary task of the Communist Parties around the world had always been to defend the Soviet Union and thus the former 'imperialist war' was now to be characterised as a 'people's war' against fascism. In Britain the Party argued for the subordination of short-term working-class demands to the needs of the war against the Nazis. Thus, for example, they opposed strike action to redress grievances. At the same time they called for the exposure of inefficiencies, poor management and 'inequalities of sacrifice' in society as bad for the war effort; their critical support for the war-time coalition government was accompanied by calls for the planned and socially just use of resources. Therefore it campaigned for the full use of requisitioning powers by all local authorities.[15] Apart from being of potential assistance in dealing with some of the worst excesses of the housing shortage, it was an opportunity to challenge the government to 'remove the growing conviction that the Ministry of Health is more concerned with protecting property interests than in the needs of the people'. The Party could also charge that local authorities were complaining about the restrictions on their powers as 'a pretext for inactivity'.

At the very end of the war an outburst of direct action prompted the government to revise its policy on requisitioning in what appeared to be more progressive directions.

The Brighton 'Vigilantes'

During the summer of 1945 a significant squatting movement emerged in Brighton. Ex-servicemen were returning to the area to find an acute housing shortage with all the consequent overcrowding, enforced separation of families and punitive rents. A core of them formed an informal and clandestine action group called the Brighton Vigilantes, who included those who had been involved in the struggles of unemployed ex-servicemen after the First World War. They identified suitable empty houses, moved families into them under cover of darkness, and then arranged for services to be supplied and rents to be paid. They eventually occupied about sixty houses in the Brighton area in this way and attracted considerable local sympathy. As the Communist press pointed out, however, the Vigilantes were not able to repair houses whereas under official requisitioning Brighton Council could. It claimed that if the council used its powers properly the Vigilantes' action would be unnecessary; the success of their movement would be judged by how much pressure they could bring to bear on local and national government. At the time of the People's Convention the Party would probably have offered the Vigilantes unequivocal support. This was exactly the type of initiative it had called for, and in the case of the London shelter campaign had itself carried out. In the context of the new approach to the war, though, their attitude was clearly more nuanced: they were asking could this action change national policy?

The Brighton events were reported at the time by Colin Ward in the anarchist paper *War Commentary*. This has led both Andrew Friend and Charlie Johnstone to assume that anarchists were involved in organising these squats. In fact the key figure, Harry Cowley, was a picaresque local community politician and 'fixer' whose politics resist any clear label. Cowley claimed never to have belonged to a political party but nonetheless he was a veteran of several political campaigns. Besides those of the unemployed ex-servicemen after the First World War he had also been an organiser of protests against meetings of the British Union of Fascists in Brighton during the 1930s, as well as the squatting there at that time.[16]

The issues were not confined to Brighton of course; they were national ones. During that July of 1945 the annual conference of the Association of Municipal Corporations in England vented its frustration. Delegates were told that its officers 'had exchanged strong words' with the government over housing and had warned that 'widespread suffering, disappointment and unrest' would arise in the coming years. Housing must be treated as 'a serious national emergency' or the 'direct action seen recently would become widespread in a dangerous and unsettling way'. The Town Clerk of Sheffield claimed that the government had deliberately misled servicemen by sending out housing application forms to them. The troops had thus assumed that houses would be available when in reality they were not.

The Brighton group had always called for council and government action on the issue of requisitioning. During that summer of 1945 they organised a rally in London's Hyde Park which attracted an audience of 2,000. The Vigilantes' Committee called on other towns to follow their example. After a march and rally in the town and an address by Cowley, Brighton Council agreed a resolution to the Ministry of Health stating that the existing powers to requisition empty properties were inadequate – due to 'inertia by the Government' – and demanding immediate steps to empower councils to requisition any empty properties they deem necessary 'in order to alleviate the distress at present prevailing'. They wanted the power to take over properties immediately. In a clear reference to the actions of the 'Vigilantes', the resolution claimed that this enhanced power was also needed to 'obviate the necessity of the application of unconstitutional methods'. A cross-party council deputation was agreed to press this case with the Minister of Health.[17]

By the end of that month the Ministry had announced changes that it claimed would strengthen the power of local authorities in England, Wales and Scotland to requisition empty properties for housing. They could, until the end of the year, requisition all empty but habitable housing for occupation by 'persons inadequately housed' and give the owners fourteen days' notice to explain their intentions for the occupation of the property. Requisitioning for housing would take place unless there was clear evidence that the owner intended to let, sell or occupy the property, and if owners delayed the Ministry would decide if there was a case for requisitioning. Only in those circumstances would councils have to refer to regional officers of the Ministry of Health, the Welsh Health Board or the Scottish Office; otherwise they were free to act on their own initiative. This was one of the last acts of the wartime coalition government before the general election of 1945.

In later years former Vigilantes claimed that it was their campaign that brought this change of legislation about. They had certainly had an effect on the Association of Municipal Corporations, as we have seen. Cabinet papers too suggest that this claim is correct. Prime Minister Churchill's view of the Brighton campaign was that 'we can't tolerate this' and that the Home Office 'should check this lawless action ... by force'. The eventual decision was that as this was a civil matter in England only action through the county courts would be appropriate. In the meantime local authorities would be 'told to use their powers of requisitioning'. Press comment at the time associated the new ministerial circular with the Vigilantes; according to *The Times*, for example, the new policy 'destroyed any possible justification for the actions of the Vigilantes':

> This movement, which began with good intentions, is already attracting the support of doubtful persons and can easily degenerate into a new type of private brigandage unless stopped forthwith.

Another newspaper, in this case more sympathetic to the human stories that lay behind the actions, commented that 'these major concessions' had been 'forced by dissatisfaction with government policy'.[18]

Activists in different parts of the country had begun to respond to delays in derequisitioning property once used by the military authorities. In Edinburgh the District Communist Party moved some families from overcrowded conditions into a large house in Polwarth that had been formerly been a base for the Home Guard. This particular squat proved premature however because the military still needed the property; the squatting family and the Communists were evicted by the police, although the family were accommodated in another derequisitioned property surplus to the military. The Ministerial circular did fall short of the powers requested by the resolution and lobby from Brighton Council. They had wanted to avoid giving the owners enough time to avoid requisitioning once notice had been given. Nevertheless the council voted unanimously to agree with the circular, a decision which incensed the Vigilante leadership; they accused the council of a cowardly backing down to the Ministry. Harry Cowley and a colleague had to be ejected from the council meeting by the police for their persistent heckling. In protest at the response of the authority two Vigilante activists stood as Independents in the local elections in Brighton in November 1945 but lost to Labour. The same Cabinet discussion that advocated requisitioning had noted that the publicity the Vigilantes were attracting would 'cause imitation'. This indeed seemed likely; but although the press tended to equate squatting actions at this time with the Vigilantes, groups such as the Edinburgh Communist Party had already been active over squatting themselves. Churchill's parting shot had been 'see that the police do stop this sort of thing' and in Brighton the police obtained injunctions on Cowley and the other Vigilante leaders to prevent them from organising further squats. The direct action this group promoted seems to have evaporated by the autumn of 1945 as the authorities developed a smooth organisation of civil court action to restrain squatters from occupying properties.[19]

Many council housing departments had themselves found the pace of derequisitioning from the military to be far too slow. In Surrey the Mayor of New Malden Council welcomed the new arrangement:

We don't want Vigilantes here. We want to do the job in a proper manner. Before D Day representatives of the invasion chiefs came to the district and requisitioned old houses. We have been trying to get them back ever since to house the homeless but instead of allowing us to take over the properties they have been handed back to their owners … we have now instructed our rehousing officer to requisition the whole of them under the new Ministry of Health order.[20]

The rejection of Vigilantism here, and the reference to 'doing the job in a proper manner' suggests that local authority leaders wanted not just to proceed within the law but to ensure that they were in charge of selecting who should be rehoused and in what order. This contention between the actions of squatters and control by local government was to surface the following year on a much larger scale.

Requisitioning extended

The circular was enthusiastically received by the national press – *The Times* for example believed that 'it will no longer be possible to charge the government with excessive leniency towards property owners, or for local authorities to excuse inaction with a plea that their powers are insufficient'. Nevertheless those charged with implementing the new powers were quick to reign in any expectations about rapid improvements. In Hull the realism that had greeted the 1943 circular did not change. The Chief Clerk stated that the existing procedures that the city used to requisition accommodation for bombed-out families were quicker than those being introduced, and like many authorities Hull believed they would prove cumbersome and cause delays. The fourteen days granted to property owners to state their intentions was more than enough for them to announce their own sale or letting arrangements. Elsewhere in Yorkshire the new powers were not expected to make a great deal of difference. Property empty for a long period, or damaged, would need to be renovated and in Leeds the Housing

Director pointed out that 'neither labour nor materials are available to make the scheme effective on a big scale, even if a greater number of houses are requisitioned than seems likely'. In Bradford the Chief Clerk believed that few suitable empty properties were available to it and that 'when everything is done that can be done under the new powers the housing position will still remain acute'.[21]

Despite these reservations there were instances of local authorities using their powers to protect tenants in changing circumstances. When the rent control legislation finally became applicable to the letting of furnished rooms there were cases in Aberdeen and Glasgow where tenants were served eviction notices after they had appealed to the rent tribunal. The Secretary of State approved the requisitioning of the properties to protect the tenants. This was particularly important because around the country councils believed that many people paying excessive rents would not lodge complaints about them because they feared eviction as a result. As the war came to an end the owners of a large block of flats in Bournemouth issued notices to quit to their tenants, wishing to replace them with summer visitors who would be charged higher rents. Again, the local authority responded by obtaining permission to requisition the property and leave the tenants in place.[22]

This sort of problem was not uncommon in British seaside towns. Owners had left their properties following invasion or air raid scares, and rented them out. Seaside hoteliers and owners of holiday homes had seen their market collapse during the war and had rented them to war workers. Now, with the end of hostilities, they wanted their old lucrative market back again. In Largs on Scotland's west coast the Town Council sent a delegation to the Department of Health for Scotland over the issue in December 1945. The council pointed out that Glasgow people, including ex-servicemen, were living in what were normally holiday lets in the town. When the holiday season started they would face eviction because the owners could make more from renting to visitors. Although Largs was, they said, 'economically dependent' on visitors it was wrong that people should be made homeless because landlords could make more profit by renting to people who after all had homes. They warned that evictions would make 'distressing scenes'. The Department wrote to the Town Clerk inviting the council to apply for requisitioning powers, and these were implemented successfully.[23]

Bristol provides an example of a local authority attempting to make full use of its requisitioning powers, and the reactions it provoked from the vested interests of the local property market. In September 1945 the Corporation Housing Committee agreed to requisition all unoccupied houses put up for sale by auction, or offered for sale by auction or private treaty with vacant possession. Thus was intended to help to alleviate conditions for the 11,000 families in the city in need of homes. The reactions from local auctioneers and solicitors specialising in house sales included terms like 'shocking', 'disgusting', 'a death blow to small auctioneers' and 'interference with the liberty of the individual'. The move attracted a great deal of publicity and interest from other local authorities; auctioneers reported that the threat of requisitioning was deterring landlords intending to buy in order to let. The Bristol Chamber of Commerce campaigned against the action for several months with public meetings and formally complained to the Ministry of Health on several occasions. The Ministry however, always unwilling to become involved with local details so long as powers were not being exceeded, did not oppose the corporation. By the middle of 1946 around 1,500 families were being housed in requisitioned properties in Bristol.[24]

Nevertheless when it came to Conservative-controlled authorities there were suspicions about how far they were taking these powers seriously. *Reynolds News*, a paper associated with the Co-operative movement, gave voice to the 'deep suspicion that while requisitioning notices are being put up to allay public criticism, a go-slow policy is being followed in order to prevent good homes being taken over. Owners of homes in the £4,000 – £5,000 range fear their use by the homeless will reduce their value.' The London District Communist Party claimed that only a few boroughs there had a large number of empty houses and flats, but when it came to requisitioning councils 'were making every conceivable excuse for not doing so'. The Labour groups on these three or four authorities did not accept 'the official excuse' that the empty properties would need too much to be spent on them to make them reasonably habitable. In response to a parliamentary question about this the Ministry of Health reported that out of 5,750 empty properties identified in the London boroughs of Westminster, Hampstead and Chelsea only 192 had been requisitioned for housing.[25]

However some councils could argue that the costs, and the availability of labour, that could be involved were a property to be requisitioned and refurbished could not be justified, bearing in mind that it would eventually be returned to private ownership.

Obstacles and opposition

The local authorities who had low expectations of the effects of the circular were proved to be correct. Also proved to be correct was the left press, who had predicted, before the new powers were announced, 'the tenacity that can be expected from property owners when their interests are threatened'. At the end of 1945 it identified Broadstairs on the Kent coast as having 300 homes suitable for rent to working-class families. The problem was that the owners preferred to take advantage of the market and put them up for sale at high prices. The Labour group on the council complained that the authority, far from using its requisitioning powers, was allowing the derequisitioning of properties which were then put up for sale. This was not an isolated example, and nor was it a grievance confined to the left press. Several English councils complained to the Ministry of Health about how the obligation not to requisition, if the owner notified the intention to occupy within a fortnight, was working in practice. There were cases of owners, given notice of requisition, personally occupying the property within a fortnight and then selling or letting at a profit when derequisitioning was automatically conferred. The shortage of property created a sellers' or landlords' market and high prices could be expected and arranged quickly if requisitioning was likely. Others simply announced an intention to let and then rented to family members or tenants they had chosen themselves. In Bristol, where the local authority had tried to make full use of its powers, it was reported that sellers were advertising houses as 'in part possession now, full possession later', thus ensuring that the property would evade requisitioning by never being unoccupied. The Ministry had no suggestions to make and believed it should 'let local authorities take whatever course they think will work'.[26]

The owners of requisitioned properties in some areas at least were able to put forward their own suggestions for tenants. This meant that the council did not have complete control over who was to be rehoused, even if their list of applicants was prioritised in terms of need. At Withnersea on the Yorkshire coast senior councillors met in private to consider applicants for tenancies in such a property, the names coming from their own list of applicants and some suggested by the owner. In the meantime 'anxious women waited for a considerable time outside the municipal buildings' to hear who the fortunate applicants were to be. The National Federation of Property Owners – and its equivalent the National Federation of Property Owners and Factors of Scotland – had defended their members' interests against the potential threat of requisition from the beginning. Requisitioning after the war was challenged in the courts too. At the end of 1947 the Court of Appeal in London gave a judgement against Blackpool Council over a requisitioning procedure following an action by the property owner.[27]

A significant legal case took place in Glasgow. Early in 1946 the Corporation requisitioned an empty private school and proposed to use it for people 'inadequately housed'. The company which owned the school obtained an interdict from the Court of Sessions to prevent this, arguing that rather than a housing issue the proposal was 'part of a political campaign to suppress fee-paying schools'. Secretary of State for Scotland George Buchanan introduced a new requisitioning system following the Court of Sessions interdict. Requisitioning proposals were now to be sent to the Secretary of State for a decision and the local authorities in Scotland would be acting as his agent. Councillors in Edinburgh described this as a reversion to the system that had been operating previously and unless it was a temporary measure they believed it 'it would just create a natural bottleneck'. In fact Buchanan effectively suspended requisitioning in Scotland until the appeal against this ruling had been heard. The Corporation's appeal was upheld the following year, but the Court commented that the case 'illustrated the dangers which attended the application of emergency powers to purposes for which they were not originally intended'.

Therefore it is unsurprising that a few years later the opinion of the Clerk to Glasgow Corporation about requisitioning was that 'the experienced owner or factor found little difficulty in evading the provision of the regulations'. Many of his colleagues across Britain would have agreed.[28]

Besides the 'experienced owners or factors' using the regulations to their advantage there was the matter of just how far Ministry officials were prepared to support requisitioning as a measure to improve housing. Having reviewed the issues raised on the subject at a Principal Housing Officers' meeting in March 1946 the response was:

> It was not thought, however, that we could give local authorities complete discretion over whether or not to release from requisitioning, because the chances are that they would give preference to people of their own list of applicants for accommodation as against the owner or the middle class or people from other areas to whom the owner might wish to let.

This suggests that the Ministry when pressed was likely to side with the property owners rather than the local authorities with 'their own lists of applicants'.[29]

In any event the progress of requisitioning after the circulars of 1943 and 1945 was slow as well as fraught. In Edinburgh for example the City Corporation was told by officers that storage space was not available for furniture and that therefore the large, furnished properties that had been standing empty for years could not be taken over. At the same time senior officers drew attention to the number of large houses that were being converted into flats by private developers. This meant that 'they were being put to good use from a housing point of view' and the practice 'should be encouraged to continue to the largest possible extent'. The Corporation was challenged on its use of requisitioning powers. In September 1945 a local trades council deputation told it that 'houses were standing empty all over the city' and where people owned more than one house and there was insufficient occupation the local authority should take them over. Three months later local Labour MPs compared the Conservative-dominated Corporation unfavourably with Glasgow, where 575 houses had been requisitioned for letting out in contrast to the mere 55 in Edinburgh. They maintained that this was because the Corporation was allowing derequisitioned properties, not required for occupation by the owners, to be sold to speculative builders who then converted them into flats for sale. This was to the benefit of the affluent and not those who had been on the housing waiting list for years; further, it was allowing those builders to become major employers of skilled labour to the detriment of the Corporation's own housing schemes.[30]

Entering peacetime

The end of hostilities in Europe and with Japan brought together a range of factors to create an unprecedented demand for housing in every part of Britain. One of the new Gallup opinion poll surveys found that in the autumn of 1945 one third of all Britons were looking for somewhere to live. People who had moved to a different area for war work might well decide to stay there, particularly in areas such as Oxford or the Midlands where the car industries offered better wages and more secure jobs than were available in the older industrial centres. This was especially the case for those who had married or otherwise settled whilst working. Private landladies, that is, those who did not normally make a living from renting property but let out rooms in their own houses for the duration of the war, often did not want children in their houses. Indeed, councillors in some areas claimed that it was impossible for families with children to find rented accommodation. The issue of wives being evicted from these sorts of lodgings because they were expecting a baby was raised in the House of Commons before the end of the war.[31]

Where rooms had been let because a family member had left them for the forces, tenants had to move when that person was demobilised and returned home. People who had rented out part of their houses for the duration, perhaps to a bombed-out family or to someone migrating or directed to war-work, wanted their houses all to themselves again once the war was over. The historian James Hinton quotes a particularly poignant example of what could happen:

When my husband went overseas ... I came and stayed with my mother ... I kept going up to Wembley Town Hall and asked what I should do when my husband came home. I told them he could not make do with a bed on the landing. When he came home in March we had a bed in a surface shelter, but three weeks ago it was demolished. We then went to a warden's post ... We were turned out of there and Wembley Council suggested we should go to a rest centre, but eventually they found there was no room ...[32]

Inevitably then squatting continued. At the end of 1945 twenty families in Broughty Ferry near Dundee occupied condemned tenements that had been empty for three or four years. There were no gas and electricity supplies; they made do with candles and paraffin, and the local Communist Party campaigned against the actions of the Sheriff's Court in fining them for trespass. The council agreed to examine such properties for potential requisitioning, rehabilitation and re-letting, although it also warned that any further squatters would not have the protection of the local authority.[33]

Individual squatting families – as distinct from those who were part of a larger organised group – seem to have fared worse, evicted even if they offered to pay rent for the properties they had occupied. Similarly where a serviceman's wife was struggling to meet the rent commitments because of the drop in the family income, eviction could happen even if, as took place in Birmingham, there was a local campaign in her support. Once again Communist branches in London and elsewhere gave practical support on occasion by finding accommodation for evicted families as well as organising deputations of protest to the council about their position. Others helped evicted families to squat in empty council properties and campaigned for the local authority to find them requisitioned accommodation.[34]

Issues

There were examples of squatting being successful – in the sense that evictions did not take place unless alternative accommodation had been found – during and immediately after the war. In such cases the squatting had either been of a large group of families in a single building, or a number of families spread over an area but co-ordinated by the same activists. They had also, crucially, been associated with a campaign and with wide support from the local community, from the labour movement or from other activists who would engage with elected local government on their behalf. Where squatters had been individual families but without such support then an eviction seems to have been much more likely.

Another issue that had emerged was the requisitioning of empty properties for those 'inadequately housed'. The administrative history of this measure should not obscure the fact that its introduction, and revision, was the result of campaigning pressure. The Brighton Vigilantes and less well-known actions elsewhere motivated the wartime government to allow some limited and temporary appropriation of unoccupied private property for the benefit of the homeless. Nevertheless, the wartime coalition government had shown a reluctance to seriously challenge powerful vested interests such as the organised property owners or the manufacturers of prefabricated houses. It remained to be seen how the new Labour government with its unequivocal mandate and commitment to reform would be prepared to do so. The problems were serious and the expectations were high. Alongside the national housing shortage and the legacy of overcrowded and inadequate housing came the accelerating level of need which the war produced.

A.E. Holman has used the term 'potential households' to refer to home-seekers, and in this context they included a large number of people who had married during or immediately after the war when one or both partners had been demobilised from the armed forces. There were also those who had married at the beginning of the war and who were now reunited. In all such cases newly-married couples and those with young children were looking to set up their own homes instead of sharing accommodation with parents, in-laws or other couples, or indeed instead of living apart. Holman estimates that whereas there were half a million more potential households than houses at the start of the war there were over two million when the hostilities ceased. As one councillor in Hull had put it two years before the end of the war, 'What it's going to be like when demobilisation starts I don't know. It will be a nightmare.'[35]

NOTES

1   Figures quoted in Alan Allport, *Demobbed: Coming Home After the Second World War* (New Haven: Yale University Press, 2009, p. 74), and Andrew Marr, *A History of Modern Britain* (London, Fontana, 2007, p. 73). David McGrory, *Coventry's Blitz* (Stroud, Amberley Publishing, 2015); *Daily Worker*, 12 July 1945.

2   Hansard, HC Debates, 1 September 1939, vol. 351 cc180-88; *Daily Worker*, 27 March, 29 May and 18 April 1940.

3   See the detailed study by Kevin Morgan, *Against Fascism and War: Ruptures and Continuities in British Communist Politics 1935-41* (Manchester, Manchester University Press, 1989, pp. 236-242). Relevant too are John Attfield and Stephen Williams (Eds), *1939: The Communist Party and the War* (London, Lawrence and Wishart, 1984) and Noreen Branson, *History of the Communist*

Party of Great Britain 1927-1941 (London, Lawrence and Wishart, 1985).

4   Bob Saunders, 'The Glasgow Squatters 1946', *Scottish Marxist*, no.7 (October 1973, p. 25).

5   *Aberdeen Weekly Journal*, 18 January 1940; *Motherwell Times*, 2 February, 29 March 1940; *Scotsman* 30 June 1941; 13 April 1944.

6   *Scotsman*, 19 January 1944.

7   *Scotsman*, 19 January and 13 April 1944; *Daily Worker*, 10 and 17 January, 20 May 1944; HC Debates 9 November 1944 vol 404 cc1531-2; *Daily Record*, 19 November 1944.

8   Kevin Marsh and Robert Griffiths, *Granite and Honey: the Story of Phil Piratin, Communist MP* (London, Manifesto Press, 2012, pp. 48-52). The authors point out that through their shelter campaign the Communist Party had probably saved a large number of lives but they are rarely given credit for this by historians.

9   HC Debates, 8 October 1942 vol.383 cc 158-9; *Daily Worker*, 28 March 1945.

10 *Scotsman*, 4 September and 24 December 1943; Richard Croucher: *Engineers at War 1939-1945* (London, Merlin Press, 1982, pp. 328-9).

11 HC Debates, June 8 1943 vol.390 cc 615-616.

12 *Scotsman*, 6 March 1942; NA: T227/816: Emergency Housing: Policy and Requisitioning 1942-1951: Ministry of Health to Local Authorities and Secretary of State for Scotland, 4 August 1943; NRS: DD.6/167: Requisitioning and Families Inadequately Housed. This last source quotes a Memorandum to the War Cabinet by the Ministry of Health 14 July 1943, acknowledging that the requisitioning policy was introduced as a response to lobbying around the country.

13 NA: HLG7/585: Requisitioning for Families Inadequately Housed 1943-1949, Circular 2845: Chief Clerk of the County Borough of Croydon to the Ministry of Health Regional Office 16 August 1943.

14 *Hull Daily Mail*, 9 August, 6 October 1943.

15 *Daily Worker*, 10 August and 28 October 1943; Kevin Morgan, *Against Fascism and War: Ruptures and Continuities in British Communist Politics 1935-41* and Noreen Branson, *History of the Communist Party of Great Britain 1927-1941*.

16 Colin Ward in *War Commentary*, 28 July 1945. Andrew Friend, 'The Post-War Squatters' in Nick Wates and Christian Wolmar (Eds), *Squatting: The Real Story* (London, Bay Leaf Publishing, 1980 p. 110) and Charlie Johnstone, 'Housing and Class Struggles in Post-War Glasgow' in Michael Lavalette and Gerry Mooney (Eds), *Class Struggle and Social Welfare* (London, Routledge, 2000 p. 142) are examples of the assumption that the Brighton Vigilantes were anarchists. An account of Cowley and his activities is in Jackie Blackwell (Ed.): *Who Was Harry Cowley?* (Brighton and Hove, QueenSpark Publishers, 2006). The CP view of the Brighton campaign is in the *Daily Worker*, 10 July 1945. When the British Union of Fascists attempted to re-organise in London after the war it formed a front called the 'Vigilantes Action League' to propagandise around housing grievances. Communists disrupted the meetings and the initiative died (NA: CAB/128/5: Cabinet Minutes, 14 March 1946). Colin Ward in *Housing: An Anarchist Perspective* (London, Freedom Press, 1976, p. 22) claims that the CP 'denounced' the Vigilantes; he must have confused the

Brighton group with the fascists.

17   *Times*, 13 and 14 July 1945; *Daily Worker*, 16 and 19 July 1945.

18   NA: CAB/195/3/46: Cabinet Secretary's Notebook, 6 July 1945; *Times*, 21 July 1945; *News Chronicle*, 24 July 1945.

19   *Scotsman*, 1 August 1945; *Times*, 8 September and 3 November 1945; NA: CAB/195/3/46: Cabinet Secretary's Notebook, 6 July 1945; *Scotsman*, 1 August 1945; Jackie Blackwell (Ed.), *Who Was Harry Cowley?* p. 34.

20   *Times*, 23 July 1945.

21   *Times*, 23 July 1945; *Hull Daily Mail*, 13, 25 July and 25 September 1945; *Yorkshire Post and Leeds Intelligencer*, 10 August and 27 June 1945.

22   HC Debates, 22 June 1944, vol 401 cc 56-59; *Bedfordshire Times and Independent*, 31 August 1945; *Daily Worker*, 7 April 1945.

23   NRS: DD.6/167: Requisitioning and Families Inadequately Housed; *Scotsman*, 16 February 1946.

24   *Western Daily Press*, 18, 19 and 20 September 1945, 4 October 1945 and 28 May 1946.

25   *Reynolds News* quoted in Andrew Friend, 'The Post-War Squatters' in Nick Wates and Christian Wolmar (Eds), *Squatting: The Real Story* (1980, p. 110); *Daily Worker*, 24 July 1945; NA: HLG7/585: Requisitioning for Families Inadequately Housed 1943-1949: Requisitioning of Premises under Circular 2845.

26   *Daily Worker*, 11 July and 1 December 1945; *Western Daily Press*, 21 September 1945; NA: HLG/101/539: Requisitioning of Unoccupied Houses 1946-1951: Proposals and Minutes 7 March 1946.

27   *Hull Daily Mail*, 25 August 1945; NRS: DD.6/167: Requisitioning and Families Inadequately Housed.

28   *Scotsman*, 22 May 1946; *Edinburgh Evening News*, 4 June 1946; *Scotsman*, 5 July 1947; NRS: DD.6/167: Requisitioning and Families Inadequately Housed: briefing paper for the Secretary of State for Scotland (Sir Hector McNeil) 6 June 1951.

29   NA: HLG/101/539: Requisitioning of Unoccupied Houses 1946-1951: Proposals and Minutes 7 March 1946.

30   *Scotsman*, 4 July, 14 September and 10 December 1945.

31   Gallup poll quoted by Alan Allport, *Demobbed: Coming Home After the Second World War*, p. 75. Allport also discusses the issues of housing the war's migrant workers and profiteering in the private rented sector. Recollections about how this affected one area can be found at OXOHA: LT900: BBC Radio Oxford, *Squatters' Delight* (1994). Examples of the problems of families with children trying to rent are in the *Derby Daily Chronicle*, 28 February 1944 and HC Debates, 20 October 1944, vol 403 cc 2793-800.

32   *Hendon and Finchley Times*, 23 August 1946, quoted in James Hinton, 'Self-Help and Socialism: The Squatters' Movement of 1946', *History Workshop*, Issue 25 (Spring 1988, p. 103).

33   *Daily Worker*, 11 December 1945; *Dundee Courier*, 25 January 1946.

34   *Dundee Courier*, 28 December 1945; *Daily Worker*, 10, 20 and 25 July 1946.

35   A. E. Holmans, *Housing Policy in Britain: a History* (London, Croom Helm, 1987, p. 93); *Hull Daily Mail*, 6 October 1943.

Chapter Four

'REFUGEES FROM OVERCROWDING':
THE SQUATTING MOVEMENT BEGINS

Bevan and the housing programme

The Labour government of 1945 was the third to be elected in the twentieth century but the first to hold a commanding majority. Their parliamentary programme included the nationalisation of the mining, railway and steel industries, some redistributive taxation, free education up to university level, and a National Health Service with no charge to the patient at time of use because it was to be funded through taxation. Further, the nineteenth century Poor Law was to be replaced by a national insurance scheme for every working adult that would guarantee the same level of unemployment benefit and state pension for all. In addition allowances for some children would be available for families and, thanks to the campaign by the independent feminist MP Eleanor Rathbone, they would be paid to the mother.

Prime Minister Attlee's government also made council housing the central theme of its housing policy. As was the case with the selective nationalisation of industry, this decision was based on pragmatism rather than ideology. It was clear that the private sector, the market, had failed to deliver good and affordable housing for much of the population during the inter-war years. It was just not plausible that the speculative building of houses for sale was going to meet the needs of the nation in 1945. Aneurin Bevan was appointed Minister for Health and as such had responsibility for the key social programmes of the new government: the National Health Service, National Insurance, and a council house building programme to meet the national housing crisis.

As a member of Tredegar Urban District Council in the 1920s Bevan had opposed building greater numbers of council houses if that would mean sacrificing quality for the sake of volume. His vision was still for houses for working people that were larger and with better amenities than had ever been provided before. He wanted permanent houses of excellent quality and not temporary measures such as the pre-fabs. The priority too would be houses built by local authorities to accommodate the lower income groups first and therefore at this stage only one in five of the building licences the Ministry granted would be for building private houses for sale. Unlike in the pre-war period the balance of funding responsibility was to lie with central government and thus Bevan aimed to ensure that, again unlike in the pre-war period, the lower-paid would not be priced out of good rented accommodation.

Serious problems appeared immediately. Skilled building workers were to a large extent awaiting demobilisation from the forces, at home or overseas, or they were still employed in war-related industries. All the materials needed for house building were in very short supply and timber had to be imported. Again, production was still geared to war industries and not the building trade and this would take time to resolve. There were also problems around co-ordinating the different ministries with a stake in the issues: the Treasury controlled finance, the Ministry of Labour still had some residual power to direct manpower, the Board of Trade was involved with currency reserves to pay for imported materials, and the Ministry of Works controlled the building trade. In addition, the Ministry of Town and Country Planning could refuse sites for housing in favour of industrial development, and Scotland of course was administered separately. In addition, Bevan deliberately refused to make use of planning targets and so it was impossible to measure progress. Although issues of administration and shortages were eventually resolved when it came to building there was no prospect of rapid progress.[1]

A political difficulty was also waiting in the wings. Whereas Stafford Cripps and Ellen Wilkinson, two other key figures of the Labour left of the 1930s, had been members of the wartime government Bevan had stayed, or been kept, on the backbenches. Again whereas both those two had been incorporated into the government machine and Ellen Wilkinson had opposed dissident popular movements during the war, Bevan had been a supporter of some. He had defended the *Daily Worker* in parliament on free speech grounds when it was banned in 1940, and defended workers who agitated for the redress of legitimate grievances. Later he had supported the Communist campaign for a Second Front in Europe to relieve pressure on the Soviet Union. According to his biographer Michael Foot Bevan had emerged as the foremost parliamentary critic of Chamberlain, Churchill and the wartime coalition. He had helped to ensure that parliament remained a forum for critical debate about the conduct of the war and to press for policies to further social justice. Churchill had dubbed him 'the snarler in chief'. In housing the levels of need were at crisis point, public expectations were high and the practical difficulties were numerous. The right wing had scores to settle besides their anger at how the government seemed to be ignoring the private housing market. It is known that the Conservatives relished the possibility of the socialist rebel failing in a position of responsibility as a Minister.[2]

Spare capacity?

The end of hostilities in 1945 had left a large number of facilities that had been used for the war effort vacant and apparently surplus to requirements. As we have seen in a previous chapter these included the properties, often large houses, that had been requisitioned by the services or a government department and were now unused. A common sight outside major urban conurbations too were complete army, naval or RAF camps lying empty, or service camps in which only a relatively small area was still in use. Young men nicknamed 'Bevin Boys' after the war-time Minister of Labour Ernest Bevin had been conscripted into coal mining rather than the forces during the war, and the hostels that had accommodated them were now often deserted. Empty too were the huts that had once housed the personnel for anti-aircraft and radar installations, coastal batteries, and the Auxiliary Fire Service.

It was to emerge during the summer and autumn of 1946 that a very large number of local government bodies – the full range, in fact, from a small Rural District Council in Sussex to a major authority like Edinburgh City Corporation – had been approaching the Ministry of War about the disused installations in their area. They wanted to discuss the use of the better-appointed huts as temporary accommodation for the families on their waiting lists, but apparently not one council had had a positive response. Edinburgh, for example, which wanted to take over an empty camp 'with ready-made accommodation for 200 families' had spent three months in negotiation with the Scottish Office and government departments in London. Finally it was told that the camp 'may be needed' for troops in transit or for building trade trainees. Sunderland Council had been told that one of its local camps would be needed for agricultural trainees. Both facilities were still vacant more than a year after the soldiers had left. Other councils such as Neath in Wales, Sheffield, and Blyth in Northumberland were to point out later that their approaches to government departments about this issue had not received any reply from them at all. Bevan himself was asked in the House of Commons about this matter very early in his tenure of office. He was not sympathetic and claimed the resources used on converting Nissen huts would be better used on the regular housing programme. His reaction is unsurprising given his commitment to good quality and permanent housing as the national priority; perhaps, too, it signalled an unwillingness to even consider using other emergency measures. In Northern Ireland in contrast the administration at Stormont approached local authorities about identifying suitable camps for housing in November 1945.[3]

There were reasons to maintain a number of unused camps under military control. Prisoners of war had still to be accommodated, along with Polish troops and rehabilitating British former prisoners of war, both awaiting resettlement into civilian life. Less than half of the 240,000 Polish service personnel in Britain chose to return home to face the exigencies of life under Soviet control. Once it had accepted that a substantial number of Polish ex-servicemen and their families would remain in Britain, the Attlee government established the Polish Resettlement Corps to provide vocational training for them before entry into British civilian life. Army camps would be needed to house them, at least in the beginning. This decision proved contentious given the housing crisis and fears about post-war unemployment, and the Communist Party – who saw these dissidents as a threat to the image of post-war socialist Poland – launched a campaign against their resettlement that did little to distance itself from more xenophobic elements. This was, in Paul Burnham's words, 'not exactly the left's finest hour' and the controversy was especially fierce in Scotland. The Communist campaign gained particular traction because the housing crisis was at its most acute there, and fears about post-war unemployment were greater, as was the influence of the CP in the labour movement.[4]

Apart from this other government departments seem to have wanted to keep camps open and in reserve for their own purposes. Agriculture believed it needed bases in rural areas for farm work trainees, and Fuel and Power wanted a reserve of accommodation for mining apprentices. Education might need somewhere to house students taking up the emergency teacher training programme. Departments looking to expand might require additional office space. A year after the end of the war most of these plans had not been realised and the government was to admit, belatedly, that it had created a problem for itself. As was noted at a Cabinet Committee meeting later in August 1946:

> There was general agreement that the greatest temptation to squatters had been the fact that the camps had been allowed to stand empty for long periods, with the result that the impression had been created that the government had no use for them.

Indeed, people all over the country who were becoming desperate for their own homes had had the sight of vacant government premises in front of them for months on end. There had also, as we have seen, been outbreaks of squatting. As regards squatting in vacant army huts the first case appears to have been near Edinburgh in December 1945, when a dozen families who had formed a 'Houseless Association' occupied empty Nissen huts. Therefore the events that erupted in the summer of 1946 should not have come as the surprise to the government that they clearly did. The two historians who have examined the squatting movement in disused army camps at this time agree that the spark was probably a cinema projectionist in Scunthorpe. Homeless since leaving the army, he had been living in the cinema with his family until he broke into an empty hut in a former army camp near the town. When he had moved in his family he gave an interview to a cinema newsreel company about what he had done and why, and the publicity that followed this interview triggered what was to become a national movement. Many thousands of homeless couples and families the length of Britain began to follow his example by moving themselves and their possessions into whatever vacant camps they could find.[5]

This chapter will focus on who was involved in the spread of squatting and why, what their objectives were and how they organised themselves; also how their actions were received by the news media and public opinion. The next chapter will examine the reactions to the movement by central government and the Labour Party, the local authorities and the armed forces. It also looks at the legal positions around the movement and what the relationship was at this stage between the squatters and political activists.

Ex-servicemen

The press reports from all over Britain at the time and those of local authority medical officers of health, the police and other observers are unanimous in their view that those occupying these empty facilities were mainly ex-servicemen and their families. In the seven occupied camps in the Bristol area for example 'to find a squatter who is not an ex-serviceman is a rarity'. Certainly those explaining their actions to reporters generally mentioned their own or their spouse's war service. It can be plausibly argued that this was not just because this group made up such a large section of the population in 1946. The ex-servicemen believed an entitlement had been conferred by their war service and the long period of separation from family that this had often involved. They were impatient with the slow pace of the change they had voted for a year earlier. As 'Homeless' wrote to a Birmingham newspaper:

All through the war we were promised this and that, but what have we come back to? To snubs if we apply for rooms, if we have children, and filling in forms and more forms. Has England really won the war?

He would have agreed with another correspondent in the northern press, 'Ex-RAF': 'The people of this country have waited patiently, too patiently, for the benefits they were promised at the last election.' There are echoes of these sentiments too in the words of one Sunderland squatter, '… it's hardly a place for heroes to live in such as we were told about when we were fighting but at least it is some sort of a home.'[6]

Paul Burnham's detailed account of the occupation of the empty facilities in the High Wycombe area makes the point that some of its leaders had served as commandos during the war and thus were used to taking risks. Certainly the large number around the country who had combat experience would have appreciated the value of decisive action in the right circumstances and this may well have had an influence. There were indeed risks involved as we shall see and the outcomes of the squats could not have been predicted in advance.

Life in service camps and Nissen huts was a familiar experience for many of the squatters, as several of them pointed out at the time. One squatter near Bristol had formerly been based in the same camp he was occupying when he had served in the Home Guard. An ex-services couple near Durham told a reporter that 'it's second nature to us to live in a hut, and we've both been in worse places'. Others too noted the irony of returning to live in the type of huts in which they had served in the forces. Therefore a move into these camps, albeit unauthorised, was not the outlandish exercise it might have been to an entirely civilian group. It was noted too of squatters near Stockton on Tees that 'their war-time experience of hutted camps has been a valuable asset in arranging a general routine'.[7]

Despite the prominent role of ex-servicemen there are several examples of women taking the initiative about squatting too. In Glasgow, as we will see, women were the prime movers in at least one camp occupation. In Watford a woman squatter told a Mass Observation reporter that 'I moved in while my husband was at sea so he'll come back to find us here'. Similarly in Blyth a woman who had taken a hut said 'I shall have to partition this myself. My husband is serving in Palestine.' Miner Bill Wilson returned from his shift at Usworth Colliery in County Durham to be told that his wife had joined the squatters, and 'claimed' a two-roomed hut at the Civilian Resettlement Unit in Washington. Another local woman who had taken the same initiative there and was anxious to confirm her claim asked: 'Tell Ted to bring a chair when he comes in from work.' In Motherwell Mrs Stephen had 'often walked past' Auchenstewart House, empty after vacation by the wartime Auxiliary Fire Service, and 'wondered what was going to be done with it' before moving some of the family possessions in while her husband was on night shift. Nottingham's first squatters included women whose husbands were soon to be demobilised from the forces and who still had no homes of their own. Women also, if sometimes by default, had a role in presenting the squatters' case to the outside world. If newspaper reporters arrived at the camps during the day when the men were at work interviews tended to take place with mothers of pre-school children because they were at home at the time.[8]

One of the squatters in an empty radar camp outside Tamworth in Staffordshire was former sergeant George Hirons, a veteran of Dunkirk and subsequent European campaigns. He explained that he, his wife and their five children had been sleeping in one room in his sister-in-law's house. A fellow ex-serviceman in the camp had been living in one room with his family of seven. Another example of what overcrowding meant in practice came from a veteran of the desert war who was part of an occupation of empty huts in a prisoner-of-war camp in Kent:

When I came out of the army I found accommodation for myself and my wife completely unobtainable, and finally managed to get one room in the town. Every night we have to move the table back against the wall to make our bed up. If we want to go out of the house we have to go through the drawing room of the other tenants who have to stand up from the table and move to one side to let us out. Naturally we want more room, more privacy, and to cause less trouble to other people.

Although this comes across as gross inconvenience there were many stories from squatters about really iniquitous levels of overcrowding. In the North East of England the first known squatters included ex-servicemen and miners with experience of family life in one room, or of having spent their first three years of marriage staying with a mother-in-law. In Berkshire early squatters included Mr and Mrs Boddy, who had been living, cooking and sleeping in one room with their two children. An ex-paratrooper in Bristol told reporters that he, his wife and two children had been among eleven people sharing three rooms. At the Patterton camp near Glasgow a squatter from Maryhill explained that she had been living in a single room with her children without heating or running water for the past four years. The Darnley camp near Glasgow was occupied by sixty families from sub-letted tenements; as one woman said of her hut, 'this is better than a miserable single room in Warwick Street with an oil lamp, for which we were paying 12s a week rent'. At Wooton Hall camp outside Peterborough a squatter explained that he, his wife and his children and been living, sleeping, eating and cooking in one room in a shared house.[9]

This was another consistent story from squatters all over the country alongside the overcrowded conditions they were enduring. Those with rooms to spare – and it seems this could include family members – were making the most of the housing shortage by charging extortionate rents. The local police reported of the squatters in huts at Tynemouth that 'the motive in most cases is to escape overcrowding frequently in expensive lodgings, e.g. man and wife and one child living in two rooms, rent 21s a week; woman and two children living in one room let by her mother at 15s a week'.

Privacy was another major issue. A number of the squatting families had been staying with in-laws, in many cases for a long period, after they had married. As Fred Armstrong, who squatted with his wife in a camp outside Oxford was to recall years later:

> ... people were desperate, and of course when the fellers came back from the war they had a choice of living with in-laws which didn't always work out; if you went to get rooms you likely couldn't afford them the prices were extortionate ...

'Living with in-laws' for newly married couples could be a particular strain, and Andrew Marr has suggested that the mother-in-law joke, a staple of radio and television comedy in Britain into the 1960s, derives from the circumstances of this period. Squatters in several locations also reported another important consideration behind their actions. 'I have never really had a home of my own', 'this man and his wife are living together for the first time in their married lives', were two such statements. Others included 'for many years, in some cases, these married couples had no place to call their own'. At Cannock in Staffordshire a squatting couple told reporters that 'we've not had a home of our own since we got married in 1938'.[10]

It almost goes without saying that although they were generally on the council waiting list they saw little prospect of a house for years to come, if at all. Many of the squatters interviewed by their local papers had stories about that, and about what they had been told about thousands being ahead of their place on the waiting list, and how the housing queue did not seem to be moving at all. As Vera Hughes in Oxford was to recall, 'we were 5,079 on the council waiting list and we thought we'd never get a place'. In London it was official that the average waiting time for a family was between seven and eight years, and even small Urban or Rural District Councils had several thousands of applicants on their lists – all observing the lethargic pace of the house building programme and the empty accommodation in their areas.[11]

Forced entry?

The occupations may have appeared to be spontaneous but they were often the product of observation, planning and discussion by local people. The miners and their families who occupied an empty hostel formerly used by 'Bevin Boys' in Consett did so after a series of 'kitchen conferences'; at Maryhill in Glasgow 'the women organised a street meeting this morning as a result of which their menfolk started looking around the district for likely prospects', which in this case were boarded-up tenements. At Cowley Marsh near Oxford, 'the possibility of moving into the camp had been under discussion among homeless families in the surrounding area for some days and when one family took the initiative others quickly followed'. A Dunkirk veteran in a camp at Burscough in Lancashire told a reporter that, 'I've been watching the place for months and since the WRENS moved out there's been no-one near. Yesterday afternoon we got together, held a council of war and fixed zero hour for 6pm.' In Cardiff prospective squatters had first toured the area and identified potential targets before they took over all the camps around the city.

Jim Tatters in County Durham recalled discussions about the empty hutments and facilities and how taking them over was discussed with workmates at Usworth Colliery:

> It was like a jungle telegraph. Wuh had a lovely grapevine and you always knew what was happening … When wuh were arl in the cage going down, arl pushed together like, you're talking to each other, that's how these things happened. 'When are wuh gannin' in like?' 'Yus'll be told.' So one night wuh invaded and took the lot! Then the civil servants that was guardin' the gates were overwhelmed. There was no violence. Wuh just crowded them out and took over. There some there, patrollin', round the place, Aa think they were a bit frightened, but they weren't in a position to stop wuh.[12]

This was one example among many of what was referred to by the Parliamentary Under-Secretary of State at the War Office of 'civilian watchkeepers being brushed aside by the squatters'. Similarly when the camps in the Cardiff area were occupied it was reported that the Ministry of Works watchmen there 'made no effort to stem the flow' of squatters. In some cases army officers condemned what they saw as forced entry and therefore criminal offences alongside trespass. In Staffordshire an army officer accused squatters there of breaking open a gate and tearing down fence wire, although those concerned claimed that the gate was open and that the wire had been broken down for some time. At Daws Hill in Buckinghamshire, however, where the mass occupation of a camp was initiated by local Communist and Labour Party activists, the vanguard cut the wires attached to the main gate to let the hut-seekers through. There seems to have been a similar situation at Norton Fitzwarren in Somerset where a local Labour Party branch chairman cut through barbed wire to allow homeless people entry to huts. Outside Glasgow at the Patterton camp 'young men from Govan and Maryhill vaulted barbed wire entanglements' to gain access to the huts. At Bebington in the Wirral camp squatters had reportedly 'surmounted formidable barbed wire entanglements' to gain entry. At Blyth in Northumberland the unauthorised occupants of ex-army huts near the beach, assisted by people in nearby houses, cut down barbed wire fences so that carts and wagons with their furniture could get through.[13]

In many places entry was straightforward for a large and determined group. At Tullichewan Camp near Balloch in Scotland the crowd 'took no heed of the naval guard on sentry duty' there and simply walked in. At West Derby near Liverpool all the 'married couples' had to do was 'race across the parade ground' to 'pick the best of 40 Nissen huts being vacated by ATS personnel'. In Sheffield a participant in just such a 'race' outside the city likened it to a 'gold rush'. Others used some guile: a Communist member of Inverness Town Council led a group of squatters through the back entrance to occupy army huts while the guards were stationed at the front gate.

Once inside the camps or installations some direct methods could be required, at least according to Jim Tatters in Washington, County Durham: 'How did Aa get that one, the hut? Aa just hoofed the door in. Of course Aa was a big strappin' young lad then so Aa just hoofed the door in.'

At Bristol however it was reported that 'some climbed in through windows; others found keys in the doors' after they walked past police and the camp warden. If this was what the squatters claimed there could well be another explanation given that at Peterborough the War Department 'had secured the doors and windows of the huts but the squatters took them off again'.[14] It seems to fair to say that a variety of means were used to gain access, and it was only to be expected that squatters would play down any suggestion of forced entry or damage when speaking to the press.

Respectability

There is clear evidence to suggest that the squatters were seeking to become mainstream council tenants and that the very term 'squatter', despite being the term used at the time and by many of those involved, may be misleading. An ex-army couple squatting at the large camp at West Derby near Liverpool were quoted as saying that 'we want to pay our way, not to live rent free. It's a home we want.' Similarly Sheffield squatters explained that 'we didn't come here to live rent free.' As soon as weekly fees were being paid to local authorities camp residents often referred to themselves as 'tenants' even if that was not their legal position with their council. This was also taken up by some local councillors who were sympathetic; at Taunton in Somerset for example one councillor believed his authority should 'take a lead' by 'obliterating the word squatter from council reports'. As the people concerned were paying rent they should be referred to as something like 'temporary residents of unused hutments.' He was told however that 'squatter' was the Ministry of Health word and was thus 'official'. At Hartley Wintney Rural District Council in Hampshire squatters' representatives were co-opted members of the council Squatters' Committee responsible for managing their huts. The Committee changed its name to the Hutments Committee because these representatives 'strongly objected' to the use of the term 'squatter' in council meetings and the press because it gave the impression that they were in the camp without authority, whereas in fact they had been recognised by the Rural District Council.[15]

Before long they took to calling their camps 'estates' with improvised street names and numbers on their doors; for example the committee secretary at the Hill Head squat in County Durham wrote to the Sanitary Inspector at Newburn Urban District Council from 'no.6 The Crescent, Hill Head Camp, Lemington Road' in September 1946. The camp at Abbots Leigh near Bristol was referred to as 'Abbots Leigh Gardens' by the residents. In a very interesting move camp occupants near Sunderland named their huts 'Liberty Villas'; as we have seen this was the very name used by squatters in virtually the same circumstances in the town after the previous world war. This suggests that the original action in the early 1920s may have entered local folklore.[16]

Respectability took other forms. The squatters shared the conventional working-class prejudice against gypsies and their keenness not to be associated with them. In Hampshire camp committees made representations to the council for action over gypsies who had set up a camp near them, and when gypsies occupied some empty huts as well the council agreed with the 'official' squatters that they should be evicted and steps taken to ensure that huts did not remain empty in the future. At the Daws camp near Wycombe it was found that gypsies had occupied a hut and were ignoring basic hygiene; therefore, in the words of a former camp committee member, 'we had a committee meeting and decided to get them out. One Sunday morning we got them out.'[17]

In the early stages squatters were keen to show how they were living to the outside world, probably an additional effort to demonstrate their respectability and ordinariness. At least one local newspaper carried a feature on cooking in an army hut; squatters at the Grangetown gun site near Sunderland planned to make their camp 'an ideal village residence', and their secretary Mrs. Birkbeck opened a hut as a show home to demonstrate to reporters what a painted, renovated hut was like. Homeliness was the key, as Joan Marriott and Vera Penman, squatters in the Oxford area remembered:

> That was our aim, to make the best of the place as we possibly could. We all vied with one another over what we could do to make it like a home. We all had front gardens and allotments. Archie and I were very proud of our chickens out the back.
>
> I had no curtains but we got some dust sheets and I dyed them and put a fringe on them, made curtains out of them. He put lovely wallpaper up even though there were those high walls and painted the kitchen area, it was lovely.

Violet Fraser spent part of her childhood in a squatted army camp at Forres in North East Scotland, and she too remembered '… Mam trying to hang wallpaper. She also started a small flower garden. Mam and Dad were both still young and optimistic and they were determined to give us a family life despite living under these conditions.'[18]

Organisation

Whether the squatters were alone, part of a group or part of a mass occupation an impromptu system seems to have been followed across the country. There was no allocation of huts as such it was first come first served, an issue that was to draw criticism later on as we shall see. Those with a hut marked their spot: this could be by chalking their name on the door, leaving a chair in the doorway, sometimes even a small object like a bar of soap. Once booked the claim was always respected, as Jim Tatters recalled:

> Not a one individual from aal them streets tried to pull a fast one on you. As soon as you saw somewhere was occupied it was like, that was the law, nobody interfered from then on. As a matter of fact they would have come and defended you.

Local newspapers were often very impressed by how the squatters, once installed, were organising themselves. The site named 'Liberty Villas' in Sunderland was described as 'a most highly organised community' and similar observations were made about other occupations: those in the camps around Bristol were said to be 'disciplining themselves very well indeed' and at Coxhoe in County Durham 'the encampment has already developed a strong community spirit'. The Nuntsfield camp near Taunton in Somerset was reported to be 'set fair to become a model community'.[19]

There were several factors at work to promote cohesive communities in these camps. The families involved had much in common: often recently married young families, a background of war service, the frustrations generated by seeking non-existent private accommodation to escape overcrowding and extortionate rents. The men may often have had shared occupations or workplaces in the area and many of the families had young children. There were common external issues they faced together such as dealing with the local authority and in some cases a government ministry or the army. They had common tasks too of cleaning and renovating their huts, sharing skills and expertise over carpentry or decorating. Almost immediately – and the reports of this are ubiquitous and suggest spontaneity – the hut occupiers organised themselves into committees and took responsibility for pooling a weekly sum of money from each family. At Washington in County Durham the squatters paid their weekly five shillings to the committee treasurer, who recorded it for them; at Sheffield the camp committee was organising a pool of rents 'so that they can be paid when needed'; squatters in Somerset paid a weekly sum 'into a central fund to meet possible liabilities'. At Bushey Park outside London a meeting agreed a camp committee to collect rent payments, liaise with the local authority, and organise rosters for using the communal cooking and washing facilities. Similarly at West Derby, described by the press as 'Liverpool's Squattersville', the camp 'had its own miniature council, which is split into various committees to deal with lighting, sanitation, and hygiene'. Some of these organisations were clearly informal whereas others like one outside Chester formally recorded the minutes of their meetings; at the Elton Hall site on Teesside the committee had an elected chairman, secretary and treasurer and the regular camp meeting agreed a 'code of conduct' for the families.[20]

These collections were to demonstrate that the occupiers were keen to pay a rent and for services and to make sure that funds were available to pay charges when their situation became official. Further, circumstances could also call for community organisation where facilities had to be shared: at a camp outside Birmingham for example 'housewives have pooled their cooking utensils and are sharing two communal cook houses'.

Colin Ward, in justly praising the high levels of communal organisation in the camps, goes on to claim that the huts were allocated by the squatters according to need so that the largest and best-appointed ones for example went to those with large families. In fact this romanticises what happened. It is clear from press accounts that in many places there were no allocations as such – occupations were on a first come first served basis and those who got there first were able to commandeer the better huts. For example at 'Liberty Villas' near Sunderland the first family on the site took the 'most comfortable' hut. Much in demand were the former officers' quarters, as Jim Tatters recalled about his own hut: 'Large, three bedrooms, bathroom and toilet, tiled fire place, officers' quarters. We had too much really. But there was no envy, or anyone trying to be in with you.'[21]

The next chapter will examine the circumstances under which local authorities began to take over these camps themselves or manage them as agents of the Ministry of Health. At this stage though it is worth noting why the camp committees had good reason for immediate negotiations with the local authority. There were the issues of the supply of services to be arranged: electricity, fuel, water, sanitation and refuse collection. Local authorities were legally obliged to ensure that there were no risks to public health arising from the camp occupations and so sanitary inspectors made visits and made recommendations which councils carried out, even if they were uncertain about what to do next. Crucial too was having the huts recognised as official addresses. In 1946 the public had to register their name and address with key suppliers such as coal merchants to buy fuel, addresses were needed for ration books and to ensure school places. All this, of course, had to wait until it was officially confirmed that the new occupiers were going to be allowed to stay. As a woman at the Bushey Park camp near London told one of the Mass Observation reporters: 'It was awful at first. Every time that somebody knocked on the door I thought that they had come to turn us out.'[22]

The physical conditions in a number of places were difficult. An example of the problems has been recounted by a participant in the camp occupation at Norton Fitzwarren in Somerset, who described the facilities they encountered at first:

> They had no water, cooking facilities or toilets. The one facility we had was electric light. We had to buy coal burning stoves etc. The brick hut at Courtlands now occupied by Apple Country Kitchens had about

nine open toilets with no segregation. Anyone using them had to make sure that no one of the opposite sex was 'in residence'. Baths were non-existent. Eventually, after some judicious 'thieving' of War Department property we managed to rig up a 'Heath Robinson' style shower.

Although some of the camps, or parts of them, were well-appointed that was not always the case. Some squatters faced broken windows, no form of heating or lighting, water supplies that had been cut off or only available from outside standpipes. Some huts were no more than the basic corrugated iron Nissen huts without wall division. Local authorities had basic public health obligations to fulfil but until they reached a formal position over what to do about their squatters – and who, indeed, was to be responsible for them – the squatters had to manage with even less than the basics. Many of the squatters put time, effort and money into their new dwellings once they had had confirmation that they were going to stay there, as Jim Tatters recalled: 'I got a nice little fireplace set up, got it from a hardware shop in Newcastle. I put a chimney up through the top and we had a lovely little fire.'

As was said by their supporters on some of the local authorities, the fact that people were prepared to take on such conditions is a comment on the circumstances they were leaving behind. In Derry when 'dozens of harassed, long-suffering families, cooped up for years in single rooms of overcrowded tenements' squatted local camps the Medical Officer of Health said of where they had left that 'from the health point of view the position in regard to overcrowding had reached the danger point'.[23]

Other buildings

Disused service hutments were by no means the only accommodation subject to 'unauthorised occupation' during 1946. In Carlisle almost an entire street of empty houses were occupied by sixty families in the course of one day in September. Rydal Street had been condemned but then requisitioned to house army personnel during the war. It had been empty for some time during the slow process of derequisitioning, and Carlisle Corporation intended to demolish the street and rebuild new housing there. However two families, helped by local people, took over one house and then as news of this spread many more families 'presenting scenes which had probably never been seen in Carlisle before' occupied the rest of the street. In County Durham too there were examples of squats occurring in condemned terraces and the families involved evicted on safety grounds.

In Scotland the occupation of empty, boarded up tenements had occurred during the war and such actions continued into the peace as well. There were instances at least in Glasgow, Wishaw and Dumbarton of squatters moving in when the original tenants were moved out to pre-fabs and the tenements condemned. These sorts of actions could be dangerous, of course, given the condition of some of the buildings, and therefore the man described as the squatters' leader, Peter McIntyre in Glasgow, organised a move of seventeen families out of condemned properties in Maryhill and into 'a thirty room mansion' in the Kelvindale Road. This house had been requisitioned for use by the military during the war and was 'equipped with all amenities'. McIntyre – who will be examined later – then 'issued orders to all squatters that they must not occupy condemned property'. There is evidence of a good level of community organisation in these other squats too. This was described by a reporter visiting the large house squatted under the leadership of Peter McIntyre's group in Glasgow. The nine families there had a committee whose chairman prepared tasks and instructions for the day, cooking and cleaning was done communally by the women while the men were out at work, and one case of 'bickering' had been resolved through a committee meeting.[24]

Events in Glasgow took a new turn when a group of 24 families occupied two empty accommodation blocks owned by the Scottish Prison Service. These were intended to be renovated and used to house prison officers working at Barlinnie Prison, but, as had happened so often elsewhere, the buildings had been empty for so long that people assumed they were not required. When the Sanitary Inspector visited the squat at the end of August he reported on a situation that was typical of the British squatting wave as a whole:

> The majority were all young married couples ... had all been living with their parents and overcrowding meant that the conditions were impossible ... most of the menfolk had been in the Services and married during the war while in the Services. Most had taken across beds, bedding, tables and chairs and intend having the remaining furniture carried over as soon as they can so manage.

They also, like the occupiers of the condemned tenements and the street in Carlisle, set about making the property habitable by extensive cleaning and by fixing locks, windows and floors.[25]

In Consett, as we have seen, 'a most orderly intrusion' of 35 families had occupied a very large house at Leadgate formerly used to house 'Bevin Boys' working in local collieries during the war. This building could accommodate all the families without overcrowding and was equipped with three central heating boilers and a shower block. Large houses that had been lying empty following derequisitioning could also be a target, as was the example above of Auchenstewart House. Near Dundee for example nineteen families from Broughty Ferry took over a '100 bedroom mansion' at Castleroy that had been a police headquarters before requisitioning. During that same week in Aberdeen groups of homeless families took over a former YMCA hostel and two hotels in the city centre, each of which had been requisitioned but which were still vacant. An attempt to occupy part of another was thwarted by hotel staff.

In both cities the local authority began legal proceedings for trespass, despite offers by the squatters to pay rent and renovate the properties, although before eviction notices were served alternative accommodation was arranged in local squatted army camps. At Buxton in Derbyshire the Empire Hotel, again once requisitioned and now empty, was occupied by homeless families at this time although in their case the legal proceedings were to prove of three years' duration. In Northamptonshire occupations took place of an empty isolation hospital and a hostel formerly used by American troops; those in the hospital defied a notice to quit and threatened to squat in the council offices if they were evicted. Eventually they were moved to the squat at the American hostel.

In Birmingham, where as we shall see the Communist Party had a significant role in the squatting movement, activists set themselves on a collision course with the local authority. A number of flats had been requisitioned and then acquired by the City Council Estates Committee which proceeded to refurbish them for letting. The CP claimed that the pace was far too slow to meet the urgent needs of the city and therefore it organised a squat of sixteen families in the properties. In Falkirk thirty people, describing themselves as 'refugees from overcrowding' occupied a large empty hostel in an action facilitated by local Communists.[26]

The mass media and public opinion

In 1946 it was estimated that one third of the whole population of England went to the cinema at least once a week, and the total attendances exceeded one and a half thousand. Even in 1950, despite something of a decline in numbers, cinema attendances in England per head of population exceeded those in every other county in the world apart from the United States. In urban Scotland this must also have been the case: Glasgow for example had had, since the 1920s, more cinemas per hundred head of population than any other city in Britain, or any other city outside the United States. All over Britain inadequate and overcrowded housing must have been a significant factor in the popularity of cinema attendance in 1946, providing as it did a cheap and convenient, if temporary, escape from it.[27]

The programmes in local cinemas always included a newsreel before the main feature. This meant that awareness of the squatting movement, beginning with the Scunthorpe interview, was almost instantly conveyed to the bulk of the British population. More to the point the newsreel coverage of the camp occupations was uniformly sympathetic; for example the British Pathe News commentary on the occupation at Chalfont St. Giles in Buckinghamshire included the view that:

This is only one of many ex-army camps taken over by the thousands of ordinary, hardworking folk who haven't a place they can call their own. Yesterday they were cold, inhospitable huts, today they're homes; a transformation which is in itself proof that the old Blitz spirit lives on and can still win through.[28]

Such commentaries surely help to explain the speed with which the movement grew in August 1946. On 20 August the Cabinet Committee was informed that 235 army camps had been 'seized' compared to 62 camps five days earlier. Other local reports around the same time provide something of a snapshot. There were around 2,000 – it is unclear whether this refers to families or individuals – in camps in County Durham and Tyneside, and that in and around Bristol 272 families were spread over twelve camps. In the Glasgow area there were 311 families in occupation of 163 hutments and four houses. There were, by mid-October 1946, 148 huts occupied in the Edinburgh area. As we have seen rural districts too were involved, some 70 families were occupying camps in the vicinity of Taunton. The Dundee area had 700 families squatting, of whom 45 were in army camps, 650 in condemned properties and the remaining five at the Castleroy mansion. The Dundee situation illustrates that homeless families were occupying whatever was available and that they could gain entry to, not just disused army accommodation. In Northern Ireland 80 families comprising 500 people ('who had been living in the slum areas') had occupied unused camps in the Derry city area and around Belfast 700 families were to be officially housed in camps converted by the Ministry of Finance. The Cabinet Committee held the cinema newsreels largely responsible for the rapid and widespread occupation of camps and installations by the homeless.[29]

The point was that those audiences were presented with information about the takeover of the camps that was broadly sympathetic, or at least not condemnatory. Crucial too, surely, was the fact the squatters were not shown to be facing any substantial threats of legal consequences. In most cases neither the armed forces nor the local authorities knew how to react and consequently they were seen to be doing nothing. This will be explored in more detail in the next chapter.

Other squatters had first heard of the movement by word of mouth, such as Jim Tatters in County Durham whose sister was in a squat outside Middlesborough; some reported that they had read about it in the newspapers, which had indeed been giving the movement front-page attention both locally and nationally. Potential squatters were not dependent on the news media for their information either, because there are several examples of how, once a camp or a building had been entered, the news quickly spread through the neighbourhood grapevine so that the initial squatters were soon joined by others in the same position.[30]

The newspaper coverage was generally sympathetic and even supportive, both reflecting and serving to influence public opinion. The Conservative-supporting national dailies saw an opportunity to attack the government, a point which will be discussed later. Here was a chance to support ordinary people who could be seen as having been let down by the failure of the socialists to deliver on their promises and frustrated by Labour government bureaucracy. Thus the *Daily Mail* praised the 'robust common sense' of the squatters and claimed that 'the "invasion" of empty service camps is a refreshing example of what ordinary people can do when they have a mind to do it ... a warning that people will not put up forever with empty promises'.[31]

Local newspapers in England, even the conservative ones, were not without some positive words for the movement. In the North East of England there was criticism, but not without sympathy, of those who 'were taking the law into their own hands' but also a view that 'Whitehall should have taken action over the use of these camps long ago'. Similarly it was pointed out that while squatting openly flouted the law and could not be commended, and in fact overturned the whole principle of allocation according to need, it was nonetheless 'a national scandal that so much useful accommodation should be left standing empty and deteriorating when housing is the country's most urgent need'. Likewise in the North West the view was taken that if using army camps 'can be done now that badly housed people have taken the law into their own hands why could it have not been done before? Someone has blundered badly – or is blundering now.' Another paper 'sympathised wholly with the squatters' but thought it right that 'they should face the risk of being moved out to make way for those in greater need if the camps were run by the Council'. This was also the line taken by the Manchester press: it welcomed the movement but called for strict supervision of it by the Ministry of Health:

Handled rightly the squatters – although hardly likely to find a place in any text book – can provide a genuine example of democracy in action, an initiative coming from the people, noted, taken up, respected and guided into the most constructive channels by the central organs of government, who are able from their special position to see the picture as a whole.

The point was made that the squatters, however desperate their circumstances, were challenging the principle of allocation by need by ignoring waiting lists and following their own principle of first come first served. Thus in Wales the conservative press opined that the squatters were 'creating new hardships for the law-abiding citizens waiting their turn for council houses'. North of the border one columnist in Glasgow, despite pointing out that the government's housing programme was obviously not 'keeping pace with the growing discomfort and discontent of the homeless', nevertheless believed that in effectively condoning their actions councils had 'set a dangerous precedent'. Later though a colleague, having already argued that 'the Ministry of Health and other Ministries should have acted sooner' claimed that squatting was a warning to 'an out of touch government', which should reflect on 'the calm way in which it has been accepted by the public … who feel it displays independence rather than defiance of the law … public opinion sympathises and worries little about the legal aspects'. Elsewhere too surprise was expressed at 'the support squatters are receiving from the press and the public throughout the country'. Another warned that the squatting movement showed that 'people are no longer prepared to wait patiently until the government's airy promises about new houses are realised'.[32]

Sympathy was also evident among some local authority members, although as we shall see in due course this was by no means universal. Middlesbrough councillors believed that their local camp squatters 'had acted unconstitutionally' but they 'would get every help'; it was an occasion, said one, 'where the will of the people has risen up in spite of governments'. Similarly the Mayor of Blyth Council said that squatters 'would have my full and complete sympathy' and when, soon enough, squatters did occupy Nissen huts close to the town he declared that he 'would have done the same thing in their position'. The MP for Houghton le Spring in County Durham worked with his local squatters' committee to lobby the council to lay on services to their camp, which was soon achieved, and the council claimed that it had been 'in sympathy with the squatters from the start'. One reason for this support, or at least lack of opposition, was simply one of pragmatism. Here was a temporary solution to what was admitted all round to be a desperate situation. As the chair of Housing at Consett Urban District Council reported after squatters occupied the empty miners' hostel: 'They are some of the genuine cases for whom we as a Council are trying to get homes for.'[33]

It was within these contexts of political criticism that Prime Minister Attlee and his Cabinet had to develop their response.

NOTES

1   There are good accounts of Bevan's work on housing in John Campbell, *Nye Bevan: A Biography* (London, Hodder and Stoughton, 1994, pp. 149-65); Nicholas Timmins, *The Five Giants: A Biography of the Welfare State* (London, Harper Collins, 2001, pp. 140-48) and Stephen Merrett, *State Housing in Britain* (London, Routledge and Kegan Paul, 1979, pp. 235-46). See also Nicklaus Thomas-Symonds, *Nye: The Political Life of Aneurin Bevan* (London, I.B. Tauris, 2015).

2   Michael Foot, *Aneurin Bevan: A Biography Vol.1: 1897-1945* (London, Davis-Poynter, 1962, pp. 300, 347).

3   See for example *Evening News*, 31 May; *Sunderland Echo*, 8 August; *Western Mail*, 17 August; *Sheffield Star*, 26 July; *Blyth News*, 1 August 1946; HC Debates, 23 August 1945, vol 413 c828. On the Northern Irish contrast see the *Irish News and Belfast Morning News*, 16 August 1946.

4   Paul Burnham, 'The Squatters of 1946: A Local Study in National Context', *Socialist History*, no. 25 (2004, p. 37). As regards Scotland the controversy is examined in Don Watson, 'Poles Apart: the Campaign against Polish Resettlement in Scotland after the Second World War', *Scottish Labour History*, vol. 49 (2014, pp.107-24).

5   NA: CAB 130/13, squatters in Military Camps: Minutes of the Cabinet Committee on Squatting, 20 August 1946; *Daily Record*, 10 December 1945; Paul Burnham, 'The Squatters of 1946: A Local Study in National Context', p. 23; James Hinton, 'Self-Help and Socialism: The Squatters' Movement of 1946', *History Workshop*, Issue 25 (Spring1988, p. 104).

6   *Birmingham Mail*, 15 August; *Shields Evening News*, 15 August; *Sunderland Echo*, 10 August; *Western Daily Press*, 14 August 1946.

7   Paul Burnham, 'The Squatters of 1946: A Local Study in National Context', p. 25; *Western Daily Press*, 15 August; *Durham County Advertiser*, 6 September; *Middlesborough Evening Gazette*, 8 August, 14 September 1946.

8   SA: MO, A1/2/48/1/A Squatting 1946 File Report 2431. The Mass Observation material covers some camps in the London suburbs. *Newcastle Journal*, 17 August 1946; Dave Simpson, *No Homes for Heroes: Post War Squatters in Washington* (Sunderland, Gilpin Press, 2006, pp. 62, 67); *Motherwell Times*, 30 August; *Nottingham Evening Post*, 24 August 1946.

9   *Tamworth Herald*, 17 August; *Kent Chronicle and Courier*, 13 February 1948; *Newcastle Journal*, 6, 15 August; *Berkshire Times and Weekly News*, 13 September; *Western Daily Press*, 14 August; *Evening Times*. 16, 21 August; *Northampton Mercury*, 23 August 1946.

10   NA: CAB 130/13, Squatters in Military Camps: Police Report on Type and Motives of Squatters, 19 August 1946; OXOHA: LT900, BBC Radio Oxford 1994, *Squatters' Delight*; Andrew Marr, *A History of Modern Britain* (London, Fontana, 2007, p. 74); *Blyth News*, 19 August; *Western Mail*, 22 August; *Northern Daily Mail*, 16 August; *Birmingham Mail*, 12 August 1946.

11   OXOHA: LT900, BBC Radio Oxford 1994, *Squatters' Delight*. A senior London County Council Housing Manager quoted in Addison, *Now the War is Over: A Social History of Britain 1945-1951* (London, BBC/Jonathan Cape, 1985, p. 64).

12   *Blaydon Courier*, 23 August; *Evening Times*, 27 August; *Oxford Mail*, 15 August; *Lancashire Daily Post*, 16 August; *Western Mail*, 19 August 1946; Jim Tatters, interview with John Suggett and Don Watson, 2013.

13   *Western Mail*, 19 August 1946; NA: CAB/129/12, Squatters in Army Camps: Memorandum by the Parliamentary Under-Secretary of State for the War Office; *Tamworth Herald*, 17 August 1946; Jack Spector, 'Occupation of Daws Hill Camp, High Wycombe', *Our History*, no.10 (November 1985, p. 9); *Somerset County Herald*, 24 August; *Evening Times*, 21 August; *Liverpool Evening Express*, 16 August; *Blyth News*,19 August 1946.

14   *Scotsman*, 13 August; *Lancashire Daily Post*, 12 August; *Sheffield Star*, 23 July; *Aberdeen Journal*, 21 August 1946; Jim Tatters, interview with John Suggett and Don Watson, 2014; *Western Daily Press*, 13 August; *Northampton Mercury*, 23 August 1946.

15   *Liverpool Evening Express*, 13 August; *Sheffield Star*, 14 August 1946. See for example DCRO: UD/CS 221, Chester le Street Urban District Council Correspondence re. squatters at Roman Avenue military camp 1946-1954:15 December 1946 letter from Mr E.R. Sinclair, Roman Avenue Camp Committee Secretary; Dave Simpson, *No Homes for Heroes: Post War Squatters in Washington* (Sunderland, Gilpin Press, 2006); *Somerset County Herald*, 23 November 1946; HALS: 59M76/DDC86, Minutes of Hartley Wintney Rural District Council Squatters Committee, 28 February 1947 (Squatters Committee Minute Book vol.1 1946-1948).

16   TWAS: U.D. NB/20/49, Squatters Occupying Hill Head Camp West Denton: letter from Mr James Ostler; *Western Daily Press*, 20 December; *Sunderland Echo*, 12 August 1946.

17   HALS: 59M76/DDC87, Minutes of Hartley Wintney Rural District Council Hutments Committee 25 October, 19 November 1947 (Hutments Committee Minute Book vol. 2 1948-1949); Paul Burnham, 'The Squatters of 1946: A Local Study in National Context', p. 37.

18   *Shields Evening News*, *Sunderland Echo* 12 August and *Newcastle Journal* 13 August 1946; OXOHA: LT900: BBC Radio Oxford 1994: *Squatters' Delight*; Violet Fraser: *Huts for Houses: A Forres Squatter's Childhood* (Moray, J & J Publishing, 2012 p.410).

19   *Evening Times*, 16 August; *Dundee Courier*, 21 August 1946; Jim Tatters interview with John Suggett and Don Watson, 2014; *Sunday Sun*, 25 August; *Western Daily Press*, 20 August; *Durham County Advertiser*, 6 September; *Somerset County Herald*, 31 August 1946.

20 Dave Simpson, *No Homes for Heroes: Post War Squatters in Washington*, p. 60; *Sheffield Star*, 24 July; *Somerset County Herald*, 31 August 1946; SA: MOA1/2/48/1/A, Squatting 1946: Mass Observation File Report 2431, p. 12; *Liverpool Evening Express*, 14 August; *Manchester Evening News*, 20 August; *Middlesborough Evening Gazette*, 13 August 1946.

21 *Birmingham Mail*, 17 August 1946; Colin Ward, *Housing: An Anarchist Approach* (London, Freedom Press, 1976, p. 24); *Sunderland Echo*, 18 June 1947; Jim Tatters, interview with John Suggett and Don Watson, 2014.

22 SA: MOA1/2/48/1/A, Squatting 1946: Mass Observation File Report 2431, p. 17.

23 SHC: A\BVF/2/4, Extract from memoirs of an ex-serviceman looking for accommodation in Norton Fitzwarren 1946; Jim Tatters, interview with John Suggett and Don Watson, 2014; *The Derry Journal*, 23, 26 August 1946.

24 *Carlisle Journal*, 10 September; *Durham Chronicle*, 11 October; *Evening Citizen*, 29 August, 2, 3 September; *Sunday Post*, 15 September 1946.

25 NRS: HH57/1080, Barlinnie Prison: Squatters in Nos. 4 and 5 Quarters.

26 *Blaydon Courier*, 23 August; *Dundee Courier*, 21, 22, 23, 28 August, 14 September; *Aberdeen Press and Journal*, 22, 23, 24 August, 25 September; *Northampton Mercury* 6, 20, 27 September; *Birmingham Mail*, 23, 24 August 1946; James Hinton, 'Self-Help and Socialism: The Squatters' Movement of 1946', p. 110; *Falkirk Mail*, 6 September 1946.

27 Ross McKibbin, *Classes and Cultures: England 1919-1951* (Oxford, Oxford University Press, 1998, p. 419); Joe Fisher, 'Leisure and Culture – The Glasgow Story' (www.theglasgowstory.com viewed October 2013.)

28 British Pathe News, 22 August 1946 (www.britishpathe.com, viewed February 2013). Some footage of the camp occupations from this and other sources is available via www.youtube.com.

29 *Sunday Sun*, 18 August; *Western Daily Press*, 4 September; *Evening Times*, 28 August 1946; CEA: SL2/2, Minutes of the Corporation of Edinburgh Housing Committee, 15, 22 October 1946; *Somerset County Herald*, 24 August, 1 September; *Dundee Courier*, 3 September; *The Times*, 24 August 1946. NA: CAB 130/13, Squatters in Military Camps: Minutes of Cabinet Committee, 20 August 1946.

30 Jim Tatters, interview with John Suggett and Don Watson, 2014; Jim Harland, *Blyth Memories, Part Four* (Newcastle on Tyne, Summerhill Books, 2013, p. 17); *Northampton Mercury*, 23 August; *Carlisle Journal*, 10 September 1946.

31 *Daily Mail*, 10 August 1946.

32 *Sunday Sun*, 18 August; *Sunderland Echo*, 9 August; *Liverpool Evening Express*, 17 August; *Middlesborough Evening Gazette*, 13 August; *Manchester Evening News*, 14 August; *Western Mail*, 18 August; *Evening Times*, 20, 26 August; *Shields Evening News*, 16 August; *Aberdeen Press and Journal*, 20 August 1946.

33 *Middlesbrough Evening Gazette*, 12, 14 August; *Blyth News*, 1, 19 August; *Shields Gazette*, 23, 24, 29 August; *Blaydon Courier*, 23 August 1946.

Chapter Five

'WE WERE SOLID AS A BRICK WALL':
RESPONSES AND ORGANISATION

The government responds

By the middle of August Prime Minister Attlee seems to have become irritated and frustrated by what was happening. He had, some weeks earlier apparently, given specific instructions that redundant camps 'should not be allowed to stand empty and provide a temptation to squatters', but this had not happened; he believed that action by the police should be explored further, and where squatters occupied camps needed by the Civilian Resettlement Unit or for other civilian training Attlee's opinion was that 'they should be evicted forthwith'. Moreover, ministers should 'explore what steps could be taken to prevent undue publicity being given to the occupation of camps by squatters'. The Home Secretary James Chuter Ede established a Cabinet Committee specifically to deal with squatting and a network of Regional Committees to which representatives from local government, Principal Housing Officers of the Ministry of Health and the armed services were to report. These Committees attempted to record and provide briefings on a rapidly changing situation: in the last week of August 520 camps had been occupied in England and Wales and this had risen to 921 camps, involving over 33,000 people, a month later. In Scotland at that time 152 camps had been occupied and 7,534 people were reported to be living in them.[1]

At the national level the different branches of the armed services made it clear to the Cabinet that they did not have the manpower to guard all the empty hutments. There were other factors too:

The Service Departments state unequivocally that they cannot find the men to guard camps effectively ... Further, the Services are unwilling to face the consequences of a clash between armed guards and a party of determined squatters. It is also pointed out that many of the men who might be employed on such duties e.g. experienced NCOs in charge of young soldiers, may themselves be potential squatters and their sympathies may well interfere with their duty.[2]

There is indeed evidence that the service personnel who were still at the camps sympathised with and supported their new neighbours. Most of them had after all been in the same uniforms until recently and those servicemen awaiting their discharge knew that they would be facing the same housing problems themselves before long. A reporter with the *Daily Worker* was with a group of families occupying a camp in the south of England when they simply walked past the sentry on duty. At his apparently half-hearted observation that 'I'll have to report this' the reply was 'All right mate, we know, we've been in the army ourselves'. An ex-serviceman in Seaham, County Durham, entered a camp where ATS soldiers were still present; they helped by watching over the hut he had claimed until he could move in his furniture. Similarly in England and Wales – the legal position in Scotland was different, as we shall see – when army officers called the police to these occupations they were powerless, and for either legal or sympathy reasons did nothing except observe the formalities. Under English law at that time trespass was a civil offence and not a criminal matter unless damage had been done by the trespasser. In the event of such allegations it would be necessary to show that damage had been caused by the squatters when entering and not vandalism occurring before the occupation. It would also be necessary to identify the individuals who had caused the damage. In short, charges of damage would be nigh-on impossible to prove in these circumstances. Press reports describe the police taking names and checking identity cards (issued under war-time regulations and still compulsory), or warning squatters in general terms that legal action might be taken against them. As a rule such visits did not deter the occupants. In Birmingham 'the police tactfully withdrew' when they saw no damage was being done to the vacant anti-aircraft sites that families were occupying. In some cases it would have taken a major effort by the authorities to prevent an occupation, for example at the Crookston camp near Glasgow when a large crowd mainly of women 'surged through the gates without hindrance from the police'. When a crowd of around thirty families assembled outside a camp near Bristol the camp warden called the police, but all they could do was warn against causing damage before the squatters 'raced over the ground to find the best huts and stake their claim'.[3]

Nevertheless when camp occupiers at Norton Fitzwarren in Somerset, in the words of one of them, 'broke into the Nissen huts' there some of the squatters were arrested and charged with breaking and entering. At the same time though the police there were very sympathetic to the position the homeless ex-servicemen were in.[4]

When empty army huts were occupied in the Aberdeen area the Scottish Command of the army stated that evictions would be necessary if the services required the huts again in the future, but in the meantime the squatters 'had their sympathy' and that 'roughly, the position is, we cannot stop them'. Further south in Lancashire when squatters took over part of a former Navy Air Station – the rest was still an Admiralty installation – the commander on the spot accused them of trespassing. Nevertheless he admitted that 'the orders I have received say that people should be told that they can't come in but that force should not be used to prevent them'. Similarly in Sunderland an army officer, having spoken to squatters at Grindon, stated that he 'had no authority to ask them to leave'. The army command in the Birmingham area was reported as admitting, 'our policy is not to worry about it, and in fact you could almost say we were sympathetic'.[5]

However not all sections of the armed forces commands or the War Department were relaxed about the occupation of their empty or partly used facilities. In Scotland telephone messages were sent to cinemas and dance halls in the Ayr and Prestwick areas 'summoning RAF personnel back to guard their camps' against possible occupation by squatters. At Greenock army and naval guards were posted at huts for deterrent purposes. In Amersham, Buckinghamshire, and the Vale of Leven in Scotland confrontations took place between squatters and Polish soldiers who had been allocated the facilities, and in the latter case it took the arrival of the police to defuse the situation. Outside Taunton in Somerset squatters left the camp they had occupied when told the army still required it, only to move to another part later the same night. Arrangements were reached here as elsewhere for soldiers and squatters to live in parallel circumstances.[6]

By mid-August 1946 the Cabinet was being advised that 'the present illegal situation cannot be allowed to continue' and that the occupations should be 'regularised' unless the camps concerned were definitely going to be needed. There were political factors at work too: for example the Parliamentary Under-Secretary of State at the War Office advised against evicting British families from accommodation allocated to Polish troops or prisoners of war because he 'did not feel it would command public support'. Where however government departments or local authorities did have 'a need for immediate possession' then proceedings for eviction were inevitable but in liaison with the Ministry of Health: 'every endeavour must be made to find alternative accommodation.' Although technically the camp squatters in England and Wales had committed trespass the government was recommended to avoid, in such cases, a legal response. A Cabinet Committee reported that 'we are advised that it would be difficult to take a large number of cases to court' and that although what it referred to as 'the movement' might suffer a setback if a few selected cases in various parts of the country were taken to court, 'generally though eviction is not designed to deal with mass trespass'.

It seems that, just as their large numbers had allowed homeless and inadequately housed families to carry out a mass entry to the camps, so their large numbers were their best defence against prosecution and eviction.

Towards the end of August the 'illegal situation' was 'regularised'. The government stated that, where a camp was going to be surplus to the requirements of the armed services or government departments, it was to be offered to the local authority for potential use as housing. The process of reaching that decision would now be accelerated. It was agreed that evictions, but only with the agreement of the Ministry of Health, could be executed if the camps were needed or were a danger to public health. In such cases the Ministry would expect that alternative accommodation had been arranged.

In the Cabinet Committee one view was that rents should not be charged to the hut occupiers because that could entail the legal relationship of landlord and tenant; a large number of the huts were uninhabitable by normal standards and if rents were charged the local authorities would be pressed for expensive repairs where permanent housing should be the priority. The prevailing view though was that the camps were in the same position as requisitioned properties where the rents charged did not carry the legal status of tenant. In any event if no rents were charged this might 'might give an incentive to the squatters' movement and attract the more undesirable section of the community'. In those camps already occupied rent equivalents and charges for council services (water, sanitation and lighting) would be made. Where a local authority was unwilling to accept huts as part of their own housing complement it was to have the option of managing them on behalf of the Ministry of Health – acting as an agent to collect charges and administer lettings or repairs. The Ministry undertook to reimburse councils for 'reasonable costs' arising from repairs and renovation to the huts.[7]

Bevan accompanied this undoubted concession – or acceptance of a popular fait accompli – by attempting a propaganda offensive against the squatters. The Ministry of Health statement outlining the policy also stated that the camp squatters were 'threatening to upset reconstruction plans' in many areas. Alternative provision would now need to be made for accommodating civilian vocational trainees, returning servicemen and so forth, and this would divert 'labour and materials badly needed for housing'. They had also forced a departure from the local authority practice of allocating accommodation according to the needs of applicants. Whilst expressing sympathy with the plight of the homeless ('Whilst I am very sympathetic – nobody, I think, could be more so – with people's housing conditions') he stated that the government was 'bound to condemn the action of squatters in taking unauthorised possession of these premises ... Further, where the camps are such as can be suitably taken over by the local housing authorities, the squatters have in many cases jumped the claims of persons higher on the local authorities' lists of applicants for houses.'

In a country so recently at war and in which shortages were prevalent and essential items still subject to rationing, the accusation of 'queue jumping' was likely to resonate. It was going to be up to the local authorities and the squatters themselves to deal with this.[8]

Labour responds

The Labour Party produced different responses to the squatting developments. The one from what might be termed the mainstream of the Party was somewhat less than positive. There were two main reasons. Firstly, and obviously, it was seized on by their political opponents and their many friends in the press, as we have seen. Critics of the government made as much of the issue as they could. At political meetings around the country both Conservative and Liberal speakers described squatters as acting 'out of contempt for the Labour Party ... they have been promised so much and been given so little' and that they were 'a product of the failure of the Socialists' housing plans ... and the Socialists' broken promises'; they were victims of 'the muddle and incompetence of the Socialist government'. In parts of South East England Conservative Associations issued press releases in which they claimed to sympathise with those forced to squat because of government housing failures. When Parliament resumed that autumn Bevan faced questions about the situation in the House of Commons, principally about the actions in London, which will be discussed in a later chapter, but also about the camp occupations. He was compelled to admit that it was only the mass outbreak of squatting – in the words of one Conservative, 'helpless people driven to take illegal action' – that had brought about the adoption of these camps by local authorities for housing. He also had to face other Tory comments:

As the term 'squatter' is rather an inelegant phrase, would the Government consider changing the name of these people who are occupying such camps to that of 'Bevan boys', in imitation of another Minister's great achievement?

Nevertheless, taxed by Winston Churchill about the standard of accommodation being provided for home-seekers in the occupied camps, Bevan reminded the Conservatives of why the housing programme had such a low base to start from:

It is quite true that the standard of accommodation in these camps is very much lower than we would consider to be desirable. However, it is very much higher than that of the slums in which the party opposite left people for so many years.[9]

This kind of pressure over an area where the government was clearly vulnerable is bound to have encouraged defensiveness among some in the Labour Party. The second reason is suggested in an article by the Clydeside MP Jean Mann, herself a pre-war Housing Convenor for Glasgow Corporation, in which she was particularly vehement. 'Groaners' she maintained, should be grateful that the Labour government was expanding services unlike after the first war, when nothing could be given but cuts because the war had to be paid for. Squatters would in fact 'do everything to hinder and nothing to help the housing problem ... People who waited ten years under capitalist governments don't appear to want to wait one year under a Labour government'. She likened squatters to pensioners jumping the post office counters and helping themselves to the increased state pensions that were being introduced:

The squatter is a queue jumper. Who selects the tenant in this organised squatting? Local councils have the authentic, including the private, information about each prospective tenant and can allocate according to the greatest need ... If a Council allocates unfairly the remedy is open to all ratepayers who vote ...[10]

This quotation expresses the foundations of the resentment clearly. There is anger at a perceived ingratitude: is this how they respond after all we've done for them, and with all we're trying to do? Added to this is annoyance that the envisioned system of orderly planning and organisation has been disrupted, and by the very people it had been designed to help. Similarly the Secretary of the Blaydon Constituency Labour Party in County Durham criticised 'queue jumping' by squatters who may not be in the greatest need; he went further, and expressed surprise that the council was preparing rent books for them and supplying services when it should be evicting them and only housing those on the waiting list. Likewise at a meeting in Hull a former councillor from Leeds declared that squatters were 'acquiring accommodation out of turn and gaining an advantage over those waiting patiently for houses'. Both of these men had ambitions to rise in the Labour Party – they were prospective parliamentary candidates – and this may have prompted their loyal response.

Labour at the local level could be more supportive. At the Hull meeting above, for example, a good many in the audience were apparently of the opinion that the squatters were 'prodding the Labour government for quicker action in the matter of housing'. In Falkirk a Labour Party public meeting attributed the squatting movement to lack of government action over requisitioning. In Bristol Alderman Hennessy had acted as the squatters' advocate, earning him censure by the City Council Labour Group, but at least one constituency party supported him. As we have seen there were a number of Labour councillors and authorities offering full support even if they had reservations over 'unconstitutional' action. Carlisle had witnessed a local Labour MP turn the mass squat in the city to political advantage. Declaring his support for them at a public meeting he blamed the housing problem on 'a City Corporation dominated by private landlords for the past twenty years'. Other Labour MPs acted in support of their local squatters, such as the member for Taunton who lobbied the Ministry of Health on their behalf. In Derry the chairman of the City Labour Party, who was also a councillor, acted as an advocate for the camp squatters and appealed for support from 'all sections and branches of the Trade Union and Labour movement in this forgotten and neglected dead-end city'.[11]

Cabinet Ministers held firm to the government's line that the squatters were not necessarily the people in the most need, they were jumping the turns of others who were a greater priority, and that they were diverting resources from the mainstream building programme. In addition Home Secretary Chuter Ede – who turned down an invitation to meet squatters in his own constituency of South Shields – made a comment that could be interpreted as ominous. Although he said that the camps were to be regarded as part of the temporary housing schemes of districts:

... the local authorities might of course consider that some persons who had entered such premises were not entitled to so high a priority among other applicants for houses, as their needs had in fact been met.[12]

Did this mean that he was advising that, since the squatters had adopted their own unofficial solution to their inadequate housing, they had removed themselves from any priority in terms of the waiting list? As we shall see in a later chapter this was the position taken by some local authorities and the consequences for the squatters could be serious.

The use of the law

The difference in the trespass legislation between Scotland and England had an effect. At the start of the camp occupation movement in Scotland nineteen people were fined at Hamilton Burgh Court for squatting in Nissen huts at the Auchenraith camp, which was required for use by Polish soldiers. There is evidence that the courts were prepared to use their discretion and to be lenient when camp squatters came before them charged with trespass. They showed some understanding of the circumstances of the accused and tried to enforce the law in that light. In some cases court proceedings would be postponed to give squatters an opportunity to resolve the issue by moving out of the occupied premises. This happened in Stirling, where the Scottish Office asked the county court to delay action against squatters at the Polmaise camp in the hope that they would go of their own accord. Generally only the minimum fine of ten shillings was imposed and in some cases admonishments. In the case of families fines would be imposed on husbands but if they were not in court the wives, obviously considered to be less guilty, would be admonished.[13]

Once the Ministry of Health had regularised the position of those who had occupied disused camps such prosecutions were replaced by those of people occupying other properties. For example in Falkirk ten squatters were fined £1 each for illegally occupying a property they claimed had been empty for two years. Where squatters in Scotland were fined in court it did not necessarily follow that they would be evicted. After the squat in the prison officers' quarters at Barlinnie in Glasgow eight women and four men were fined £1 each in the Sheriff's Court after admitting contravention of the Trespass (Scotland) Act 1865. Nevertheless, after representation by the Labour MP Margaret Herbison the following month the Secretary of State for Scotland forbade their eviction unless alternative accommodation was available. Squatters were to remain in these premises for almost ten more years.[14]

At Westminster the Glasgow MP John McGovern raised the issue of the discrepancy in the legal responses to unauthorised occupations in England and Scotland. He pointed out that in a number of districts 'it appeared that their occupation was afterwards legalised by the Government, and that that was a direct encouragement to a large number of people to seize other camps'. How did Bevan 'square that with the fact that certain men have been placed in court for seizure, while others were legalised in a proper manner?' The reply was simply that 'it must inevitably happen that quite a number of anomalies were created in this matter ... we did not want to expel large numbers of people from camps in these circumstances'. As we have seen the fact of the matter was that the Cabinet had been advised that it was neither legally nor politically practical to 'expel large numbers of people from camps' in England and Wales. This fact had played a more significant part in the government's decisions than sympathy for the position of the squatters. Evictions of some camp squatters were attempted in both England and Scotland but not until the camps were required by the military or were a danger to public health. In buildings in England other than camps or requisitioned premises squatters were not fined but could be evicted; for example in Northamptonshire, squatters in the American hostel were finally served notice to quit. Despite public meetings organised by their Communist supporters they were transferred to a squatted army camp.[15]

Even when a camp was on a military required list there was at least one case of determined squatters remaining in place. The occupation of the planned Civilian Resettlement Unit at Washington, County Durham, was a particularly contentious one because the War Office maintained that it was required for current and future use. The first squatters had in fact occupied while the ex-prisoners of war were on leave and they had returned to find themselves sharing with local homeless families. The Parliamentary Under-Secretary of State for the War Office informed Attlee's office that this was 'a serious situation' and that he was seeking action to evict. The military authorities, threatening court action, did try to persuade the squatters to leave and several of the squatters later recalled various attempts by the army and the police to intimidate them into leaving. However as one of the participants, miner Jim Tatters, recalled in 2012:

The' was threats an' that, but we were just solid. Aa divven knaa what would happen wi' modern day youth, but we were as solid as a brick wall ... an' wuh were adamant. 'But where yuh ganna put wuh?' 'If yuh chuck wuh oot, where yuh ganna put wuh?' 'Where wuh goin?' Yuh knaa, arl things like that! An' the' gave in an' wuh started t' pay rent.[16]

The local Urban District Council had been one of those that had been approaching government departments over the use of disused huts for housing, only, like many others, to receive no reply. It now effectively came on to the side of the squatters by making an approach to take over the occupied huts as housing again, whilst agreeing only to provide sanitation services until this was resolved. The War Office pursuit of eviction proceedings did not materialise in this case. Looking back Jim Tatters had his own interpretation of why the council were supportive:

> The council were mainly pitmen, what was on the council. Wuh'd see them at work an' down the club. If they'd have been saying 'yuh shouldn't be in there' wuh'd have challenged them. Aa think the' just looked the other way.[17]

As we shall see in the next chapter evictions or the threat of eviction were used effectively in several areas later when squatters were in private or council owned properties.

Local government and the waiting lists

Bevan maintained that local government was best placed to manage the occupied huts once ministries had passed them over. However as we have seen a very large number of local authorities had already tried, without success, to raise the issue of using surplus wartime installations to relieve the pressure on housing resources. Several councils now repeated that had their original requests been granted they could have ensured that the camp occupants were the high priority cases from their waiting lists. There were also some expressions of resentment about having to take responsibility for resolving an issue that had been created by unresponsive and uncoordinated ministries. There was one claim at least that 'Town and County Councils are getting sick of being told by London what they must do'.[18]

The response by the local authorities to the new position was, predictably, varied. Some, like Gateshead Council, took charge of the situation, adopting what the local press called 'a common sense approach to the squatter problem'. Having posted police at an empty anti-aircraft gun site and 'thwarted many attempts to gain possession of the huts' the council took the huts over, adapted and equipped them, and then moved in thirteen priority families from the waiting list as tenants. Cardiff too moved families from its waiting list into camps which it managed as an agent of the Ministry; this was on the basis that 'no more squatting was to be allowed' there. In Edinburgh the City Corporation took over the Craigentinny Camp on condition that the occupants were local residents and that there was no more squatting there; however, as the camp committee explained a year later, they were not able to prevent others from moving in. Aberdeen Council had criticised those who had 'rushed the queue for houses' by squatting, especially as it was claimed that they 'were not the most necessitous cases'; this last group were considered to be large families living in overcrowded sub-lets. Aberdeen was one of many authorities who resented the 'first come first served' effect of squatting as opposed to the orderly queue in order of priority. Therefore when it, like Gateshead, took over Hayton Camp and refurbished it for official tenants, they were to be 'the most necessitous cases' from its own waiting list.[19] Supporters of the squatters such as Oxford Communist Party pointed out that they were not getting accommodation that others in greater need could have had; the camps would still have been lying empty if they had not entered them and by so doing had opened more places up.[20]

In Wales Newport Council organised 'blocks of lavatories, shower baths and wash houses' to be 'divided and converted to civilian use' as well as a canteen. As was explained:

> The minimum of labour is being diverted to the camp but materials in the form of breeze blocks, cement and sand (none of which is in short supply) are being supplied to enable the occupants to build their own partitions and generally to make the huts habitable.[21]

This supplying of materials to the squatters themselves to carry out their own refurbishments was proposed elsewhere, as will be seen, although often ignored by the authorities. In contrast to Newport there were councils, including major ones like Bristol, who were unhappy from the beginning. The ruling Labour Group there criticised the local squatters and disassociated itself from the dissident Alderman Hennessy who supported them. Besides being concerned at 'mob rule' and 'disregard for law and order' it clearly saw what the movement represented as an implied attack on its housing programme. Further, it had decided that the camp huts were not appropriate for family accommodation and that it would be uneconomic in terms of labour and materials to convert them. A large number of councils, like Bristol, were not prepared to take over their local camps or invest any resources in them.

Instead they chose the option of acting as agents for the Ministry of Health. In one case, Chester le Street in County Durham, the authority would only act in this way 'to a very limited extent'. As was explained to the squatters:

The Council, while holding the opinion that the hutments – in one of which you are living – are unfit for human habitation, realise that to take measures to evict you would be unfair in view of existing circumstances, and have therefore attempted to mitigate the hardship of the position by the provision of water, electrical energy, and sanitary facilities.[22]

'Existing circumstances' likely meant that no alternative accommodation could have been found. This particular decision to act as an agent and provide basic services was taken four or five months after the occupation took place and until it was made the squatters would have had to manage without the services and live without confirmation about their future.

It was clear that eviction was not a weapon that could readily be used against the squatters. However once responsibility for them was passed to the local authorities another threat could be brought into play: the security of their position on the council housing waiting list. Squatters did not see their huts as a permanent residence and therefore the major issue for them was assurance that they were still on the list for council housing, that their action had not effectively removed them from the list or otherwise harmed their applications. At the same time spokesmen for the camp committees often stressed that they were not seeking special treatment or to move themselves up the waiting list. 'Queue jumper' was an accusation often made about the squatters and it was one to which they were clearly sensitive. Local authorities too were well aware of the impression that could be created when they effectively made the camp occupations official by co-operating with them.

The government's view was that when it came to the waiting lists for permanent accommodation squatters 'should receive neither advantage nor disadvantage from their actions', in other words squatting should not give them a higher priority for housing but nor should it prejudice their position on the list. It was aware that at least one authority had placed the squatters in its area at the bottom of the waiting list for council housing but in the view of the Cabinet 'local authorities should not thus seek to impose punishment for actions for which the law provided no penalty'.[23]

Conservative Tynemouth Borough Council took this view. It made it clear, indeed it stressed, that squatters in the camps in the borough were to be included in the points system for new houses; the council had unanimously decided that the camp squatters 'should not have their claims prejudiced' because they had occupied disused camps. In the Nottingham area one local authority caused controversy when it moved some camp squatters from a camp that was still required into flats in a requisitioned house: they were seen to have received preferential treatment. This was contrasted with another which had acted quickly to take a camp over and install tenants from its waiting lists, thereby 'ensuring preference for people who have been waiting for years'. Similarly Manchester Corporation 'was determined' not to allow any family to 'force its hand to give them alternative accommodation' and thereby 'jump the claim of those already on the waiting list'.[24]

Aberdeen Council tried to halt further attempts at squatting in empty private property in the city through a policy whereby those squatting illegally would 'forfeit all priority on the Council waiting lists'. This was modified somewhat after a campaign by the occupants of civilian huts at Balangask ensured that they would not be penalised in this way. Similarly in Derby the council, which like most had taken over or acted as an agent for camps and moved tenants in, decided that those occupying huts without council permission would be struck off the housing list and not be considered for council housing. This had followed a stand-off between officials and squatters in huts at a former anti-aircraft site. Health officials had condemned these huts as unfit and the local authority had offered to store the squatters' furniture while they moved them out. The squatters' response, when officials, workmen and the police arrived, was to barricade themselves in their huts and threaten to resist unless a court order was produced. They also lobbied a Housing Committee meeting – at which an alderman complained that they'd called him 'a dictator' – to request leave to stay. Eventually the authority agreed to re-house them in other huts which it had renovated and refurbished for the purpose.

A similarly robust attitude was taken at a conference of members of the Association of Durham Urban District Councils, who agreed that squatting was 'in defiance of the law and contrary to public health', those involved 'should have no illusions that their action would help them rise up the queue'; in fact some councillors were of the opinion that squatters should be removed from the housing list or at least move down it. One of the member bodies was keen to reject 'the idea that had got about' that the council would provide alternative accommodation for squatters. In the Vale of Leven in Scotland the campaign by the Dunbartonshire Homeless Tenants' Association for the supply of basic services to the camps also resisted 'those who declare that squatters should now go to the back of the Council housing list. We seek no advantage, just our rights. Our members should not be penalised for having the guts to do something for themselves.'[25]

There were authorities who had other considerations. Although the Unionist Derry City Corporation adopted the major squatted camp in the city it refused to do so for one outside it. Ostensibly this was because it lay outside the city boundary, even though the squatters were Derry residents. However the local press reported an 'uneasy feeling in Unionist circles concerning the effect on the Unionist voting strength in the rural area of a drift from the city'; the City Labour Party later used this refusal as an example of 'gerrymandering' by the Unionist establishment.[26]

Role of activists

The role played in these events by local political activists is worth some attention. There are brief accounts of the squatting movement of the summer of 1946, influenced by the anarchist perspective of Colin Ward that present it as essentially a spontaneous movement and dismiss the idea of Communist Party involvement until the events of September that year. In contrast the official history of the Party states that, 'in many localities it was the Communist Party that took the initiative'. There is certainly evidence to support this last claim. Archie Marriott in Oxford has recalled how his own involvement was sparked by a local militant:

> I worked at the Pressed Steel. During the dinner hour one day in the summer when we had our sandwiches and went outside there was a man, we'd all heard of him, Abe Lazarus the Communist, he said why don't we go and squat in these huts out at Worminghall. So we decided to go out there and see them so we did, and squatted, left a chair to mark our place.

Abe Lazarus – who was to become, with his family, a squatter himself – was indeed a well-known Communist campaigner in the Oxford area. In the 1930s a private housing developer had built a wall to insulate a new private housing scheme from a nearby council estate in Cutteslowe; Lazarus had been involved in the campaign against this and the unsuccessful direct action to break up the wall.[27] During August 1946 the Oxford Communists, the local camp committees, trades unions and the City Council agreed a procedure whereby prospective squatters would contact the council before taking action. This was to avoid occupying buildings that were planned to be used. This led to the Oxford Joint Squatters' Committee which sifted information about possible empty sites and then, by agreement with the council, organised their use by the homeless. The Communists claimed that this would deal with the matter in an organised way, through 'the local authority backed up by public initiative'. As a local response to the squatting wave this seems to have been rare.[28]

In Blyth Communist councillor Ned Breadin urged people to squat in the local empty camp as a temporary measure to ease overcrowding; he pledged that the housing committee, of which he was a member, would give full support. Breadin himself had been an elected member of Blyth Council since 1934, largely as a result of his role as a leader of the local branch of the National Unemployed Workers' Movement. Further down the North-East coast of England on Teesside it has been recalled that the occupation of huts surrounding an anti-aircraft battery was led by the Communist Pat Durkin. In Buckinghamshire according to Paul Burnham an alliance between local Communist and Labour Party activists was the motor behind the organisation of the camp occupations and the subsequent negotiations with the local authorities.[29]

In England the area that seems to have had the most Communist involvement in the squatting campaign was Birmingham. Here some of the protagonists in both the Labour and Communist Parties were the same individuals who had joined political forces during the great rent strike in the city during 1939. In the post-war world however Jessie Eden and Sam Blackwell were to be the opponents and not the allies of Councillor Bradbeer and his Labour colleagues. What began initially as an occupation of disused army camps by homeless people spread into properties that had been requisitioned by the City Council for conversion into flats. The Birmingham Communist Party was behind this from the outset. It pointed out, accurately enough, that the camp squatters were pleased with what they had and that this illustrated 'the scale of the appalling housing problem in the city'. The Party declared that if no immediate steps were taken by the council to requisition properties it would 'assist the homeless to take them over'. Senior councillors stated that they had evidence that the CP was 'directing the squatting of empty houses' – something surely obvious to everyone in Birmingham – and refused to meet a deputation that included Sam Blackwell. They then tried to persuade squatters on council property to move out and thereby avoid court proceedings. As James Hinton comments, the Birmingham situation became intertwined with the national one after the London squats of September that year, and this will be discussed in a later chapter. Once squatters had taken over the camps activists had roles too. At Teddington the local CP branch provided legal advice to camp squatters and in many occupied camps in the London area such as Stratford, Cricklewood, Sutton and Primrose Hill local Communist branches helped with approaches to the local authority and the organisation of camp committees, as was the case also in Reading and Lincolnshire.[30]

As we have seen once the camps were occupied there followed a period of negotiation with the local authority and other bodies over sanitation arrangements, the restoration of power and water supplies, and payments to the councils in lieu of rent. There were also the efforts to persuade councils to take over camps as part of their own housing establishment and to protect the position of the squatters on the housing waiting lists. Here again activists – principally although not exclusively Communists – had a role. In Blyth Communist councillor Ned Breadin and his Party colleague Councillor Waters argued unsuccessfully for the Town Council to take over occupied huts, while in Chelmsford the International Brigade veteran Alf Cooper led a refusal by hut residents to pay the rates the council proposed to charge them until gas and electricity services were provided and the sanitation improved. After the empty prison officers' accommodation at Barlinnie was occupied Communist Bob Saunders led a deputation of three men to the prison governor requesting that gas, electricity and water supplies be reconnected in the interests of public health and the welfare of the young children in the squat. The reconnection was arranged the following day.[31]

At a former gun site outside Sheffield a confrontation took place when the local authority served a notice to quit on the camp occupiers. The eviction was due to insanitary conditions in the camp but the squatters felt that the period of notice was too short for them to find somewhere else to live. Councillors, officials, council workmen and a large body of police arrived but even after a two-hour stand-off the squatters could not be persuaded to leave. Their resolve had been strengthened by speeches from one of their leaders, Mrs Jane Arkhill, and the local Communist councillor Howard Hill. Eventually the council workmen refused to demolish the huts until alternative accommodation had been arranged. This was then done, and the squatters moved to a former Civil Defence camp where the conditions and services were in fact far superior; they had 'technically won their battle against eviction'.[32]

In Scotland the Communist Party congratulated itself on the role its activists played with the occupation of the camps and other buildings, 'in which our members have played an outstanding role in defending squatters in courts, and in putting families into vacant premises.' The Party reported that its councillor Arthur Henderson in Clydebank had represented the families squatting in an empty manse when they had been charged with trespass by the Church authorities. He had also organised a community campaign to ensure that temporary alternative arrangements were made for them. At Carluke in Lanarkshire families seeking homes had approached the branch secretary and the outcome had been the occupation of an ex-RAF camp at Burnwood. The Party was also active with the squatters in Inverness, as we have seen, Cambuslang, Dundee, Edinburgh, Aberdeen and Dunbartonshire. It had been instrumental in organising Homeless Associations in several areas to pursue housing issues. In Falkirk thirty people occupied a large empty hostel after a CP member had entered through a window and opened the door. The squatters then moved in their furniture, describing themselves as we have seen as 'refugees from overcrowding' and began to clean up the premises. As was to occur repeatedly all over Britain in the near future, the local branch of the Party called on the local authority to use its requisitioning powers over this and other similar properties. In the meantime the Falkirk CP claimed to have its own 'waiting list' of families interested in squatting.[33]

In Glasgow a participant has recalled how a 'continuous stream of people' came to the Communist Party offices to seek help with their housing problems, 'many of them families in heartrending circumstances'. The responses of a Party team led by Johnny Gold could be inventive:

> His masterpiece was a building that had once been a workers' hostel but had been taken over by the Admiralty during the war and was then empty. He was unable to gain entry in the normal way but, nothing daunted, he went home for his tools and spent the greater part of a night cutting his way in through the back wall and later opened the doors from the inside and admitted a large number of squatters.[34]

The Party also had its share of rebuffs from the authorities in Scotland when it tried to support squatters. In Glasgow the activist Bob Saunders attempted to bring a deputation of the Barlinnie squatters to a Corporation meeting but councillors turned him down, as they did Bob McIlhone and squatters from huts in Kelvingrove Park. Corporation meetings also refused to meet deputations of Communist-led tenants groups to discuss housing issues the following year. Similarly when three men who had squatted with their families spent a night in gaol and then received a nominal fine for trespass in Falkirk Sheriff's court George McAllister of the CP was refused permission to speak on their behalf. Nor did the CP have things entirely their own way when it came to campaigning for squatters in Scotland. Outside Edinburgh the Craigentinny Camp was one of those that had been occupied and when 'delegates elected by the residents' lobbied the City Corporation about the restoration of electricity they were accompanied by 'ministers from the churches in the district.' The Corporation agreed to restore electric light and inform the Fuel Overseer that the council had taken over the camp, so that the residents could buy coal. Until this intervention it appeared that the Corporation did not wish to take this responsibility.[35]

The main challenge to the role of the CP came in Glasgow. An organiser and unofficial advocate for the local squatting movement emerged in Peter McIntyre, a former Communist who during the early 1930s had been a candidate for the Party in local elections in the city. By 1946 he had not only left but turned against the Party in no uncertain terms and his own politics could be described as a kind of left populism. As an experienced speaker and organiser he had encouraged the Crookston Camp occupation in August 1946, stating that he was acting on behalf of the Govan Tenants' Association. He debated the squatting issue with Corporation councillors in the press, lobbied both Bevan and the Secretary of State for Scotland and, as we have seen, played a role in the squatting of large empty private houses in Glasgow.[36]

When Glasgow Unity Theatre staged its play about the Glasgow housing crisis, *The Gorbals Story*, in September 1946 McIntyre attended the opening night and was invited to speak by an actress. It seems he delivered what amounted to 'an impassioned prologue' about housing conditions in the city to an audience which included 'the Lord Provost of Glasgow and many other squirming dignitaries'. It seems to have been political pressure that forced the Glasgow Labour Group to defend its record in a pamphlet, *Glasgow's Housing Progress*. This pressure was not just from the Communists, McIntyre and the camp squatters generally but from the City Corporation too. The 'Progressive', or, loosely speaking, the Conservative councillors had succeeded in getting a motion passed protesting at both delays to the housing programme and the 'failure to keep citizens informed of progress'.[37]

Glasgow's Housing Progress adopted the familiar stance of the Scottish official or politician under pressure: it pointed out that things were worse in England. Compared to Liverpool, Manchester and other English cities Glasgow was 'well to the fore' when it came to requisitioning, and it had a better record than any in England when it came to building permanent houses during the war years. Further, it had not 'placed restrictions on the building of temporary houses' and was lobbying the government to ensure that building workers were available. In a final swipe at the Corporation's critics the pamphlet concluded that it was a 'cruel deception' to 'ignore the real facts of the situation and make political capital out of the house-starved condition of the people'.[38]

Elsewhere too the activists involved were not necessarily Communists. In Hereford a city councillor and former chairman of the housing committee led two separate groups of squatters into empty local camps following meetings at the town hall. Later he was instrumental in persuading the local authority to requisition property and take over a prisoner-of-war camp when it was empty. At the village of Norton Fitzwarren, near Taunton in Somerset, two Labour Party activists, veterans of the First World War, assembled a party and led them through the churchyard to empty hutments, where as we have seen they cut the wire for them. In Stafford the Labour MP Stephen Swingler told a public meeting that the squatters were 'morally justified' in taking the law into their own hands, and he urged ministers to allow the use of camps for temporary housing. Apparently his speech immediately led to squatting in aerodrome huts nearby. In Bristol, the city where the local authority had taken a robust approach to requisitioning empty property for housing purposes, Labour's Alderman Hennessey actively supported the camp occupations. He organised a meeting that seems to have precipitated the camp occupation by thirty families described earlier, and he spoke at mass meetings at other camps where he told the crowds that rumours of police action to evict them were unfounded: 'they cannot turn you out.' He continuously supported what he called this 'requisitioning by the people' and defended their case to the City Council. In this, as has been mentioned, Hennessy was isolated, at least on the council; his Labour colleagues issued a statement disassociating themselves from his activities.[39]

At this time the Independent Labour Party was reduced to only a few councillors, mainly in Glasgow, and one Member of Parliament, again in Glasgow, whose death in 1946 ended the ILP's presence at Westminster. The ILP had been refused re-affiliation to the Labour Party when it applied in 1946, and within two years it would dissolve itself. Nonetheless there are examples of ILP members who were actively supporting the squatters. In Essex the ILP and a member of Ashington Rural District Council established a 'People's Housing Committee' whose members came from Labour and the ILP, the Co-op, the British Legion and the Farmworkers' Union. This committee surveyed empty properties in the area and made recommendations for requisitioning; it also helped families to occupy empty army huts. Besides directly organising squats ILP activists lent their support in other ways. On Teesside National Chairman Bob Edwards spoke up for the local squatters and took part in a round-table discussion with local Labour councillors about them. Edwards stressed that the disused services accommodation was in fact public property and 'should not be standing idle'. Some progressive MPs in the Liberal Party also lent their support, such as Wilf Roberts in North Cumberland. Roberts had campaigned against the appeasement of fascism in the 1930s and been a leading figure in campaigns for the Spanish Republic. Now, speaking of the occupation of the former

RAF aerodrome at Silloh, he declared that it was 'wonderful that people should occasionally act on their own and not wait for official decisions'. There is evidence that the squatters' committees included people who had political awareness even if they were not associated with an organisation. In Carlisle a reporter was told by one of them that 'we've had a lot of support from people in Carlisle. The elections are in November so no party dare come out against us.'[40]

Building an organisation

It is not always easy to ascertain what the relationship actually was between the camp squatters and the political activists who were supporting them. This can be seen from some of the efforts to build representation for the squatters. Besides the Homeless Associations supported if not initiated by the Communist Party in Scotland there were other efforts to build representative organisations of camp squatters. A Mr Callaghan, who chaired the committee at the West Derby camp near Liverpool, stated that he was contacting other camps with a view to forming an area committee. Somewhat less ambitious, although along the same lines, was the meeting between two squats in Tynemouth to agree a common approach to the local authority. Similarly at the Elton Hall camp on Teesside the committee sought to 'contact various camps with a view to the formation of a squatters' union to strengthen their position generally in the event of any future action that may be taken against them'. This has been recalled as the initiative of the Communist Pat Durkin. In Bristol a camp secretary, Ernest Yeo, organised a meeting of delegates from all the other camp committees in the area for a 'general review of policy, welfare and conditions'; this he hoped, would lead to an organisation he proposed to call the Bristol and District Homemakers' Federation. In Yorkshire also there was an attempt to establish a county-wide squatters' organisation when more than twenty delegates from camp committees around Doncaster met to seek support. In this example they were approaching trades unions for help, a move which suggests some involvement from the traditional left and labour movement.[41]

Birmingham is a particularly interesting example of an attempt to organise the camp squatters' committees into a cohesive body; here, as in several cases in Scotland, the initiative came from the local Communist Party. More than 250 families who were squatting in and around the city were now members of the Birmingham and District Squatters' Association, chaired by Sam Blackwell of the CP; there were echoes here of the Birmingham Tenants' Federation the CP had initiated before the war. The committee of this group would negotiate with the council over further work that was needed for the camps and other issues. During the following month however the politics of squatting in Birmingham changed, as they did in Britain as a whole, following the actions that will be examined in the next chapter. It seems to have been as a result of this that the BDSA experienced a split over claims that it was 'a political body, affiliated to the Communist Party'. In contrast the breakaway Birmingham and District Camp Residents' Association promised to be non-political' and focus solely on those in the ex-army camps; it is interesting too that it eschewed the term 'squatter' in favour of 'resident', in line with the aspirations of camp occupiers in the rest of the country. This suggests that relationships with activists were not necessarily static but sensitive to changes in the wider political environment.[42]

In Glasgow Peter McIntyre shared a platform with an ILP councillor and tenants' association representatives at a mass rally in St Andrew's Hall in support of the squatters. Later he led a delegation with three other men, described as 'spokesmen for the squatters in the West of Scotland', to meet the Secretary of State for Scotland George Buchanan. Their purpose was to press the case for joint management of the camps by the Scottish Office and the camp committees. In this they were unsuccessful, as we shall see, and at the meeting Buchanan expressed surprise and disappointment that no one in the delegation was in fact a squatter. In this case it seems that that men with political experience, even if they had no affiliation, together with seasoned public speaking and organisational skills could by default assume leadership roles even if the cause did not affect them personally. Possibly these roles were granted by formal agreement at a meeting. Possibly McIntyre's clear distance from the Communist Party also cleared him from suspicions of political opportunism; keen to distinguish his campaigning from that of the Party, he maintained that 'we have no political axe to grind. All we want is to get people homes.' The squatters were presumably content that someone with the necessary knowledge and self-confidence was prepared to advocate for them with the local and national authorities. Unfortunately the available sources cannot clarify these questions although it is significant that in November that year McIntyre was elected as an independent member of Glasgow City Corporation. This presumably reflected local support for his agitation in the city over the housing crisis.

Buchanan had made an interesting point about the deputation, and the same point could have been made about the deputation that attempted to meet Birmingham City Council. It seems that only in some cases were the political activists who were acting as squatters' leaders or advocates actually squatting themselves. In Dumbarton Communist Town Councillor

John M'Gandle was chairman of the Homeless Tenants' Association and indeed as a camp squatter he was in their situation himself. In England Abe Lazarus in Oxford was squatting and so was International Brigade veteran Alf Cooper in Chelmsford; Pat Durkin in Middlesborough was another. At the Daws Hill camp in Buckinghamshire Communist squatters were the key members of the camp committee. In these cases they and their families were squatting in army huts for the same reasons as the others who were there. Apart from such exceptions the squatters' advocates had not been produced by the movement itself but had adopted it as a function of their established political activism.[43]

So what were the Communist Party's objectives at this stage? The role of the CP in these events will be discussed in detail in the next chapter, which concerns the squatting the Party directly organised in London, Glasgow and elsewhere in September 1946. During that month the role and motives of the Communists came under scrutiny from the left as well as the national and local press. In the two months or so before that the attitude of the Party seems to have been that this new direct action was 'an excellent record of the people's initiative and independence' that would prompt authorities to 'speed up the housing programme' to relieve the overcrowding that had led to the squatting movement. In Scotland Bob Cooney, on behalf of the North East Area Committee of the Party, stated that the squatters were only doing what the local authorities should have done already and therefore they were performing a public service. He urged a speeding-up of the requisitioning process and called on councils to publish lists of properties they intended to requisition for housing purposes; otherwise Communists would continue to assist squatters as they were already doing.[44]

Therefore the squatting movement was seen as a popular initiative that should prompt the government to an urgent approach to the housing problem, one that should also take requisitioning more seriously. In the same way that it had argued a few years earlier, the Party promoted wholescale requisitioning of empty property as a socially equitable support for homeless families. There is also the issue of what role the Party saw for itself in these events, and this is among the themes to be considered in the next chapter.

NOTES

1   NA: CAB/128/6, Conclusions of the Meeting of the Cabinet, 14 August; CAB/129/12, Squatters in Army Camps: Report by the Chairman of the Official Committee, 31 August; CAB/129/13: squatters in Army Camps, Memorandum from the Home Secretary to the Cabinet, 28 September 1946.

2   NA: CAB 130/13, Squatters in Military Camps: Minutes of the Cabinet Committee on Squatting, 20 August 1946.

3   *Daily Worker*, 14 August; *Sunderland Echo*, 9 August; *Birmingham Mail*, 15 August; *Evening Times*, 16 August; *Western Daily Press*, 13 August 1946.

4   SHC: A\BVF/2/4, Extract from memoirs of an ex-serviceman looking for accommodation in Norton Fitzwarren, 1946.

5   *Aberdeen Press and Journal*, 21 August 1946; *Lancashire Daily Post*, 14 August 1946; *Sunderland Echo*, 9 August 1946; *Birmingham Mail*, 14 August 1946.

6   *Liverpool Evening Express*, 17 August; *The Scotsman*, 17 August 1946; Paul Burnham, 'The Squatters of 1946: A Local Study in National Context', *Socialist History*, no. 25 (2004 p. 26); History of the Vale of Leven Project – www.valeofleven.org.uk; *Somerset County Herald*, 24 August 1946.

7   NA: CAB/129/12, Squatters in Army Camps: Memorandum by the Parliamentary Under-Secretary of State at the War Office, 13 August 1946; NA: CAB 130/13, Squatters in Military Camps: Minutes of the Cabinet Committee on Squatting, 20 August 1946.

8   The Ministry of Health statement was widely covered in the press; these quotations are from the *Scotsman*, 19 August 1946. HC Debates 10 October 1946 vol 427 cc337-43 337.

9   *Blaydon Courier*, 27 September; *Somerset County Herald*, 24, 31 August; *Cumberland News*, 7 September; *Essex Newsman*, 13 August 1946.The parliamentary debate can be seen at HC Debates, 10 October 1946, vol 427 cc337-43 337.

10   'Jean Mann Defends the Government' *Forward*, 21 September 1946.

11   *Blaydon Courier*, 27 September; *Hull Daily Mail*, 14 September; *Falkirk Mail*, 30 October; *Western Daily Press*, 24 August; *Carlisle Journal*, 17 September; *Somerset County Herald*, 24 August 1946; *The Derry Journal*, 23 August 1946.

12   This interview was widely quoted in the press; the quotation here is from the *Sheffield Star*, 7 September 1946.

13   *Scotsman*, 23 August; *Evening Times*, 6, 9 September; *Stirling Sentinel*, 12 November 1946.

14   *Scotsman*, 17 December; *Evening Citizen* 14 October 1946; NRS: HH57/1080: Barlinnie Prison: Squatters in Nos. 4 and 5 Quarters: telegram from the Secretary of State for Scotland to the Home and Health Department, November 1946.

15   HC Debates, 10 October 1946, vol. 427 cc337-341; *Northampton Mercury*, 6, 13, 20, September, 14 December 1946

16   NA: PREM 8/227: Prime Minister's Office, Squatters in Army Camps; Dave Simpson, *No Homes for Heroes: Post War Squatters in Washington* (Sunderland, Gilpin Press, 2006, pp. 33-6); Jim Tatters, interview with John Suggett, 2012.

17   Jim Tatters, interview with John Suggett and Don Watson, 2014.

18   *Somerset County Herald*, 31 August; *Western Mail*, 17, 20 August; *Lennox Herald*, 7 September 1946.

19   *Gateshead Times*, 13 September; *Western Mail*, 20 August 1946; CEA: SL/2/2/3, Minutes of the Corporation of Edinburgh Housing Committee, 26 November 1946, 25 February 1947; *Aberdeen Press and Journal*, 27 August, 3 September 1946.

20 *Oxford Mail*, 23 August 1946.

21 Letter from the Chairman of Newport Council Housing Committee, *Times*, 19 September 1946.

22 *Western Daily Press*, 14, 17, 20 August 1946; DCRO: UD/CS 221, Chester le Street Urban District Council Correspondence re squatters at Roman Avenue military camp 1946-1954, letter from the Clerk of the Council to each squatted hut, 26 November 1946.

23 NA: CAB/128/6, Conclusions of the Meeting of the Cabinet, 17 August 1946.

24 *Shields Evening News*, 27, 30 January1947; *Nottingham Evening Post*, 29, 30, 31 August; *Manchester Evening News*, 13 August 1946.

25 *Aberdeen Press and Journal*, 20, 23 August; *Derby Evening Telegraph*, 16 August, 30 September 1946, 11 January 1947; *Durham County Advertiser*, 13 September, 18 October; *Lennox Herald*, 7 September 1946.

26 *The Derry Journal*, 30 August 1946, 1 January 1947.

27 These accounts are criticised in James Hinton, 'Self-Help and Socialism: The Squatters' Movement of 1946', *History Workshop*, Issue 25 (Spring1988, p. 118); see also Noreen Branson, *History of the Communist Party of Great Britain 1941-1951* (London, Lawrence and Wishart, 1997, p. 120). OHC: OXOHA: LT900, BBC Radio Oxford, *Squatters' Delight* (1994). On the Cutteslowe Walls campaign and Lazarus see Peter Collison, *The Cutteslowe Walls: A Study in Social Class* (London, Faber and Faber, 1963). Lazarus as a squatter is referred to in the *Oxford Mail*, 30 August 1946.

28 *Oxford Mail*, 17, 19, 23 August 1946.

29 *Blyth News*, 8 August 1946; Bert Ward quoted in Noreen Branson, *History of the Communist Party of Great Britain 1941-1951*, p. 20; Paul Burnham, 'The Squatters of 1946: A Local Study in National Context', pp. 20-46.

30 *Birmingham Mail*, 21· 26 August, 3 September 1946; James Hinton, 'Self-Help and Socialism: The Squatters' Movement of 1946', p. 108; *Daily Worker*, 16, 19, 22 August, 2 September 1946.

31 *Blyth News*, 16 September; *Essex Newsman*, 10 September 1946; on the International Brigade generally see Richard Baxell, *Unlikely Warriors: The British in the Spanish Civil War and the Struggle Against Fascism* (London, Aurum Press, 2012); NRS: HH57/1080, Barlinnie Prison: Squatters in Nos. 4 and 5 Quarters.

32 *Sheffield Star*, 23, 26, 27 August 1946.

33 LHASC: CP/LOC/SCOT/01/02, *Report of the Scottish Committee of the Communist Party January 1945-June 1946, and Resolutions of the Scottish Congress September 1946*; also LHASC: CP/LOC/SCOT/01/03, Scottish Committee of the Communist Party, *Bulletin* no. 193, August 1946; *Falkirk Mail*, 6 September 1946.

34 Bob Saunders, 'The Glasgow Squatters, 1946', *Scottish Marxist*, no.7 (October 1974, p. 27).

35 ML: C1/3/114, Minutes of the Corporation of Glasgow Housing Committee, 28 August, 11 September, 18 December 1946; 9 January, 26 February 1947; *Falkirk Mail*, 13 September 1946; *Evening Times*, 16, 20 August, 5, 6 September 1946; CEA: SL/2/2/3, Minutes of the Corporation of Edinburgh Housing Committee, 26 November 1946.

36 For McIntyre's early CP candidature see *Glasgow Herald*, 4 November 1931.

37 Linda Mackenney, 'Introduction' to Robert McLeish, *The Gorbals Story* (Edinburgh, 7:84 Publications, 1985, p. 14). This invitation to McIntyre suggests that the Communist Party was not as embedded in the Glasgow Unity Theatre as it was in its London counterpart, Unity Theatre. ML: C1/3/113, Minutes of the Corporation of Glasgow Housing Committee, 27 April 1946.

38 ML: Glasgow Trades Council, City Labour Party, and Co-operative Association, *Glasgow's Housing Progress* (Glasgow, no date, circa 1946/47).

39 *Western Mail*, 22, 27 August; *Somerset County Herald*, 24 August; *Birmingham Mail*, 17 August; *Western Daily Press*, 14, 17 August 1946.

40 *Socialist Leader*, 7 September; *Middlesborough Evening Gazette*, 14 August; *Carlisle Journal*, 6 September; *Cumberland News*, 14 September 1946.

41 *Liverpool Evening Express*, 17 August; *Shields Evening News*, 20 August; *Middlesborough Evening Gazette*, 13 August; Bert Ward quoted in Noreen Branson, *History of the Communist Party of Great Britain 1941-1951*, p. 20; *Western Daily Press*, 2 September; *Daily Worker*, 20 August 1946.

42 *Birmingham Mail*, 26 August, 12, 14 September 1946.

43 *Glasgow Herald*, 16 September; *Newcastle Journal*, 16 September; *Scotsman*, 19 August, 6 November; *Lennox Herald*, 7 September 1946; Paul Burnham, 'The Squatters of 1946: A Local Study in National Context', p. 34. Birmingham City Councillors refused to meet the deputation to discuss squatting because it was made up of Communists – *Birmingham Mail*, 3 September 1946.

44 *Daily Worker*, 17 August; *Aberdeen Press and Journal*, 28 August 1946.

Chapter Six
THE 'LUXURY SQUATTERS':
OCCUPYING EMPTY MANSIONS

In Scotland as we have seen there were several examples of squatting in empty premises besides camps during 1946, just as there had been during and immediately after the war. In May the Edinburgh Houseless Association installed nine families in a house in the centre, one the City Corporation had requisitioned but then left empty. In Glasgow during August families were squatting in empty mansions in the West End and the Great Western Road, formerly requisitioned properties which were now up for sale; also in buildings belonging to the City Corporation. At the end of the month the Glasgow homeless made 'their most ambitious attempts at occupation so far' by 'turning their attention' to hotels in the city. Thirty families entered the Grand Hotel at Charing Cross and another party occupied the Imperial Hotel in Buchanan Street, both vacant and in the city centre. In Woodside Crescent a large group of families led by Communist Party members took over and installed their furniture in an empty house owned by the Co-operative Society.[1]

Occupying desirable private properties and hotels was a clear escalation from much previous squatting. It was also designed to make the point that these de-requisitioned properties were being put on the market rather than used for the benefit of the homeless. There was also a significant Communist Party involvement which was inevitably controversial. Peter McIntyre for example claimed that his own group were simply out to find accommodation and not 'to go out on stunts'; he continued that 'those who advise people to go into hotels are not the friends of the homeless'. The CP repeated its demand dating from the war years for the full use of requisitioning powers and claimed that there was a homeless family for every empty house in Glasgow. As regards private hotels the ownership of a property 'was a secondary consideration to the fact that it is empty'. The authorities in the city were quick to react and make use of the Scottish legislation available to them. At several squats including the hotels the police successfully threatened the occupants with legal action unless they left; the City Corporation began legal proceedings against the squatters in its properties; at the Co-op owned hotel the police evicted the squatters following a stand-off and their furniture was removed by Co-op employees, who attracted a barrage of heckling from a crowd of observers. In Kelvindale Road, where a 'mansion' had been squatted under McIntyre's leadership, eviction proceedings were also set in motion.[2]

It was in London only a week after some of these events that the occupation of empty private property took the squatting wave to a new level and with it the political dynamics involved.

'Luxury squatters'

The London District Committee of the Communist Party included several activists who were veterans of pre-war housing campaigns. Among them were 'Tubby' Rosen and Ted Bramley, who had also been involved in the direct action to open the London underground stations as bomb shelters. Bramley's 1945 pamphlet on London's housing problems had invoked the rent strikes and tenant struggles of the 1930s, in which his Party had a prominent role, and gave the central place to popular action: 'The lessons of the past are clear. All obstacles created by landlords, Building Societies and others can be swept away by the collective action of the people themselves.'[3]

Bramley was an elected member of the London County Council while fellow District Committee members Bill Carritt, Joyce Alergant and Joan McMichael were members of Westminster City Council and Tubby Rosen had been elected to Stepney Borough Council. In later years they recalled the desperate situations of many of the constituents who approached them with housing problems; also that the Party itself was being approached by the homeless, and that local Party branches 'were under pressure to do something' about the housing crisis in London. On 6 September 1946 the Committee agreed to use its councillors and Party Borough Secretaries to identify empty buildings such as blocks of flats or hotels and to contact families, known to be in dire housing circumstances, willing to occupy them as squatters. This meant, as has been recalled, 'people who would be prepared to squat with no guarantees about anything'. The *Daily Worker* had reported the eviction following the Communist-led squat in a Glasgow hotel at the end of August but there is no indication that the London District Committee had the Scottish examples in mind when they planned their own action. The Communist initiatives in the two cities seem to have been independent of each other despite the Party link. These were the two cities in Britain with arguably the most desperate housing problems but with empty camps on their peripheries rather than within easy reach, so that additional sites for squatting were needed. There was no central co-ordination but what appears to be a simultaneous response by different cadres of experienced activists with a shared background in direct action and tenants' struggles. As was suggested in an earlier chapter the experience of key London District members of organising successful direct action during the war would have been a background to their decision. Further, there were common opportunities to contrast the conditions of the wealthy with the conditions of many working people and to promote requisitioning as a tool to help to close the gap.[4]

James Hinton suggests a wider political motive too, one concerned with the Party activists' need to rebuild an independent political identity for themselves in the circumstances of 1946. At the Communist Party Congress of 1945 the leadership had faced unprecedented levels of criticism from the local activists for the position it had taken towards the end of the war and immediately after it: opposing strikes, supporting the continuation of the wartime coalition government, and misjudging the mood of the electorate were held to be factors in the Party's disappointing electoral performance in 1945. A month before the eruption of squatting in camps the Labour Party Conference had rejected the CP's application to affiliate to Labour, and done it so decisively that no further applications were ever made. Therefore, Hinton argues, the identity the Party was seeking was as a broker between popular discontent with Labour and government policy; by channelling that discontent constructively the result could be self-confident popular movements able to push the government in more progressive and socialist direction. The squatting movement was an ideal opportunity to pursue this approach. As we have seen the *Daily Worker* had already described the camp squatting as an independent 'peoples' initiative' that could prompt the authorities to 'speed up the housing programme'; the call for the full use of requisitioning powers by local councils and for the government to act where they refused to do so had been a Party call since the war years.[5]

The initial target of the London Committee was Duchess of Bedford House in Kensington. This large block of flats had been requisitioned during the war and subsequently offered to Kensington Borough Council for temporary housing. The council had turned down the offer and so the owner, the Prudential Assurance Company, now proposed to re-let them at upmarket rents. It was a classic example of what the Party and some London Labour boroughs had campaigned against as soon as requisitioning had been introduced during the war. Hilda Lewis and her husband had been living in one room and on a housing waiting list for a year since he had left the army; they had been told that they had no chance of accommodation because they had no children. As she wrote later:

> On Sunday 8 September 1946 my brother-in-law Dave Lewis, who was Borough Secretary of the Hammersmith Communist Party at that time, came to say that there was squatting taking place in Kensington that day. He warned us that there was a risk of being arrested and possibly imprisonment, but we were prepared to take that chance. The instructions were to go to Kensington High Street, where we would see helpers who would direct us to the appropriate building.

As they reached Duchess of Bedford House 'others began to pour in and lorries packed with men, women and children and their bits and pieces, were converging on the area'. In the course of that Sunday more than a thousand people were helped to occupy this building and then, because of the swelling numbers, an 'overspill' block and some other flats in Marylebone. During the following 24 hours the Abbey Lodge block near Regent's Park and Fountain Court on Buckingham Palace Road were occupied too, as was the Ivanhoe Hotel in Bloomsbury. Entry was achieved through unlocked doors or by climbing over roofs and through skylights to open doors. On one famous occasion, reminiscent of the attitude of some military sentries at the camps, the police actually came to the aid of families who were lifting prams over railings by opening the doors of a building for them. Altogether some 1,500 people were involved in these squats and they were the largest single episode of direct action that year. It had been a rapid but meticulously planned and executed manoeuvre.[6]

At Fountain Court Communist Councillor Joan McMichael began the liaison with the housing authority:

> We were in a peculiar position, of course, because I was a member of Westminster City Council and we agreed to call an official from the Westminster City Council to come down and meet the squatters and discuss what we intended to do. It was a remarkable meeting at which the official laid down all the threats about writs and possible eviction and about breaking the law and so on. We gave him about twenty minutes and then we put the squatters' case, and what they felt about it, and then we had a break for twenty minutes while everyone discussed among themselves what their reaction would be. We took a vote, and it was absolutely unanimous that we stay; there was a tremendous feeling.[7]

As was seen in the case of the camp squats, the activists who were assisting – presumably the 'we' referred to in 'we put the squatters' case' – were again rarely squatting themselves. Among those Communists who were later prosecuted only Stan Henderson, Hammersmith Branch Secretary and chair of the committee at Fountain Court, was actually squatting there although it is not clear whether this was only for the duration of the action. Certainly the Attorney General stated that Henderson 'was himself a person living in the most deplorable housing conditions'; or, as the man himself put it many years later, living with his family in one room where 'it was hard to tell where the decay stopped and the war damage started'. Indeed such conditions and the never-ending council waiting lists explain why there were no problems with recruiting participants for these actions.[8]

These squats featured high levels of community organisation, just as the camp occupations had before them. Management committees were agreed, ration book registrations dealt with and lookouts rostered for the doors. Fountain Court organised a crèche so that the women with jobs could go to work. Nevertheless life for the hotel squatters was very different from that of the camp squatters, as the volunteers with Mass Observation noted at the time. In central London, with newspaper reporters, police, spectators, passers-by and supporters constantly outside, their circumstances must have resembled a goldfish bowl. At least one of the squats organised a press conference so that regular intrusions by reporters would stop. Neighbours and the Women's Royal Voluntary Service contributed food, primus stoves for cooking and camp beds where needed, reflecting, as Hinton suggests, the current public sympathy for ex-forces squatters.[9]

Another example of a Communist-inspired squat occurred at Whickham in County Durham. On 11 September in what was described as 'a highly organised swoop' six families including four expectant mothers occupied a twelve-bedroomed mansion for which the Urban District Council was responsible. 'Prominent in the organisation of the squatters' was Enid Ramshaw, a district nurse and midwife in a nearby colliery village. Ramshaw was a well-known local Communist who had stood as a council election candidate for the Party; she had also served with the medical staff of the International Brigade during the Spanish Civil War, and been an active speaker at Aid for Spain meetings in North East England on her return. The building had been under discussion as a potential maternity hospital to be run by the UDC for some time, and Ramshaw's election manifesto had given a prominent place to the need for better maternity facilities in the area. It seems that they had occupied the building to hasten the council's decision.[10]

The case for squatting

This squatting initiative was accompanied by a political case, principally over the issue of requisitioning property. This was set out in a London District flyer headed 'The Case for Squatting'. The Party as we have seen had campaigned over the Circulars of 1943 and 1945 for local authorities to make the maximum use of their power to requisition property for those with no homes. It argued that it was still crucial to do so under the Labour government and once more it was a class issue. It was 'evident that Tory-dominated West London authorities were acting as though the housing emergency was over and that property developers could go ahead irrespective of the conditions in which many thousands of families were living'. The government too had been lax; when service departments derequisitioned blocks of flats it had not pressed councils to requisition them again to rent to working families. It estimated that there were around half a million on the London waiting lists for housing and there was enough empty accommodation for at least ten thousand of the worst cases; however when empty blocks of flats were released for sale or let to the highest bidder 'only the most wealthy would get consideration'.

The flyer raised the issue of the Duchess of Bedford House as a 'flagrant case' of this problem and called on the government to back full requisitioning to relieve the housing crisis and 'remove the possibility of further squatting taking place'. Other calls were for the immediate requisitioning of the properties currently squatted and the provision of essential services to them. The London District tried to send a deputation – consisting of Bramley, Communist MP Phil Piratin and the squatters' committee secretaries – to meet Bevan and to discuss these issues, but he refused to meet them. This refusal set the tone for the Minister's response.[11]

The government reacts

A scheduled Cabinet meeting took place on the day after the Sunday occupations and Bevan was clearly furious at this 'organised attempt and entry by force', and also at the fact that the police had helped some of the families to move in. He complained that 'the government will be in the hands of others soon'. He requested, and got, approval from his colleagues to insist that no cooking or other facilities should be supplied to the squatters, and Home Secretary Chuter Ede would ascertain through the security service what the future plans of the organisers were. It was also agreed that it might be 'necessary to use a certain amount of force to secure respect for property' in these cases, but any 'difficulties' this might cause would be acceptable because there would not be the same public sympathy for these squatters as there had been for those in the camps. The Attorney General would investigate the legal procedures that could be followed.[12]

If newspapers had shown sympathy in many cases for the camp squatters the reverse was now the case. The occupations in London involved, as the *Sheffield Star* put it, threats to 'the sanctity of private property' that 'if left unchecked could only result in chaos'. Other verdicts were that they were 'a plain case of trespass and forcible entry' and 'if such unauthorised action is not stopped quickly all efforts to house people in an orderly fashion will be upset'. It was clear that 'an element of lawlessness had been introduced'. The *Oxford Mail* had been sympathetic to the camp squatters but now maintained that 'squatting is not a solution to any but personal problems … it is selfish queue beating … we are in danger of losing sight of one of the primary responsibilities of citizenship'.

A crucial factor in this reaction – apart from the threat to private property – was the leading role of the Communists. These squats showed that 'a movement of desperation by innocent sufferers has been seized upon by agitators as an opportunity for subversive politics'; newspapers saw that 'behind the London flats move is the sinister hand of Communist organisation … political capital is being made out of tragic circumstances'. In Scotland the press identified this 'manoeuvre by the Communist Party' and claimed that 'public opinion will not stand for lawlessness'. A paper in the south of England was clear that 'no credit whatsoever can be due to the Communist Party for trading on the misery of others to further their own political ambitions'. It would have been for these reasons that the Government were confident of less public sympathy for the London squatters.[13]

At least one newspaper observed that 'Government supporters particularly resent the fact that the Communist Party organised the latest seizures'. In Birmingham, where the local Party had organised squatting in council properties before the London events, this was clearly the case. Whereas the local Labour press had sympathy for those occupying army huts it condemned the 'Communist-instigated law breakers' and 'the actions of a small minority of queue jumpers illegally occupying houses'. It was a basic tenet of Labour's policy that when things were in short supply they should be 'shared fairly and on the basis of need'; if accommodation was to be 'taken illegally and out of turn' then the whole structure of local government would fall. In a somewhat confused phrase it accused the Birmingham Communist Party of 'organising anarchy'.

In Glasgow the Communist initiatives gave Peter McIntyre another opportunity to put distance between his campaigns and theirs. At a mass meeting on Glasgow's housing crisis, he and some colleagues shared a platform with ILP councillors and made a vigorous defence of squatting. He stated though that he would not work with the Communists 'if they were the only party in the world', and despite heckling from women in the audience accused the CP of 'sacrificing women and children for political propaganda'.[14]

The chagrin of the Labour Party was apparent when Bevan and Michael Foot used the left weekly *Tribune* for a particularly scathing attack on the Communist Party and the 'luxury squatting' in London, 'luxury' being a newspaper reference to the upmarket accommodation that had been occupied. It was careful not to attack the squatters themselves – 'from whom', as the editorial put it, 'no decent person could withhold his sympathy' – and admitted that the contrast between the housing of the poor and the housing of the rich was 'vulgar and glaring'. It argued too that the Conservative press, having systematically distorted or misreported the government's housing policy and record, had seized on the camp squatters as a weapon to use against Labour. However 'once the homeless began trespassing near their property the Press Lords woke with a start'. Nevertheless the luxury squatters risked disrupting the whole building programme by seeking to divert resources and labour to renovate the properties they had occupied. The effect of this would be that other families 'who have to wait longest and whose need is most urgent will have to wait longer'. The Government could not allow such 'disruption to the careful ordering of priorities' and could definitely not gave way to illegal action so that 'the law breaking citizen would have stolen the advantage over the law-abiding citizen'.

These actions were akin to anyone who was hungry just helping himself to a leg of lamb from the local butcher's; such 'revolutionary remedies had as much to do with socialism as Al Capone'. In organising this action the Communists had in fact joined forces with the *Daily Mail* and the *Daily Express* in damaging the reputation of the Labour Government, and done so simply to make capital for themselves and with no regard for the legal or other consequences to the squatters. Consequently it was the duty of socialists 'to repel this attack just as much as it was to counter the lies of the Tory press'. Other Cabinet Ministers joined the chorus, with Ellen Wilkinson stating that 'Government has to govern and cannot be faced with anarchy of this kind which is the negation of everything the Labour Party stands for – the organised meeting of peoples' needs'. Minister of Fuel and Power Emmanuel Shinwell added that 'we couldn't have such chaos and anarchy', and that 'enough problems had been left by the war without squatters'.[15]

Clearly the 'luxury squatting' initiative had struck several Government and Labour nerves. The attack by the MP Jean Mann, already discussed, was published after the *Tribune* editorial and used the post office and pensions grab in a similar way to the leg of lamb analogy. Such departures from the orderly prioritising of need, the queue in order of priority, and the provision of service by those in authority who had assessed needs was anathema to their vision of a planned society. It was also a step beyond the unauthorised occupation of redundant public property and into the occupation of private property, and the illegality was blatant.

Enter the law

After the Cabinet meeting gas, water and electricity supplies to the squats were cut off, and presumably under instructions from the Home Office the attitude of the police changed overnight too. Cordons were formed to prevent further squatters from entering the buildings and this had the effect of preventing those already there from leaving, or from goods arriving. The squat committees appealed for candles, paraffin stoves and water, and food; these were supplied by supporters and surreptitiously hauled into buildings by pulleys attached to neighbouring houses. Men who had to get to work did so often by climbing over roofs and then down the side of adjacent buildings. Almost simultaneously the legal challenges arrived. On September 12 Henderson and the committee at Duchess of Bedford House were served with writs for possession by the Ministry of Works (who still had the premises under requisition) and then a requirement to leave by September17. Two days after the writs Henderson along with Councillors Bramley, Carritt, Rosen and Alergant were arrested: the Attorney General had resurrected the crime of 'conspiring to trespass', an offence which dated from the reign of Richard II.[16]

Bevan issued Circular 174/46 to local authorities in England and Wales on 13 September, the day after the criminal charges had been made against the five Communists. An identical version was communicated by the Scottish Office at the same time. This circular explicitly referred to 'the recent seizure and occupation of premises, especially in London, by unauthorised persons' and made the official response clear:

> … allocations should be made by local authorities, as the elected representatives of the people, to families in the greatest need, and this responsibility cannot be usurped by private individuals, we cannot permit the claims of the most needy who have been waiting a long time for houses to be over-ridden by violence and lawlessness, and moreover

the seizure of accommodation must hinder the progress of housing operations.

This was re-stating what the government's response to squatting had been: that it was up to local authorities, and no one else, to allocate houses, and on the basis of need; queue-jumping was to be condemned, and with it diversions of resources from the housing programme; the interests of the law-abiding must be protected. The circular was also a pre-emptive measure in response to security services information that further Communist-inspired squats in private property were likely around the country. Therefore, where squats occurred in properties over which councils had control, the Minister 'expressly requested' that councils 'summon the police if the suspicion of an attempted seizure arises', refuse to provide electricity or gas services and cut them off where they were already available, and immediate action should be taken to ensure the removal of the squatters, including by the legal process of eviction. In Glasgow Peter McIntyre questioned the legality of cutting off electricity and gas supplies to households unless the bills were not being paid, and threatened to take legal cases all the way to the House of Lords, although this threat was not carried out.[17]

Support campaign

A support campaign for the London squatters moved quickly into action. The practical aid described above was accompanied by petitions, poster parades and two demonstrations in central London. The refusal of the police to allow in supplies and food, including food for babies and children, was met by a demonstration and sit-down protest that was eventually cleared by mounted officers; as a result, however, the police cordon allowed essential supplies through to the squatters.

Communist Party General Secretary Harry Pollitt and Phil Piratin MP addressed a rally of 3,000 people after which Pollitt's speech was printed as a pamphlet. As has been observed by James Hinton, the many re-drafts Pollitt made to the speech suggest how ambivalent the Communists were towards Bevan and the government at this time. This was a function of the 'brokerage' role that Hinton argues that the Party was seeking to play in regard to popular discontent and the Labour government. This meant on this occasion that Pollitt was not hostile to the government. He claimed that the squatters led by his Party had made a point of 'not going in to council properties so as not to embarrass the authorities'. This was true of London but not, of course, of Birmingham and Glasgow. He explained that, 'This fight for homes is not a fight against the government ... This initiative of the people will strengthen the government.' This would happen if it spurred on building production, council requisitioning and if the government over-rode recalcitrant councils over requisitioning for housing. He appealed to Bevan not to 'sully your splendid record of fighting on behalf of the working class'. Instead he should understand that the squatting movement was there to be used as an argument for accelerating the housing programme. The speech called for the immediate supply of utilities to the occupied premises; for councils to requisition all suitable premises and for the government to over-ride those who did not; there must be no evictions from currently occupied premises and therefore the withdrawal of writs and warrants, including 'against those people who have fulfilled their civic duties by assisting the workers to obtain this accommodation'.

Finally Pollitt went on to warn against any possible plan to evict the squatters: 'If the Government want reprisals it will get them. The working class is in a fighting mood. It will not stand idly by and see its fellow workers brutally thrown into the street. The action of the Stirling miners in striking against the arrest of six of their comrades for squatting will be followed all over the country ...' This reference to the example of the Stirlingshire miners was included in reports of the speech in the Scottish press, and in a subsequent pamphlet, but not the *Daily Worker*; how relevant the action of these miners was will be discussed later.[18]

Local Communist Party branches organised demonstrations and public meetings in different parts of the country and there appeared to be some momentum for a major national campaign. Resolutions of support were being carried by trade union organisations – an issue that will be discussed below – but the Executive Committee of the Party and the squatters' leaders took the decision to obey the legal writs and bring the action to an end. It was clear that the government was immovable: services would not be restored, the prosecutions and if necessary evictions would be carried out, and that the Party had considerably over-estimated its ability to influence government responses to the housing crisis. As Hinton no doubt accurately concludes, a serious confrontation with the government was not what the CP was seeking. The Cabinet had also offered alternative temporary accommodation to the squatters together with a pledge that they would not forfeit their places on council waiting lists if they accepted it. Henderson believed that the squatters would resist eviction if that was the recommendation put to them but also believed that it would be a mistake to do so:

The argument was, you see, that we should possibly try passive resistance. I made the point that I could not see these returned warriors from the Second World War sit passively by whilst coppers mauled their womenfolk and kids about; you knew that it would end up in a bust-up.

Nevertheless Henderson found when he reported the decision that several squatters were still prepared to resist, and it took an argument before they accepted it. On 20 September, twelve days after they had occupied the buildings, the squatters left in an organised march with banners and a piper to be bussed to their hostels. The situation there was to say the least confused and it took determined action by the squat leaders to ensure that the accommodation spoken of was actually prepared and ready for the large number of families involved. These hostels were designed as halfway houses for the bombed-out, and they were basic; rooms divided by curtains and communal living areas. Once more action was needed to secure improvements. The CP activists continued to liaise with the families for some time until they were eventually re-housed. Three days after the exit squatters took part in a rally organised by the Communists in London on the theme of 'Demand the Britain You Voted For'. The five defendants came to trial over two days at the end of October; Bramley represented himself while the others had the services of the leading barrister Sir Walter Monckton. Bramley in particular took every opportunity to make political points and the judge often tolerated these contributions. These sections of the proceedings were published as a pamphlet to raise funds for the defendants, although they were sentenced to be bound over. This indeed was leniency; they were expecting to be gaoled, the result that would be expected when the charges included 'conspiracy'. Observers at the time assumed that this was due to a desire to avoid creating political martyrs out of the defendants.[19]

Evictions

Evictions took place around the country where empty private properties had been occupied. In Birmingham as we have seen squats in council properties had been organised by the Communists before the London action; the authorities there had also begun legal proceedings before the Cabinet responded to the 'luxury squats'. By the end of August sixteen families had taken over flats in properties requisitioned by the City Estates Department for conversion into flats. According to the CP these had been lying empty for too long; according to the council, including Alderman Bradbeer, the one-time ally of Birmingham Communists during the rent strike of 1939, the squatters should 'take their places in the queue' and their action was 'unfair on law abiding citizens on the housing register'.

The situation escalated during the first two weeks of September when 25 writs were issued to squatters. The Birmingham and District Squatters' Association announced that 'a decision had been taken not to encourage the taking over of any more empty houses requisitioned by the Estates Department' although it would support those who were still there. After a display of defiant rhetoric the squatters agreed to move to a recently vacated army camp and were assured that their places on the waiting list would not be affected. The 'Birmingham and District Camp Residents' Association' which as we have seen broke away from the Communist-led group at this time was clearly a reaction to these events. Their move was highlighted by the Labour–supporting *Daily Herald* as an example of squatters realising that they were 'being used to play someone else's game'.[20]

At a meeting of Whickham UDC six days after the occupation there a deputation from the squatters presented a petition and offered to pay rent and charges for services if they could stay. However Circular 174/46 had recently arrived and when it was read to the meeting the council unanimously 'endorsed the contents of the Circular' and voted to take action against the squat, including the legal procedure to effect eviction if necessary. It appears that the squatters then moved out of the building. Elsewhere in County Durham three families of miners were evicted from a squat and had to seek emergency accommodation in a church hall, and local authorities warned that attempted squatters would get short shrift. In Liverpool police and Corporation officials removed two families who had moved into 'an empty mansion' in Aigburth.[21]

In Scotland, where legislation to criminalise squatting was readily to hand, and where Property Owners' and Factors' Associations had already been pressing for the law to be enforced, similar action soon followed. Glasgow City Corporation, despite protests from its ILP members, voted to begin eviction proceedings against the squatters on its property and refused to meet a deputation from them. It also refused a written request from Glasgow CP that these families not be evicted until alternative accommodation had been arranged for them. It refused representation too from both the Communists and McIntyre's group; the latter had pledged that at the squatted house in Kelvindale Road 'we are ready for a showdown. No matter what happens the house will be held.' In the event the police surmounted their barricades and evicted the squatters amid violent scenes and arrests. Fourteen families were forcibly evicted by the police from a squat at Park Circus Place, again with rough handling and arrests. It was at this time too that the evictions and arrests for squatting in Falkirk, referred to previously, took place after what was described as a 'midnight swoop' by the police.

The meeting between Secretary of State for Scotland Buchanan and squatting campaigners Peter McIntyre and colleagues has been described. It was at this same meeting that Buchanan rebuffed the suggestion that the squatters' committees in Scotland run their own camps or be involved in managing the camps as partners with the authorities. He told them that their proposal would be unacceptable to the government, who insisted that public bodies, the local authorities, should be the sole managers of the camps. It is not clear how much administrative autonomy from Westminster Buchanan actually had in the matter, or how far he would have been inclined to use it if he had. This Under-Secretary of State for Scotland had learnt to be wary of Harry MacShane's campaigning in Glasgow before the war and would have shared Bevan's approach to countering squats in private property.[22] His approach was interpreted by the press as a 'hardening of the government's attitude towards squatting', probably because the meeting took place during a crucial stage of the London occupations.

James Hinton states that Pollitt instructed Party Districts by telegram that there was to be 'No More Squatting'. Certainly local Communists now changed tack over squatting in private property with an abruptness that bears this out. In Manchester for example Party activists had threatened that 'if the Housing Committee does not start emergency requisitioning in the next few days we shall move into the empty houses', apparently prompting 'growing fears about mass squatting' in the city. Nevertheless during the same September week as this threat appeared it was subsequently reported that 'squatting is now unlikely to take place in Manchester' because 'Communist officials have decided that any such move is out of the question.' At the same time in Leeds the Yorkshire District Secretary Bert Ramelson stated that if the City Corporation persisted in leaving requisitioned property empty and failed to requisition all eligible vacant accommodation, 'our Party will feel justified in offering to assist those needing homes to occupy empty properties'. This was not carried out.

At the Communist Party Executive Committee meeting where this was discussed the only record is that General Secretary Pollitt proposed and was given agreement to a motion congratulating the London District on 'their services to London's citizens requiring homes' and pledging full support 'to those comrades against whom action has now been taken'. As regards any discussion Pollitt is recorded as 'emphasising' that 'in view of the very serious situation both at home and abroad' the Committee must 'allow no single aspect to take all our attention'. This somewhat cryptic reference may mean that he wanted to draw a line under the squatting episode in terms of a tactic.[23]

Although there seems to be no evidence of the Communist Party initiating or leading any more squats after the conclusion of the events in London, Glasgow, Falkirk and elsewhere as we will see its activists continued to help the camp squatters.

'Put the roofs on' and housing campaigns

There was some sympathy around the country for the London squatters despite the universal press hostility and the prominence of the Communist Party in the events. In the North East of England for example Newburn UDC passed this unanimous resolution to be sent to the Ministry of Health:

> While fully recognising the illegality of the squatters' action in seizing and occupying the premises known as the Duchess of Bedford House and Fountain Court, the sympathies of this Council are with them in their desire for housing accommodation, and the Council regrets that it will be necessary to eject them in order to make the buildings available for luxury flat dwellers and suggests that the premises should be requisitioned and converted into workers' dwellings.

Bevan aligned himself with sentiments like these when he argued in Cabinet that, in view of the severe housing problem in London some hotels due for de-requisitioning should be handed to local authorities for housing purposes. He pointed out that councils like Holborn had been making strong arguments for this policy. He did not point out that his had in fact been the Communists' argument too, and that the Holborn example had been cited in the *Daily Worker*, although the CP proposals had been for more far-reaching action. Bevan agreed that government and service departments were not de-requisitioning properties fast enough either. However the argument seems to have been carried by Chancellor of the Exchequer Hugh Dalton and President of the Board of Trade Stafford Cripps: there was a 'very serious shortage of hotel accommodation in London' and 'for the purposes of the export drive it was most important that buyers should be able to come freely to London'. Accommodation too would be needed for the planned arrival of tourists who would spend 'a substantial amount of foreign exchange'. North of the border it had already been recognised that hotels would be important to support the Scottish tourist industry. Four months later Glasgow Corporation applied to requisition the Grand Hotel, from which squatters had been evicted, for housing and protested in vain when the Secretary of State permitted its return to use as an up-market hotel.

The Cabinet accepted this order of priorities, apparently believing that the release of high value accommodation from requisitioning would indirectly relieve pressure on the accommodation available for lower income groups. This in fact was another version of the old 'levelling-up' assumption of the past. Despite Bevan's arguments the 'vulgar and glaring' contrast between the accommodation of the rich and the poor was set to continue.[24]

The Ministry of Health announced a package of new measures on 21 September. A 'Put the Roofs On' initiative would aim to have 30,000 of the new homes that were under construction completed by Christmas 1946. As the Cabinet had agreed with Bevan, more requisitioned properties no longer needed for government business were to be made available for housing, and an additional 6,000 of these were released in London in the course of the next year. Licenses for private building work in London were reduced, and pledges made about action against the black market in repairs. Decisions about responsibility for the squatted camps – and therefore over funding for essential services and refurbishment – were clarified more quickly. Both at the time and later Communists claimed that the London squats had 'galvanised the entire housing programme of the Government', listing for example the seven local authorities, five of which were in London, which had changed their policies and were now requisitioning properties for people on their waiting lists.

Whereas historian John Short has concluded that the squatting movement led directly to an acceleration of housing repairs, construction and a new pre-fab building programme this may be making too much of its influence. However it was not just the political left at that time who saw a connection; Bevan denied that his new housing campaign had been prompted by the squatters but, as the *Oxford Mail* editorial drily observed, '... to say the least, there is an element of coincidence about the two events'.[25]

The focus of the Communist Party now switched from direct action to campaigning over requisitioning. This issue had been part of the campaigns against inequalities of sacrifice during the war years and it had also been central to the demands of the London squatters' leaders. The government had extended the timescale for the 1945 requisitioning powers circular and local branches of the Party campaigned for them to be put to sweeping use. In Hull for example the Communists organised a public meeting where speakers argued that the government had 'failed to give local authorities strict instructions to requisition empty homes'. A Housing League was formed, the objective being to campaign for the requisitioning of all suitable empty houses in the city. Elsewhere in Yorkshire Bert Ramelson, a regular outdoor speaker in Leeds, accused the City Corporation there of 'complacency' over requisitioning, claiming that there was a 'mass of empty houses' in the city; the Corporation should publish its intentions towards them. In Felling-on-Tyne the CP secretary defended his Party against accusations of 'irresponsibility' over leading the London squatters and claimed that after fifteen months of peace scarcely more than two thousand homes had been erected in the North East, and three-quarters of them were temporary ones:

> Yet I can point to scores of large houses in Newcastle and other places in the North East which still stand empty while local authorities hesitate or refuse to exercise their requisitioning powers. All sorts of excuses are put forward for the delay, but it is well known that the root cause is the failure of the Government to tackle the job resolutely and sweep aside the monopolists in land and building materials who are now holding the country to ransom.

He continued that the Churchill coalition had not regarded private property as sacrosanct during the war, and that any charge of 'irresponsibility' should be levelled at 'those who fail to act in the face of such urgent need.'[26]

In Manchester delegates to the Executive Committee of the Manchester and Salford Trades Council proposed an emergency motion claiming that the City Council was not making full use of its requisitioning powers to make more properties available for rent to working-class families; it urged them to publish a list of unoccupied properties suitable for requisitioning and speed up the whole process. A deputation to the Housing Committee was agreed to discuss these issues. What the deputation heard and reported back however was that only 27 per cent of recently surveyed empty properties were suitable for adaptation; the remainder were decayed properties that could only be taken over at a prohibitive expense. The Chief Clerk had explained that the Ministry of Health would only grant a maximum of £500 per house or £400 per flat for renovating requisitioned property. This was poor economic value given that properties would revert to the original owners eventually and so both money and labour would be better used on the housing programme. The Trades Council accepted that the Corporation was doing all it could over requisitioning given the difficulties of the system. As was shown in a previous chapter these difficulties were numerous. Further, the Trades Council were in no doubt about the political origins of the motion, which was described as the 'posthumous and still born child of the politically organised squatting campaign'; or as one delegate more bluntly put it, the resolution had been 'a CP stunt to help their candidates at the municipal elections'. Council elections were indeed due in November, and the requisitioning campaign was described in Bradford too as 'the first steps by the Communists into municipal electioneering'. Other local authorities responded to the Communists with a defence of their activity; the Chairman of Northampton's Housing Committee, for example, described how he and the Housing Manager had toured the town and served requisition notices where they were appropriate. If the Communists had information about other suitable properties he would be 'pleased to act' on it. Others still, such as Leeds City Corporation, were dismissive, stating that they had requisitioned a number of properties and they would be ready as soon as the Corporation was able – 'we don't need any campaigns by the Communists to help us'.[27]

Elsewhere there could be sympathy with the objective of strengthening requisitioning although not with the Party that was promoting it. As has been shown, in Birmingham the Labour paper the *Town Crier* had consistently attacked the Communist-inspired occupations of properties in that city and in London. Nevertheless at least one Labour councillor believed of the squatting campaign that, 'the present events are a judgement on us as councillors for not using our existing powers' and he argued for more energetic requisitioning and the use of property already requisitioned. An 'opinion' column went further, arguing that whereas 'the CP will exploit every opportunity to divide the Labour Party' the fact remained that 'empty property is a scandal … instead of illegal anarchistic squatting, municipally organised squatting should begin as never before'.[28]

Just as the Mayor of New Malden Council had welcomed requisitioning whilst distancing himself from the Vigilantes the previous year, so some on the Birmingham Labour left wanted to 'do the job properly' whilst distancing themselves from the Communist campaign. In Birmingham Labour did not control the City Council and would not do so until after the elections of November 1946. Therefore the councillors who were advocating extensive requisitioning may have been unaware of the issues discussed, for example, by Manchester Trades Council. As local authorities had been pointing out since 1943, underneath the rhetoric the practical realities of carrying out requisitioning under the terms laid down by the government were another matter. As we have seen many local authorities in Britain had been critical of the requisitioning process from the beginning; they would have agreed with the opinion given by the Chief Clerk of Glasgow Corporation in 1950 that the requisitioning procedure was 'ineffective and uneconomic'. In any event properties requisitioned under the wartime legislation and its successors were due to be returned to their owners in 1952 and so by the late 1940s the Government expected that requisitioning would only take place in exceptional circumstances.[29]

Activists took up other aspects of temporary housing besides requisitioning, one of which was the provision of the most widespread temporary housing of that time, pre-fabs. Some local authorities were reluctant to make full use of them because they disliked the appearance of large schemes of pre-fabs. The Communist housing activist Harry McShane came across this in Glasgow:

> On the council Jean Roberts said she had seen temporary houses and she would wait for permanent ones. I pointed out that she would do her waiting in Moss Park where she was well housed.

Much further south the Birmingham and District Squatters' Association did act on its pledge to keep up the pressure on housing, albeit in the form of the Birmingham and Midlands Tenants' and Residents Association. Amongst its leaders was Bill Milner, the Birmingham Communist veteran of rent strikes, squatting and the requisitioning campaign – who was also challenging the reluctance of Leamington Council to build pre-fabs. In this his group was supported by the local Trades Council and Labour Party. At a public meeting it was claimed that the town was being run by a clique of 'estate agents, solicitors and shopkeepers' who were more interested in maintaining the value of desirable properties than in the housing of ordinary people.[30]

Was a different tactic possible?

Although there were good practical reasons for bringing the London squats to an end in this way the contrast between the acceptance of defeat and Pollitt's earlier rhetoric was noticeable. Unsurprisingly it is seen as a climbdown by Paul Burnham, who concludes that, like the Grand Old Duke of York, Pollitt had marched his troops to the top of the hill and then marched them down again. Could the London squats have had a different and more successful outcome? James Hinton points out that the legal proceedings could have been continued for some time, and to this it should be added that the Communist Party had access to good legal advice and support, for example from one of the leading radical barristers of the day, the pro-Soviet MP D.N. Pritt. The Mass Observation reports suggest that public opinion was not favourable to them although their reports can hardly be said to be a proper survey; they were based on conversations at one squatted camp in the south of England and a 'random sample' of passers-by in London. Perhaps unsurprisingly they did point to more sympathy for the squatters among younger working-class people seeking accommodation than among older, more middle-class people with settled homes.[31]

Perhaps the most important consideration comes from reports carried in the Communist press during that September fortnight. These were of trade union branches in London passing resolutions in support of the 'luxury squatters', and even that 'the leaders of the building trade unions have been inundated with messages of support from the branches expressing support for the squatters'. Similarly workers at the De Haviland aircraft factory in West London had organised a petition on behalf of the London squatters, and the London Trades Council – representing 600,000 workers – had also pledged support. Elsewhere the national acting council of the Engineering and Allied Trades Shop Stewards' National Council – which included delegates from the shipyards at Harland and Wolf, Cammell Laird Birkenhead and Rosyth dockyard – expressed support for the London squatters too. Their resolution described empty mansions as 'a provocation' and called on the government to requisition property for those in most need. It urged all shop stewards to 'mobilise the utmost support throughout the trade union and labour movements behind the homeless who have rightfully occupied luxury flats earmarked for wealthy parasites'. It concluded that the government 'cannot expect engineering workers to back the production drive if their workmates are thrown into the street to make way for rich idlers.'[32]

These supporting voices from the trade union movement were of a somewhat general nature, but they have been used as evidence by Andrew Friend to argue that a major factor in the sudden conclusions of the London squats was that the Communist Party, 'having placed itself in a position of leadership, had failed to mobilise popular or trade union support'. He states that there were examples of squatters and organised workers being overlapping groups, for example miners in County Durham, and that during the summer of 1946 trade unionists had blacked demolition and other work designed to thwart squatting in several northern towns. There was 'widespread public sympathy', the 'potential for workplace action in support of the occupations of residential property' and the CP had a relatively large membership. Yet at no time did the Party 'call for industrial action to get services connected or to further the demand for wider requisitioning'. By confining tactics to demonstrations and deputations, he concludes, the campaign was conducted on the government's terms. Industrial action on the other hand could have defended the London occupations and pursued their wider aims with more success.[33]

This argument is worth examining. Firstly, to what extent was the working class 'in a fighting mood', as Pollitt claimed, over housing and squatting? And what bearing did the government's own tactics have? There had been speculation in the press that the law would be applied leniently because of the 'apprehension in both government and trade union circles that shop stewards and other extreme elements among trade unionists should be lending their support to this illegal movement'. A lack of leniency would give 'agitators the chance to exploit the situation'. This possibility had indeed been anticipated by the government. The Attorney-General had pointed out however that there would be less chance of Communist 'reprisals' through 'industrial disturbance' if the conspiracy charges against the Communist leaders were pursued 'in order to establish the law and not to obtain penalties'. In other words the law of property would be upheld but any action that could be seen as repressive, and with the potential to create political martyrs, was to be avoided. The court sentences reflected this position. The Cabinet was also careful to ensure that there would be no question of the squatters being put into the street; emergency accommodation was arranged through the London County Council together with the assurance that if they accepted it their places on council housing waiting lists would not be affected. The Government had done what it could not to provoke 'reprisals through industrial disturbance'.[34]

There certainly had been occasions where workmen arriving to dismantle squatted huts refused to carry out their instructions. One had been in Sheffield in 1946, as we have seen, and there were to be others, for example in Portsmouth and Scotland in 1950 and 1949. In these cases it had been because no alternative accommodation had been arranged for the squatters, who were required to leave their huts, and the demolition did not continue until both squatters and workmen had been assured that other accommodation had been organised. This was not the case with the London squatters as alternatives had been arranged for them and so such action to prevent their evictions cannot be readily assumed.

The case of the Stirlingshire miners, whose example had been invoked by Pollitt, was not a particularly appropriate one as a closer examination of the issue there makes clear. The management at Plean Colliery had sought to attract new miners from outside the area by offering pre-fab houses as an incentive to move. The local miners objected, arguing that local men in sub-lets should have priority. The management then offered colliery housing as an incentive but local miners thwarted this by squatting in the empty houses to stake their own claims to priority. When they were prosecuted for trespass and received a nominal fine their colleagues declared an unofficial strike in their support. It did not take long for the miners' union to secure a commitment from the management that local mine workers and their families would have priority for colliery houses, and the strikers returned to work. Therefore this was not so much an example of industrial action in support of squatting as such but of organised workers supporting local colleagues over an action. In fact in coalfields where colliery housing was provided – County Durham for example – disputes over eligibility for the housing were not unusual. The Plean Colliery episode is better understood in that light rather than the one of a new militant mood that Pollitt had presented.[35]

Finally it should be borne in mind that the most assertive resolution – albeit one in terms of 'mobilising the utmost support' rather than explicitly suggesting industrial action – came from a committee of union activists. Any decision to stop work to support the London squatters would have required the active approval of a large number of workers but in contrast resolutions passed by trades councils or shop stewards' committees only required the passive consent of the union members concerned. Unless they are activists themselves they may even be unaware of the resolution being agreed in their name. It cannot be assumed then that a 'major factor' in the end of the London squats was the failure to call for industrial action, nor can it be assumed that the readiness for it was there. Friend does suggest that action might have been called to secure the re-supply of electricity and water supplies to the squats, and certainly this could have been couched in purely humanitarian terms given the number of children who were involved. This was not done of course and so we cannot know what the outcome of any such more limited action might have been.

What of Scotland? There do not appear to have been any suggestions, however cryptically worded, of industrial action against the several cases of evictions that had taken place. Protests and attempts to delay or prevent these had indeed been confined to deputations to the local authorities. In the past activists in the National Unemployed Workers' Movement had helped to prevent evictions in Scotland and elsewhere, but these had been over rent arrears and negotiations with landlords and factors were possible. Evictions for trespass were another matter and if legal routes were to no avail confrontations with the police would prove fruitless and counterproductive. In at least one instance in Woodside Crescent such a confrontation between police and squatters was headed off by the Party activists involved.[36]

As we have seen, during the war David Kirkwood had dissuaded

Clydebank shipyard workers from token industrial action against their housing conditions. In that example it should be remembered that the entire town had been affected by the Clydebank blitz, and that had any such action actually happened those involved would have been acting for their own community and not for others. The same holds true for the Plean Colliery example. There may have been a better opportunity when Glasgow Corporation rejected the deputation's proposal to delay the evictions from the Corporation's properties until alternative accommodation had been found for the squatters. Here were squats with a common link to the Corporation and a proposal to act on humanitarian grounds that was within the Corporation's power to carry out. Could a call for protest action by Corporation staff have had any effect? Once more, of course, this was not done and so we cannot know what the outcome might have been. Nevertheless in Scotland too it does not seem plausible to explain the success of the authorities simply in terms of failures by the CP to call for industrial action.

A different criticism of the Communists and the London squats has come from Colin Ward, again based on articles published in the anarchist press thirty years earlier when the London actions had just ended. He accuses the CP of trying to exploit the squatting movement as it developed and then compromising it by offering the government the 'legal handle they needed'. He also comments that: 'But for the opportunist intervention of the Communists, it seems likely that the seizure of hotels and luxury flats would have forced even more significant and spectacular concessions from the authorities.'[37]

This underestimates the intention of the government to curtail squatting in private property. It also assumes that without the Communist intervention or that of other activists large scale occupations of hotels and so forth would have happened anyway. In Scotland, where the 'legal handle' was already available there had been no hesitation to use it even when camps were originally squatted. Piecemeal seizures by small groups, including seizures of hotels and mansions, had been countered through the law without difficulty.

The impact of 'luxury squatting'

Any dissatisfaction with the government's record on housing does not seem to have found clear electoral expression at this stage, although housing was to remain a key issue for the public throughout the decade. Local elections were held across Britain in November 1946 for one third of council seats and in general the Labour vote stood up across the country with them taking control of major cities like Aberdeen and Birmingham for the first time. Labour consolidated what was to be a long dominance in the major North East England conurbations of Newcastle and Sunderland. It is more difficult to interpret these results in terms of any public judgements about local authorities, council housing and the squatting movement. Certainly there were some signals about the impact of housing issues. In Blyth the British Legion, standing on the policy of giving priority to ex-servicemen for council housing, captured a seat from Labour. In Glasgow, 'where housing has been an outstanding feature of the election campaign', Labour lost a few seats and in the Govan ward Peter McIntyre was elected as an independent member of the City Corporation, taking a seat from Labour. Presumably this was on the strength of his record as a housing campaigner and organising role with the squatters. On the other hand Howard Hill, the Communist councillor who had advocated for squatters in Sheffield lost his seat, and his Party colleagues in Birmingham were unsuccessful too. Similarly in Scotland Communist Party activists had often been in the forefront of the squatting movement but this did not bring electoral success. It won no seats in Glasgow for example and the Party admitted that its results in the Scottish councils 'did not come up to expectations'. Therefore although housing remained crucial there is no national evidence that Labour paid any serious electoral price at this stage, although there are diverse and isolated local examples to the contrary. It was not unusual for Communists to find that their community activism did not necessarily translate into votes.[38]

The Communists who organised the London squats, and at least one who was a similar organiser in Glasgow, remained convinced that theirs had been a valuable initiative. Their comments in 1984 included 'I think it was a tremendously positive achievement which rebounded to the credit of the Party'; 'I think, in the final analysis, positive'; '… a magnificent job in giving a lead to Londoners.' Stan Henderson in particular was upbeat:

> What I am absolutely certain of is that the movement itself jabbed the Labour Movement into life. There was such a change after it with the requisitioning of empty properties. I look back on it and say, it was a damn good thing for a hell of a lot of people.

Similarly Bob Saunders said of the hotel occupations in Glasgow that:

... although the squatters were subsequently evicted by the police, the occupation did have an impact as it brought to the notice of the general public in a dramatic way the dreadful plight of the homeless in our city and lent impetus to the movement.[39]

At the time the Party drew attention to the revival of requisitioning in London as local authorities retained properties for temporary housing. Although Bevan had recognised the symbolic as well as the practical role of requisitioning hotels and upmarket flats, as we have seen such a move was thwarted by his Cabinet colleagues. However further de-requisitioning for housing purposes certainly did take place as a result although not on the scale that would have had a real impact on housing need in London and the major cities.

The accusations of political opportunism that were levelled at the Party over its role came from the left as well as the mainstream press. Besides *Tribune* and Jean Mann in *Forward*, and the pieces in *Freedom Press* used by Colin Ward, the Independent Labour Party also added its voice: the Communists were using 'their usual political chicanery' and the fate of the squatters was of no importance compared to 'resuscitating the fading fortunes of the Party'. As we have seen sections of the trade union movement saw the Party's actions as an attempt to split the Labour Party.[40] The idea that people in desperate need were being manipulated by political extremists for their own ends was a familiar one in the Party's history, and indeed was a charge that could always be produced against any left activists involved in any popular struggle. In London the leading Communists were elected councillors who had a background of organising direct action and who were being approached by constituents in desperate housing circumstances. In a context of squatting already happening all over the country it was predictable that they would follow that option and also to try to force the pace over requisitioning. The strategic error was to over-estimate their ability to force the government's hand. Finally, two of the Communists involved later provided these abiding memories of the 'luxury squatters', observations that could be made about the movement as a whole at this time:

Their behaviour still gives me a warm feeling of admiration and respect. They learned how to manage together; they elected and were led by their spokesmen and women. They worked out necessary disciplines. The greater part was played by the women, the 'mums' as the men went off to work each day. I recall several of them as gifted leaders and organisers, who did on a bigger scale what they had been doing all their adult lives.[41]

NOTES

1   *Scotsman*, 6 May, 24, 30 August; *Glasgow Herald*, 30 August and the *Daily Worker*, 29 August 1946.

2   *Evening Times*, 30 August; Scotsman 15, 19, 21, 30 August and the *Daily Worker*, 29 August 1946.

3   Ted Bramley, *The Battle for Homes* (London: Farleigh Press, 1945, p. 64).

4   Noreen Branson (Ed.), 'London Squatters 1946', *Our History*, no. 80 (August 1989, pp. 21, 24).

5   James Hinton, 'Self-Help and Socialism: The Squatters' Movement of 1946', *History Workshop*, Issue 25 (spring 1988, pp. 102-3.); see also Kevin Morgan, *Harry Pollitt* (Manchester, Manchester University Press, 1994, pp. 131-47).

6   Branson (Ed.), 'London Squatters 1946' pp. 18-23.

7   Branson (Ed.), 'London Squatters 1946', p. 23. Sue Bruley quotes Joan McMichael as an example of how women activists were an integral part of the squatting movement in her *Women in Britain since 1900* (London, Palgrave, 1999, p. 141).

8   NA: CAB/129/12, Squatters in Army Camps: Attorney General to Cabinet, 16 September 1946; Branson (Ed.), 'London Squatters 1946'p. 15. Henderson has left a fascinating memoir of his political activity in a Japanese prisoner of war camp, *Comrades on the Kwai* (London, Socialist History Society, 1990).

9   Branson (Ed.), 'London Squatters 1946', p. 23; SA: MO Archive File Report 2431, Squatters 1946 p. 21; Hinton, 'Self-Help and Socialism', p. 111.

10   *Blaydon Courier*, 13 September 1946; On Ramshaw in Spain see Linda Palfreeman, *Salud! British Volunteers in the Republican Medical Services during the Spanish Civil War 1936-1939* (Brighton, Sussex Academic Press, 2012, p. 250); also *Blaydon Courier*, 9 October 1937.

11   Leaflet by the London District of the Communist Party, *The Case for Squatting* (1946). A copy is included in file NA: CAB/129/12 above; see also 'The Case for the Squatters', *Daily Worker*, 11 September 1946; the letter from Bramley to Bevan dated 9 October 1946 is included in NA: CAB/129/12 above.

12   NA: CAB/195/4, Notes from the Cabinet Meeting, 9 September and CAB/128/6, Conclusions of Cabinet Meeting, 9 September 1946.

13   *Sheffield Star*, 10 September; *Newcastle Journal*, 10 September; *Liverpool Evening Express*, 12 September; *Oxford Mail*, 18 September; *Evening Times*, 12 September; *Essex Newsman*, 13 September 1946.

14   *The Town Crier: Birmingham's Labour Weekly*, 31 August, 14 September; *Glasgow Herald*, 16 September 1946.

15   *Newcastle Journal*, 10 September 1946; 'Help Yourself to a Leg of Lamb', in *Tribune*, 13 and 20 September 1946. According to Paul Burnham, Foot wrote the *Tribune* editorials at this time and Bevan was a regular visitor to the editorial office to agree the stance of the paper ('The Squatters of 1946: A Local Study in National Context', p. 29); *Newcastle Journal*, 13 September 1946.

16   Branson (Ed.), 'London Squatters 1946', pp. 23, 25. The case of the initial response by the police had been raised in the House of Commons and the Government had assured MPs that the Commissioner of Police had 'issued

an instruction to his officers to prevent any future misapprehension'. (HC Debates, 10 October 1946, vol.427 c330-350).

17   The circular was widely quoted in the local and national press; these quotations are from the Tyneside paper *Heslop's Local Advertiser,* 19 October 1946. NA: CAB/128/6, Conclusions of Cabinet Meeting, 9 September 1946; *Glasgow Herald,* 16 September 1946.

18   *Daily Worker,* 12, 13 September; *Scotsman,* 13 September 1946. The pamphlet version is Harry Pollitt, *The Squatters: Pollitt's speech at the London demonstration 12 September 1946* (London, London District Communist Party, 1946). His draft version is in LHASC: CP/IND/POLL/66/06, *Speech in support of the squatters in Cranbourn Street, London 12 September 1946.* The reference to the Stirlingshire miners appears in the draft and the *Scotsman* but not the *Daily Worker* or the pamphlet.

19   See the contributions to Branson (Ed.), 'London Squatters 1946', p. 17; *Daily Worker,* 20 September 1946; Hinton, 'Self-Help and Socialism', p. 115. *Daily Worker,* 23 September 1946.Ted Bramley, *Bramley's Speech at the Old Bailey: The Trial of the London Communists Arrested for Action on Behalf of London's Homeless, September 1946 (*London District Communist Party, November 1946); Joyce Alergant's contribution to 'London Squatters 1946', pp. 26-28.

20   *Birmingham Mail,* 9, 18 September 1946; See also Hinton, 'Self-Help and Socialism', pp.113-14; *Daily Herald,* 13 September 1946.

21   TWAS: UD.WH/A/1/40, Minutes of Whickham Urban District Council, 17 September 1946. *Durham Chronicle,* 11 October and *Blaydon Courier,* 18 October; *Liverpool Evening Express,* 12 September 1946.

22   ML: C1/3/114, Minutes of the Corporation of Glasgow Housing Committee 20 September 1946; *Evening Times,* 13, 19, 20 September; *Glasgow Herald,* 6, 20 September; *Newcastle Journal,* 12 September 1946. *Scotsman,* 16 September 1946; see the entry for George Buchanan in Joyce Bellamy and John Saville (Eds.), *Dictionary of Labour Biography Vol. VII* (London, MacMillan, 1984, pp. 50-52). Some of McShane's pamphlets about Glasgow housing at the time are reproduced in Robert Duncan and Arthur McIvor (Eds), *Militant Workers – Labour and Class Conflict on the Clyde 1900-1950: Essays in Honour of Harry McShane* (Edinburgh, John Donald, 1992, pp. 25-51).

23   James Hinton, 'Self-Help and Socialism', p. 115; *Manchester Evening News,* 14, 16, 18 September; *Yorkshire Evening Post,* 16, 18 September; *Yorkshire Post and Leeds Intelligencer,* 17 September 1946. LHASC: CP/CENT/EC/01/04, Minutes of the Executive Committee of the Communist Party of Great Britain, 14, 15 September 1946.

24   TWAS: U.D. NB/1/25, Minutes of Newburn Urban District Council, 1 October 1946. NA: CAB/128/6, Conclusions of Cabinet Meeting, 17 September 1946; on hotels in Scotland see the *Evening Times,* 4 June 1946, and on the Grand Hotel the *Glasgow Herald,* 10 January 1947.

25   See 'The Consequences of the Squatters' Movement', in *Bramley's Speech at the Old Bailey,* pp. 3, 14; Branson (Ed.), 'London Squatters 1946'. The 30,000 target – Bevan's first public target – was not met due to the materials shortages: see John R. Short, *Housing in Britain: The Post War Experience (*London, Methuen, 1982, p. 42); *Oxford Mail,* 23 September 1946.

26   *Hull Daily Mail*, 18 September; *Yorkshire Post and Leeds Intelligencer*, 17 September; *Heslop's Local Advertiser*, 21 September 1946.

27   Issues of *Labour's Northern Voice*, for October and November 1946 and January 1947; *Yorkshire Post and Leeds Intelligencer*, 17 September; *Northampton Mercury*, 20 September; *Yorkshire Evening Post*, 16 September 1946.

28   *The Town Crier: Birmingham's Labour Weekly*, 14, 21 September 1946.

29   NRS: DD.6/167, Requisitioning and Families Inadequately Housed: briefing paper for the Secretary of State for Scotland (Sir Hector McNeil), 6 June 1951. *Glasgow Herald*, 31 August 1949.

30   Harry McShane and Joan Smith, *No Mean Fighter* (London, Pluto Press, 1978, p. 242). *Royal Leamington Spa Courier*, 2 September 1948. Their success in improving local housing in the town seems to have been somewhat limited though, given that Leamington's nineteenth century slums were not properly cleared until 1970. On the Leamington slums see Colin A. Maynell, 'Nineteenth-century Slums in Leamington Spa and the Introduction of Public Health Reforms', *Warwickshire History*, vol. xvi no. 2 (winter 2014/15, p. 96).

31   Paul Burnham, 'The Squatters of 1946: A Local Study in National Context', p. 30; James Hinton, 'Self-Help and Socialism', p. 115; SA: MO Archive File Report 2431, Squatters, 1946, pp. 25-26.

32   *Daily Worker*, 11, 12, 14, 17 September 1946. The Shop Stewards' resolution was widely reported; these quotes are from the *Nottingham Evening Post*, 17 September 1946 where it appeared as the front page headline.

33   Andrew Friend, 'The Post-War Squatters', in Nick Wates and Christian Wolmar (Eds), *Squatting: The Real Story* (London, Bay Leaf Publications, 1980, p. 119).

34   *Glasgow Herald*, 18 September 1946; NA: CAB/195/4, Notes from the Cabinet Meeting, 17 September 1946.

35   *Stirling Sentinel*, 25 June, 10 September; *Scotsman* 13, 14, 16 September 1946. As regards County Durham the issue of disputes over eligibility for colliery houses before 1914 is covered in Lewis Mates, *The Great Labour Unrest: Rank and file movements and political change in the Durham coalfield* (Manchester, Manchester University Press, 2016).

36   *Scotsman*, 30 August 1946.

37   Colin Ward, *Housing: An Anarchist Approach* (London, Freedom Press, 1976, pp. 23, 27).

38   *Blyth News*, 4 November; *Scotsman*, 6 November; *Times*, 5 November; *Newcastle Evening Chronicle*, 2 November 1946. LHASC: CP/LOC/SCOT/01/02, *Report of the Scottish Committee of the Communist Party October 1946-August 1947*.

39   Branson (Ed.), 'London Squatters 1946', pp. 14, 18, 24. Bob Saunders, 'The Glasgow Squatters, 1946', *Scottish Marxist*, no. 7 (October 1974, p. 26).

40   *Socialist Leader*, 21 September 1946.

41   Bill Carritt in Branson (Ed.) 'London Squatters 1946', p. 20.

Squatters entering huts at Chester le Street, County Durham 1946 (*Beamish Museum Photographic Archive*)

Interior of hut at Chester le Street, County Durham (*Beamish Museum Photographic Archive*)

Squatters outside a hut at Alexandra Park, Manchester, 1946 (*Manchester Library, Information and Archives, Manchester City Council*)

Interior of a hut, Alexandra Park, Manchester (*Manchester Library, Information and Archives, Manchester City Council*)

Chapter Seven

'SUCH DESPERATE NEED OF ACCOMMODATION': CONDITIONS AND PRIORITIES

By the end of autumn 1946 the spotlight of publicity had moved from the squatters to other matters. The national press turned its attentions elsewhere and the squatters in the disued camps went largely unreported. Thus, according to one historian, the squatters' movement 'captured the headlines for a month or so and quickly died down', apparently written off at the time as a flash in the pan. Another comment is that 'the movement quickly fizzled out'. Once the financial appeal for the London squatters' leaders was completed the Communist Party and its paper moved on as well, although activists continued to be involved in housing campaigns. By 1950 an Edinburgh theatre reviewer could remark that 'little is heard of squatters nowadays'. Those historians who have written about the movement conclude that in due course the camp squatters were gradually absorbed into the local authority housing programmes, although it is recognised that some local authorities used the camps for emergency housing in the coming years.[1]

It was not, however, anywhere near as simple as that. The squatting phenomenon and its aftermath did not necessarily end in the way that several of the writers on the subject have assumed. The camp squatters continued to campaign but their struggles were local ones with their councils and regional officers of the Ministry of Health. A good number of the camps concerned continued to be occupied well into the 1950s or even early 1960s, and the account reveals much about public and official attitudes to the squatters, their continuing battle for decent housing and the local politics that could be involved.

The squatters had initially sought confirmation that they could remain in the huts, secured the provision of services, and then sought the status of bona fide tenants who would receive equal treatment on the council house waiting lists. These last two points will be explored in the next chapter but another issue was the condition of the huts the squatters had occupied, and what was to be done about them by local authorities and the Ministry of Health during the slow progress of the housing programme.

Costs and conditions

When the squatting movement began officials at the Ministry of Health advised their Principal Housing Officers not to 'take a high standard about the adaptations needed' to the occupied camps. Where a camp was likely to be 'occupied in some force for some months' the local authority should accept the situation, 'spending as little labour and materials on it as they decently can'. In those camps which could not be made fit for continued occupation it was hoped that winter conditions would help to clear them.[2] An example of 'not taking a high standard' is a report by the Senior Regional Architect at the Newcastle on Tyne Region of the Ministry of Health, who stated that:

> Experience so far proves that only in very rare cases can a hutted camp be brought up to the standard of a Temporary House. The majority of camps examined to date show signs of deterioration and are therefore only suitable for a short period of possibly one, two or three years at most. Therefore expenditure of say £70-100 should be the maximum limit per family in such cases. ... few camps have slipper baths but batteries of showers are common ... Lack of bathing facilities is not considered serious as few squatters have come out of houses with a bath.[3]

Nevertheless, a senior civil servant at the Ministry of Works confessed that:

> ... until squatting began nobody in his right senses could believe that families would be content to live in dormitory huts of this nature. The squatting epidemic has shown that large numbers of people are in such desperate need of accommodation that they are only too glad to squat in empty and unpartitioned huts ...

Local authorities had been reluctant to divert resources to adapt huts into rooms, supply electricity and so on, but 'it is quite clear that the homeless are content with a good deal less than this, and of course the less local authorities have to do to make camps habitable for squatters the better'.[4] Bevan was briefed by his senior official that 'it was a bit of a worry' that when squatters 'have been in for a week or two they are sure to press for improvements which would involve substantial materials and labour.

I have taken the line that these must be kept to a bare minimum to avoid interference with the housing programme.' Indeed, Clement Attlee assured Labour MP Joan Davidson that the condition and location of many of the occupied camps were such that local authorities would have rejected them had they been offered for housing purposes. However as he explained:

Now that it is clear that people are willing to put up with fairly rough accommodation the local authorities are, of course, more willing than they have been to take over camps for housing and the transfer of camps for housing has been speeded up.[5]

These comments reveal the thinking of senior civil servants in the key Ministries of Works and Health. As little resource as possible was to be spent on renovating the camp huts but, it was believed, the occupants were prepared to tolerate bad conditions and so they would probably find this acceptable. There was a wide variety in the quality of the huts that had been squatted and in the worse ones the conditions frequently became a source of complaint and campaign rather than acceptance.

As we have seen the press coverage of the early occupations of the empty camps was positive and the attitudes of their new residents were reported to be upbeat. In those camps that were well built to start with, and where local authorities had carried out adaptations, conditions have been looked back on favourably. Vera Penman said of her hut in Oxfordshire almost 50 years later: 'Honestly I think to myself, really and truly, I know you want a house and things but that hut, I'd like that hut back, if I could have it back again …'

At the Slade Camp, also in Oxfordshire, Louie Sherlock remembered how:

The council made a good job of converting the huts, it was very good indeed. We found most of the people around to be very friendly because they were mainly ex-services people. It's surprising how wonderful people made them, they were homes … It was a home, a real home. I've got good memories. We were there about eight years, we were among the last to leave.[6]

At the other end of England in Washington, County Durham, miner Jim Tatters recalled that the colliery house he had his name down for and eventually moved in to in 1951 was much inferior; he actually described that move from his hut as 'a big mistake'. Similarly the first family to occupy a former anti-aircraft site at Grindon, near Sunderland, moved into a four-roomed bungalow that had previously been officers' quarters. The family had been living in the attic of a small cottage belonging to in-laws for nearly a year. In Scotland's Vale of Leven 84 families occupied the Tullichewan Camp which was described as 'built by the Americans, and probably one of the most comfortable in the country'.[7]

There is bound to be a strong element of nostalgia in accounts such as these. People are looking back on their younger days, their early married lives and their first real homes as a family. Nevertheless conditions in the better camps, which were almost invariably the ones that were formally taken over by the local authority, were often welcomed by this first wave of occupiers. In the Hartlepool area for example the squatters in the Easington Road Camp were grateful to local councillors for their help in securing water, sanitation and electricity and said that 'we're a lot better off than we were previous to our move here'. Another factor was the open conditions and sheer space of an abandoned camp. One woman squatting in the Darnley Camp outside Glasgow told a reporter that 'I lived in a room in Bedford Street and my wee girl has never seen grass before this morning'. Again, a childhood memory of life in the squatted camps is of 'a vast amount of space in which to roam freely … a great big adventure playground'. Outside Sheffield as we have seen squatters were relocated from insanitary huts to a Civil Defence Camp with electricity, gas, water supply and central heating, prompting one of them to declare, 'I've never lived in a place like this before. I could be here the rest of my life … we are well satisfied with what has been done for us.'[8]

However a closer examination shows there was a wide variety in the quality and condition of the huts. Those built primarily for American or Canadian forces were better constructed and with more brickwork than those built for British personnel. Those had often been erected as quickly and as cheaply as possible, not infrequently with just one outer skin of corrugated iron and a brick or concrete floor and course. At the outset of the squatting wave some officials at the Ministry of Health had warned that the huts would not be suitable for winter under any circumstances. Therefore they had been confident that the weather would be enough to clear the huts of their new residents. Certainly some of the huts, despite refurbishing by their new occupants, were still in such poor condition or of such inferior construction that the winter would be difficult. As it turned out the months from December 1946 to March 1947 were the coldest on record, with much of Britain experiencing exceptionally heavy snowfalls and then persistently heavy rain. In addition a national coal and fuel shortage reached crisis levels that raised queries about the competence of the government; both the weather and the disruptions to transport and supply also hindered the progress of the building programme.[9]

Those winters are recalled by people who spent part of their childhood in a squatted hut, particularly those with a concrete floor, single-skin brickwork and a corrugated iron roof, and with the cooking stove in the living room as the sole source of heat. They remember the thick film of ice on the inside of the windows, and sleeping weighed down by every possible quilt, blanket, rug and overcoat on top of them. In February 1947 a camp committee chairman in South Shields, County Durham, complained that huts 'have frost on the inside walls and gaps through which snow and wind enter'. Occupants had spent £20 trying to stem leaks with cement and painting the outside walls and they intended to protest to the council about an increase in charges. This they duly did, but although sympathetic councillors proposed that 'the rents at military camp sites (excluding water and electricity charges) be reduced to 7s a week' this motion was defeated.[10]

Nevertheless at the end of that first winter squatters at Longbenton, near Newcastle on Tyne, do not appear to have been deterred. They still found what they had to be preferable to what they had had before, and claimed that the huts were better than many of the old colliery houses in the area. They were drier, had electricity and were well situated for the miners to travel to work when buses were not running. There were plenty of open spaces for children during the summer. On the other hand the washing and sanitary facilities were inadequate, they relied on a single outside tap for water, and although the miners had the pit-head baths the others had to heat water over combustion stoves to fill tin baths. Like so many other camps too it was inconvenient for shops and bus routes. Despite this the young couples 'declared that they would not go back to live with parents or in-laws for worlds. We have our own home now.' Again, plans for the year included new furniture and laying out gardens.[11]

As time wore on though the living conditions in some of the occupied camps attracted attention and so did the complaints of the residents. In the summer of 1950 *The Times* ran some features on 'Rural Slums' in the south of England, contrasting the rural landscapes with the squalid living conditions in the ex-services hutments. At a former aerodrome near Basingstoke one of the tenants said that:

I have lived in a hutment for 18 months with my wife and baby daughter. We have put up with the condensation. We have watched the green mould creep over the furniture and build itself around the brick courses.

We have seen our linoleum rot under our feet, put up with the rats in the winter, and have watched the effects of continual rust.

In villages like Theale in Berkshire, a country area that had attracted many to work in key industries nearby, a continual housing shortage again meant that the camps, 'badly-lit and leaky structures of corrugated iron and weatherboard', were still home to 200 families. Work was plentiful in local factories and the nearby town of Reading, and there were hut residents who were earning enough to buy a house on instalments, but none were likely to be available. One family of four were sleeping in one bedroom and had no window in the section of the hut partitioned off as a living room. Overcrowding meant that the residents 'of these new slums ... are prone to sicknesses from which the other villagers are comparatively free.' Alongside the slow progress of the housing programme was the reluctance of local authorities to spend scarce resources on shoddy accommodation that it hoped soon, in theory at least, to demolish. Hartley Rural District Council in Hampshire for example had spent £62,000 on such huts since 1946; it wanted to keep such money for its permanent houses.[12] Four years after the squatting wave then two crucial issues were still dominant: the slow pace of the general housing programme relative to need, and the reluctance to divert scarce resources into adapting substandard huts for what was officially to be temporary use. Unfortunately in so many cases the concept of 'temporary' had no clear definition and certainly no timescale attached to it.

Generally speaking those camps with the worst problems were those where the local authority had decided not to take them over but to act as agents for the Ministry of Health, the Welsh Health Board or the Department of Health for Scotland. In these cases the huts were markedly inferior and the conditions in them were likewise. The huts occupied at Polmaise Camp outside Stirling for example were reported to be in a bad condition, so much so that the Department of Health for Scotland advised the County Council to take no action in the hope that the squatters would leave. However when a councillor described their huts as 'squalid and dirty' there was a response from the camp; objecting to this description they challenged the councillor to come and see for himself that they were not, and see the refurbishments, including toilets, that the occupiers had built for themselves. The councillor, they believed, was prejudiced against working-class people, just assumed they would be dirty, and wanted them to go. The Dunbartonshire Homeless Tenants' Association was engaged on a similar struggle, and there seems to have been a comparable situation in the Highlands. Here some camps were vacated by former prisoners of war in 1948 and promptly occupied by local home seekers, showing that in Scotland at least the camp squatting movement had by no means 'quickly fizzled out' in 1946. Forres Town Council refused to take them over and described the conditions there as 'a public scandal', provoking the squatters' committee to an angry defence of their homes and a challenge to the councillors to come and see for themselves.

It was described in an earlier chapter how in many camps, and indeed in condemned tenements, the squatters were actively carrying out repairs and improvements to the huts for themselves; the occupants at Forres stated that they were perfectly willing to do likewise if the Town Council would confirm that they could stay there. Similarly Peter McIntyre, representing squatters in the Glasgow area at a meeting with the Secretary of State for Scotland, proposed a solution to the problem of deploying scarce building workers from the housing programme to their camps. They had a good range of tradesmen among their number, he said, and so why not deliver the plaster, glass and so on to them and let them carry out their own repairs? He had already discussed arrangements with a firm of bricklayers and was confident that given the material the squatters could make their huts up to the necessary standard at a lower cost than that quoted by the government. His proposal was not taken up.[13]

There is some surviving correspondence between Chester le Street Urban District Council in County Durham and the camp committee at the Roman Avenue squatted huts. It demonstrates too that, contrary to the up-beat newspaper coverage during summer 1946, life in some camps was proving difficult and uncomfortable. This must have been particularly so during the long and harsh winters of the late 1940s. As was stated in an earlier chapter this UDC had deemed these huts unfit for human habitation when they were first occupied. Nevertheless the camp residents continued to protest at what they saw as a neglectful attitude on the part of the council and to press their case for improvements. A resident appealed to the Ministry of Health Housing Division in Newcastle that 'I am living in an ex-army camp of huts and they are in bad order outside. We have asked the Council for help but it is hopeless. And we have been in 2 years and the Health Doctor has been in once that was the week we went in and he has not been in any more. I am writing as an ex-service pensioner.' The council's reply to the ministry repeated that their position from the outset had been that the huts were not fit and could not be made fit for habitation. The Chief Clerk explained that they had '... therefore, done as little as possible, viz: making water and electricity supplies available and removing refuse only ... The huts are worse than they were when the people took possession, and the Council hope their condition will eventually compel the occupants to find rooms somewhere. They came from outside the Urban District in the first place.'[14]

Another letter on behalf of the Roman Avenue 'tenants', as they described themselves, to the Housing Division in mid- December 1946 requested improvements to the services they were being charged for. The toilets apparently were 'an insult to human decency.' There was one water tap in the centre of the camp providing the whole supply, and they suggested a more convenient height for it, 'but the ideal solution would be for a tap in each hut.' As regards food preparation:

There are no facilities apart from a communal oven which proves totally inadequate for the needs of everyone, besides being impractical due to the meagre coal ration and the extreme inconvenience of carrying food a distance of fifty yards in some cases. We ask if it is possible to provide each hut with an oven and top on which food can be cooked. The stoves at present in the hut cannot be used for anything except heating and boiling a small kettle.

Finally:

Bearing in mind the shortage of houses and realising that it will probably be quite a time before we all get houses, we ask that you do all in your power to obtain for us the few repairs requested and stress the dire need for cooking facilities.

Chester le Street Council does not appear to have done anything except respond to the request about the height of the communal water tap.[15] In Scotland the secretary of the Dunbartonshire Homeless Tenants' Association campaigned in the local press about the occupied camps in his area, complaining that in most of them 'the conditions are primitive: bad lighting, no cooking facilities, little or no heating, rats, smoking chimneys, two families sharing a hut with no partition ... Are they to be left as they are for years?'[16]

At Leadgate near Consett, where 55 families had occupied a former Bevin Boys' hostel during the wave of summer 1946, the conditions there appear to have deteriorated by 1951. Whereas the Ministry of Health had originally agreed to pay for the installation and maintenance of several central heating boilers and individual fire places it had reduced its support to the running of one part-time boiler. As time had worn on and the running costs of 'temporary accommodation' had continued the ministry was seeking economies. In January the only Conservative member of Consett UDC attracted publicity by claiming that cold and damp conditions in the hostel had been responsible for the deaths of babies from pneumonia. The councillor painted a lurid picture of what he found during his visit to the hostel with the council sanitary inspector, but he did not convince his colleagues. In other parts of the country camp occupiers made full use of the local press to draw attention to their conditions and the continuing effects of the housing shortage. In Essex for example residents at the former Boreham Airfield achieved extensive coverage for two weeks in 1949; they were able to voice their complaints about their dilapidated huts, the illness brought there by winter, and their struggle to motivate Chelmsford Rural District Council to make the huts 'even remotely habitable'. Where squatters were represented on council committees they used every opportunity to press their case for improvements, particularly regarding the problems caused by damp in the huts.[17]

An issue to be explored here is how far were the responses of local councils influenced by their attitudes towards the squatters as well as by economics. Did prejudice as well as the pace of the housing programme delay the rehousing of squatters? These questions will be examined in the next chapter. In the meantime the next section shows that by the late 1940s Parliament was aware of the conditions that residents in some of the camps were experiencing.

National and local government

At the end of 1947 the Parliamentary Under-Secretary to the Ministry of Health reported at Westminster that, in England and Wales, 694 camps had been taken over by local authorities and 379 were being managed by local authorities on behalf of the Ministry. He explained that:

There has, however, been considerable reluctance on the part of a number of local authorities to assume responsibility for camps that have been occupied by squatters. At the time of the outbreak of squatting, the government decided that families should not be evicted from camps unless the camps were required for government purposes. A good number of camps occupied by squatters were subsequently declared redundant by Service Departments and became a housing responsibility. The local authorities concerned had to be persuaded that the problem rested with them as housing authorities and in some cases very much against their will, or at least against their first inclinations, they were persuaded to take the camps over in due course. I can understand their anxiety. In some cases, the squatters came from outside their district; in other cases, they had jumped the queue; and as everybody knows this causes very considerable local trouble. Most local authorities have now realised that the problem is not only one of housing but one of good local government, and they have either agreed to take over the camps occupied by the squatters or, as I said earlier, in some 379 cases, they have agreed to manage them on behalf of the Minister of Health.[18]

As we have seen in a previous chapter when the squatting wave first broke out a number of local councils blamed government departments for the situation they found themselves in. They had also resented the fact that the suggestion so many of them had made about using empty camps for temporary housing had been rebuffed by the government. This parliamentary statement suggests that a year later Westminster was presenting the issue as essentially one for the local authorities.

In Scotland the Secretary of State George Buchanan had reported two months earlier that 143 camps had been occupied and that about 6,800 people were involved. As regards his reaction to this he explained:

May I repeat what I said when I met local authorities in Scotland on the matter? If the camp is for a short term, say a period of less than two years, in other words, if it is pretty bad and would be difficult to make semi-permanent, or even equal to a temporary house, the whole cost falls on the State. That relates to the great bulk of the camps—an overwhelming number. There the State meets the cost, but if it is a camp about which, after review and proper survey by the local authority and us, we come to the conclusion that it can be made into the equal of a temporary house, the matter proceeds on the same basis of finance as does a temporary house.

This explanation of the funding suggests that in Scotland 'the great bulk of the camps' were not considered to be in a good enough condition for use as accommodation for longer than two years. Buchanan expressed impatience with local authorities who protested at having to respond to squatters who had come from outside their areas, as this reminded him of pre-war arguments over the Poor Law; 'We have enough trouble in running the borders of the world. Do not let our borders in Scotland become too parochial and narrow'. Nevertheless, as will be seen, Buchanan's impatience was well founded. The issue of entrants to the council housing lists coming from outside the councils' areas was to continue to be contentious, and not only in Scotland.[19]

The Under-Secretary's report to the Commons at the end of 1947 was the occasion for a debate about the use of service huts for housing, and this time with the benefit of fifteen months of experience. MPs from around Britain described the conditions they had seen in some of the occupied camps in their constituencies; Willie Gallacher, the Communist for West Fife, said that:

> In my constituency, in Leslie, I was round visiting some huts occupied by squatters who were living in conditions that were appalling. There was an appalling lack of amenities, so far as sanitation was concerned, that would horrify any Hon Member who saw it.

The member for Brecon and Radnor reported on shocking sanitary conditions and wastage of water and electricity at Gilwern camp, and how the Rural District Council there could get no response on the matter from the Welsh Health Board and two government departments. In the Aberdeen and Kincardine constituency there was the argument that the Scottish Office should take more responsibility for ensuring that the huts for which it was charging 10s a week should be more habitable – for example 'weather-tight for winter … made waterproof and there could be a few dry places in which to put beds.' Similarly the member for The Wrekin in Staffordshire said that 'having accepted the circumstances of being a landlord, the Ministry must accept the responsibilities of a landlord, and I am sure that if some effort is made it will be found possible to make these huts far more habitable than they are'.

It was impossible to say how long families would have to live in these camps and so more effort was needed to bring the huts up to standard. The MP for London's Ealing West described how the local council, 'frantic because of the difficulties caused by the housing shortage', had supported the squatters in occupying a camp and then included the MP in a deputation to the Ministry of Health:

> At that time, the people were wandering about in the mud, during a terrible winter, in an effort to collect water from pipes in a field sometimes two or three hundred yards away from the huts. In very hard weather, women with child were carrying water under those conditions. We protested, and the council wanted the money to be spent. The case put by the Minister of Health was that it would be better, instead of drawing building materials and labour for that purpose, to get on with the housing scheme. The Minister said that, in some cases, the huts were

on the sites which would be used for building permanent houses, and that it would be better to get on with the job of providing the permanent houses instead of spending considerable sums of money on utterly unsatisfactory huts. The local council have got on with the job.

In contrast, other members praised their local squatters for the work they had put into renovating their huts, 'which have been converted extremely well, and they have made extremely good temporary houses'. There was a consensus that no one in the occupied camps should be evicted, but otherwise no solutions were offered either by MPs or the Parliamentary Under-Secretary to the Ministry of Health. It was recognised that decent homes and not huts were the answer and the danger of putting families into inadequate temporary accommodation at a time of shortage was that they could still be there years later. It was also pointed out that deplorable though conditions in some of the camps might be local authorities could not be seen to give them priority over others who had not entered a camp.

Labour MPs stressed that they were not blaming the government, who were doing their best in difficult circumstances, but equally, in the words of the member for Cardiff Central, they warned that 'we do not want any tinkering with or cutting down of the housing programme and that we have a grave responsibility for seeing that the programme has a high priority'.[20]

This debate did not lead to renewed government action on the camps, nor, indeed, to any successful challenge to the 'cutting down of the housing programme' following the budget of 1947.

The budget of 1947 and housing

The Budget proposals of 1947 represent a defining moment for the Attlee government, in terms of choices, priorities, and the circumstances in which they had to be made. This is worth some discussion here because of the crucial impact that Budget was to have on the housing programme. This was to be, as Stephen Merrett has put it, 'the crux of British housing history between 1945 and 1951'.[21]

Foreign Secretary Ernest Bevin was insistent that Britain should remain as far as possible one of the great powers of the world: maintaining sterling as the major trading currency, continuing with the political domination of Africa and Asia, and retaining the appropriate levels of armed forces to sustain this eminence. The rise of nationalist movements throughout the Empire and the perceived expansion of world Communism were a clear threat to this and a further motive for continued high levels of military spending. As a result historians have seen the foreign policies of the Attlee governments as essentially ones of continuity with their predecessors. Although Attlee and Chancellor of the Exchequer Hugh Dalton often disagreed with this view of Britain's post-war world role, and expressed concern at the high levels of military expenditure that it involved, they were rarely able to mount an effective challenge to Bevin and the weight of the Foreign Office establishment that was behind him.

The Attlee governments were therefore engaged on a number of state policies each of which would make a substantial demand on the available economic resources. They were in fact competing. Those resources as a whole were in turn challenged by the immediate post-war circumstances. The end of the conflict had left Britain with a substantial trade deficit and a high level of deferred debt to Commonwealth countries as a result of the war. In addition the American government abruptly ended the Lend-Lease arrangement which had assisted Britain throughout the war instead of phasing it out, as the Attlee government had expected. This led to a dependence on economic aid in the form of loans from the USA, one of the prices of which was the end of the British trade monopoly with the Empire and the demise of sterling as the principal world trading currency.

Politically the consequence was an alliance with the USA in the emerging Cold War, although it is more than likely that the leaders of the Labour Party would have entered that alliance in any case. Although the world war had left the Soviet Union in too devastated a state to mount the attempt at world domination which the Cold War assumed, its political rhetoric, its creation and manipulation of client states in the east of Europe, and the success of the Communists in China gave some credence to that view about its aims.[22]

As a result public expenditure on social programmes began to slip down the agenda of priority compared to defence spending. The results of this can be seen in the table below: the statistics for council house completion, and also the fall in the number of houses councils had permission to build and the numbers they actually began to build.[23]

Local authority building programme in Britain 1946-49

	1946	1947	1948	1949
Local authority completions	25,013	97,340	190,368	165,946
Local authority dwellings approved		101,000	42,000	

This also shows that despite the shortages and a slower pace than the scale of need demanded, substantial progress was being made up to this point. The Attlee administration had inherited a very complex series of problems yet in its first two years built more houses for ordinary people than any previous administration. Despite the criticisms of Bevan that may be made this fact must be recognised.

Nevertheless the reduction in the housing programme alongside rising armament expenditure presented a good target for local Communist Party branches. In Gateshead for example continued housing shortages produced the Gateshead House Hunters' Association: although styling itself a 'non-political' body it lobbied the council over its housing and housing allocation policies through deputations and public meetings. Local Communists in attendance blamed the housing cuts on the government policy of 'squandering the nation's wealth on imperialist adventures' and instead advocated 'construction not destruction'. The Party as a whole seems to have gained some members outside the traditional trade union sector through activity such as this. It had a membership category of 'housewives' (which also included students) and this increased between 1945 and 1955. Nevertheless the progress of the Cold War meant a period of isolation and a decline in membership and influence.[24]

MPs continued to raise the issue of conditions in the squatted camps in their constituencies for several years. This seems to have been especially true in Scotland if it gave Conservative MPs the opportunity to criticise Labour administrations. In 1950 the MP for Ayr 'asked the Secretary of State for Scotland whether he is satisfied with the conditions of the hutted camps as now in use for living accommodation around Ayr; and what action he proposes to take to secure a reasonable standard of decency for their occupants.' On being told that the camps provided 'only emergency accommodation' and that they could not be brought up to modern standards 'even with a considerable expenditure of labour and materials,' he replied that 'these tenants have been forced to live in these cold, damp, dark, insanitary houses for upwards of years, and that it is not possible to do anything to them because the outer wooden walls have perished.' Three years later another Conservative, the member for Glasgow Kelvingrove, pressed the case for the 'miserable hovels' in Kelvingrove Park, former gas decontamination shelters that had been squatted in 1946:

> In those hovels sit, sleep and work men who go into the shipyards and build the finest ships in the world. They wire and fit those ships with every kind of equipment, and then come back to Bunsen burners and small

oil stoves. That was done under the aegis of the right hon. Gentleman opposite, backed by the Labour majority of the time.[25]

In Lanarkshire Conservative MP Peter Maitland took up the case of the tenants of the Burnwood Camp at Carluke, pitting himself against the Labour County Council. Claiming that he was 'far from sure that the tenants are getting a square deal' by having to live in huts where 'the conditions are an absolute disgrace' he spent a weekend as a guest in one at the end of 1952. This exercise generated a great deal of publicity, controversy, and a Department of Health inquiry that was debated in the county during the summer of the following year. The tenants' grievances were about more than their conditions, as will be seen in the next chapter, but Maitland's controversial involvement was part of a continuous lobbying for improvements by the Burnwood occupants.

Clearly the camps, which in Scotland were known to be good for no more than two years, were lasting far longer than that and the conditions in them continued to be primitive. A Conservative government was elected in 1951 and its MPs, in Scotland particularly, pressed for a quicker reduction in the number of camps still used for housing. It was reported that in May 1952 2,838 families were housed in 129 camps, but by May 1954 that number had been reduced to 1,196 families in 78 camps. The Secretary of State for Scotland hoped that it would be possible 'to see the last of these camps' by 1956, but MPs in Scotland were still raising the issue of closing the camps and re-housing the residents in 1958.[26]

The slow progress of the housing programme was one reason for the persistence of these camps; another was the cost of the rents of new council houses. Unskilled and lower paid workers could struggle to meet the rents. Violet Fraser, a child in a squatted camp near Forres in Scotland remembered that her parents were offered a new council house but could not afford the rent at that time, and so they continued to remain in a hut until they could. Prospective council tenants in her part of Scotland were protesting about high rents. Indeed, the council house building programme was accompanied in several parts of Britain by organised tenants' groups campaigning against the high rents that could be required to help to pay for it. In South Shields for example a deputation representing the tenants' groups of four council estates organised a petition and lobbied the council over proposed rent rises; in the same month Dunbartonshire County Council received a deputation after 'public meetings held throughout the county to protest at the high rents of the temporary houses'. Similar protests were being made in Fife, and elsewhere the target for protest included the

Scottish Housing Association. In 1948 5,000 council tenants in Bristol were threatening a rent strike in protest at proposed rent increases. All this was a feature of a national trend; it has been observed that two or more households sharing a dwelling was 'very widespread' in Britain until around 1951, due not only to the shortage of housing but because 'large numbers of households could not afford the rent of a single house or flat'. Just as with the slum clearance programme of the 1930s it appeared that tenants were being housed in accommodation where rents was stretching the income of lower-paid workers.[27]

The Treasury takes action

When the Conservative government took over in 1951 the Ministry of Local Government and Planning became the Ministry of Housing and Local Government. The new Minister, Harold Macmillan, had a target agreed by his party conference to build 300,000 new council houses in five years. This pressure for more council housing came from the Tory activists of the conference floor, an illustration of the consensus at the time that this was the immediate solution to the housing problem. Macmillan managed to make housing the chief priority for domestic public spending. The target had been reached by 1953 and comfortably exceeded by 1954. However, as Nicholas Timmins notes, crucial to this success was the reduction in the size of council houses as Bevan's original emphasis on quality rather than quantity was almost reversed. Cheaper construction methods were used to by-pass the persistent shortages, and smaller, two-bedroomed council houses with proportionately lower rents were encouraged. Licenses for private house building were removed and in 1952 Macmillan attempted to generate more capital for housing by allowing some council house sales. This was fiercely resisted by many Labour authorities; in Glasgow, when the Conservative- dominated Corporation attempted to sell properties built in 1946 it was met by a mass campaign of resistance that united trades unions, the left, tenants and community groups.[28]

Nevertheless the amount still being spent on what was classed as 'emergency accommodation', both the legacy from the homelessness generated by war and the results of the squatting wave of 1946, exercised the Treasury during the 1950s. There was a quandary: the sums being expended would be better used on the housing programme, but until houses were available the emergency accommodation – squatted army camps, hostels for bombed-out families and so forth – could not be cleared. As regards Scotland the Secretary of State informed Chancellor of the Exchequer Rab Butler that emergency housing arising from the war was not really an issue.

However 'the camps used for emergency housing purposes represent a more difficult problem, because local authorities are reluctant to rehouse the squatter families in them out of turn'. A civil servant was later of the opinion that although the number of families concerned had reduced to about 2,000, 'it is clear, if we are to rely solely on the local authorities, that the camps which are likely to become increasingly costly to maintain as time goes on may not be cleared for a long time to come'.[29]

The issue of local authorities and rehousing squatters will be examined in the next chapter. In 1952 the government established, for England and Wales, the Working Party on Requisitioned Properties for Use in Housing. Its terms of reference included preparing a report on 'measures necessary for relieving the central government from the financial responsibility for the housing of families in requisitioned properties at an early date'. By the time of the Working Party's Third Interim Report its scope included families living in the camps.

The report drew a distinction between those camps actually taken over by local authorities and those merely managed on behalf of the Ministry of Health or the Welsh Health Board, a distinction that had been clarified in the House of Commons in 1947. This was because the former 'compared favourably in terms of quality of construction, amenity and durability' with the wartime prefabs. The latter group did not meet those standards, and it was noted that there were 1,300 such camps in England and Wales housing 22,000 families; they ranged from a few huts to settlements of around 250 families. The numbers quoted here are very significant: they indicate that there had been a marked increase in the use of the camps since the Parliamentary statement in 1947, always assuming that the ministerial report had not been based on an under-estimate in the first place. This probably also showed the effect of the 1948 National Assistance Act which placed a duty on local authorities to provide emergency accommodation for people made homeless in their areas.

The Working Party had visited a representative sample and talked to officers of the managing authorities together with residents in their huts. They had found that the quality of the accommodation was wide in range also. The best of them provided accommodation that was inferior to that found in most of the requisitioned flats and houses, and 'in the worst camps the conditions – physical, sanitary and social – are such that they should not be tolerated'. Speedy closing was essential here, and in other cases the huts were deteriorating steadily and likely to incur heavy and uneconomic expenditure.

The interim report urged that the Principal Regional Officers of the

Ministry of Housing and Local Government work, urgently, with local authorities to bring about the clearing of the camps 'in order of priority corresponding to their degree of undesirability for housing'. A proportion of the new council lettings becoming available each year could be reserved for camp dwellers. Those with the wherewithal could be encouraged and supported to seek their own tenancies or mortgages; there were also those whose history of rent arrears or general behaviour meant that councils would be reluctant to take them on as mainstream tenants. In these cases the Working Party recommended that authorities actively manage the camps as they would their own council estates, with the same systems of incentives and sanctions. The interim report seems to suggest, between the lines, that a number of councils had not sought to manage the camps in this way. Possibly they had been reluctant to have anything to do with the camps that were in a poor initial state in the first place and that arms-length attitudes had persisted.[30]

In any event material prepared for the House of Commons Public Accounts Committee in March 1956 contains an explanation of why the pace of rehousing from the camps began to accelerate. The briefing stated that in England and Wales there had been a 33 per cent reduction in the number of families living in camps between the financial year 1950-1951 and the end of 1954. As a result the running costs to the Treasury had reduced from £27 per family in 1953/4 to £21 10s per family in 1954/55. This was because the Treasury was now offering a differential subsidy to local authorities 'for the purposes of rehousing persons coming from such camps or other unsatisfactory temporary housing accommodation as the Minister may designate ...' In other words once councils and housing authorities had a financial incentive to rehouse they acted.[31] In Scotland too incentives were offered:

A number of local authorities do manage ex-service camps on requisitioned land as clearing houses into which they put people on waiting lists until their turn comes. The whole expense falls on the Exchequer who therefore is anxious to reduce the number of families in the camps as quickly as possible ... allocations of houses should be conditional on the proposed numbers to be rehoused from the clearing house camps and the demolition of the huts.

An example of this was Stewarton Town Council which took over a camp for seventy families in 1949 and three years later accepted an offer of an additional forty houses on condition that they were used to help to rehouse families from the camp, and that vacant huts would be demolished.[32] Nevertheless local authorities did not always respond to this incentive in the way that the Treasury assumed they would. Often this was because they had responsibilities to provide emergency accommodation under the 1948 Act, for which the huts were a useful resource, and quite simply because of the persistently slow construction of affordable housing to rent relative to need. In 1950 in Edinburgh for example the City Corporation was made aware of the Secretary of State for Scotland's 'concern at the deteriorating condition' of the emergency camps it managed. Lochinvar, for example, was an inland naval installation taken over to house 200 families in 1946. This was intended to be for only two or three years with no family living there for longer than six months. Some of the huts were in a bad state of repair and the cost of maintaining them in a reasonably habitable condition could not be justified by the unsatisfactory condition of the accommodation. There was also the issue of the labour diversion from the housing programme that would be involved. He wanted the Corporation to demolish huts as vacancies arose. However there were 1,272 families on the City's waiting list for emergency huts and so the Corporation could not meet this request 'so long as the housing emergency remained in its present acute stage'. A year later their response to the Department of Health for Scotland's advice to demolish huts when residents were rehoused was similar, pointing out that they had over a thousand applications for housing in the huts besides the long conventional housing waiting list. Yet again, as with the situation in England, the numbers being quoted show that occupation of the squatted camps was still high.[33]

These issues were not confined to Edinburgh or cities in general. When a prisoner of war camp near Northallerton in Yorkshire became vacant in 1948 – again, indicating that the movement did not end in 1946 – squatters occupied it before the council were able to demolish the huts on the ministry's instructions. Belper Rural District Council in Derbyshire had a policy of making huts uninhabitable when occupiers moved out, only to find that new squatters took over before their workmen could act. Nonetheless even when central government was able to address the camps issue there could be local difficulties. The Department offered Edinburgh Corporation an additional allocation of 100 houses for the rehousing of families in the four camps, including fifty houses for the Craigentinny residents. The Department appreciated the objection to rehousing families before others having a prior claim because of their higher position on the waiting list, but they submitted that the present was a special case, particularly in regard to Craigentinny Camp, and 'the desirability of terminating the social problems which the continued use of emergency housing camps' set up. As we have seen in an earlier chapter, in October 1946 the Corporation had not wished to take over Craigentinny and its acquiescence with the squatting there, by supporting the supply of basic services, had followed pressure from the local clergy and others. At the beginning of 1952 it resolved to accept the Department's offer of an additional allocation of 100 houses 'but not subject to conditions'. It believed that as the pace of the housing programme was determined by resources the addition should be incorporated into the general allocation the Corporation received.[34] This major local authority at least did not accept that its housing allocation policy should be determined by central government.

Housing action

In 1952 a journalist for the *New Statesman* visited one of the four 'clearing house' camps on the outskirts of Edinburgh. It would have been at Sighthill, Duddington, Lochinvar or Craigentinny; between them these four ex-service camps were housing 700 families in 1951. This was the first report about the squatters to appear in a national progressive journal since 1946, and it presented a grim picture of the living conditions in the camp and also of the depressing atmosphere he seems to have found there. Families were living in Nissen huts with concrete floors, internally separated for different families by breeze blocks, and with metal skinned walls and roofs. As in the camps in rural areas of England, the metal was old and corroded and very few repairs were done. The huts were damp, leaking, and extremely cold in the winter and plagued by flies, smells and rats in the summer; with just a metal skin roof 'You can hardly hear yourself think when it rains.'

The communal kitchen was too small for the numbers using it and trying to make sure that their husbands had a hot meal when they came home from work. All food had to be carried from the kitchen to the individual huts when cooked. A few families had very low standards regarding the use of the communal kitchen, lavatories and wash houses. The camp was intended as a temporary inconvenience until houses or 'pre-fabs' became available but there were delays, so that 'weeks or months of tenancy have lengthened to two or three years'. He found there were camp committees, just as the original squatters had established, 'spokesmen to deal with municipal officers and clerks who vary from the helpfully friendly to the acidly supercilious.' This particular camp committee reported that they had used to look forward to polling days but they had now lost interest; their focus was not on a candidate's political party but what kind of effort they would make to get repairs done in the camp. The local MP had had to campaign on their behalf in order to get separate and lockable doors fitted on the toilets in the huts. The author stated that 'life is a fight, not only against authority, dirt, cold, damp, heat, illness and rats, but against one's own growing apathy'.[35]

Nevertheless at the time this article was published there is evidence that the residents of the Edinburgh camps were agitating to improve their circumstances, not relapsing into apathy. Further, this was the case too in other parts of Britain. The Duddington Camp Committee told Edinburgh Corporation that it was 'obvious that people would be homeless for many years to come and was it the intention to keep people housed in the fast deteriorating huts all the time they were waiting for a new home?' The influence of political activists can be seen in their point that ex-servicemen could be recalled ('given the world situation and the defence measures the present government are taking') and be forced to leave their families in those conditions. They were told, as had been the Secretary of State that the camps would be kept on out of necessity. An earlier request from the committee for quarterly reports on housing progress had been turned down, but a year later 'a largely attended and helpful meeting in a friendly atmosphere' took place at the camp between councillors, housing officials and residents at which the housing allocation system was explained. Complaints were also received about it and investigations promised. This meeting took place a few hours after a demonstration at the City Chambers and the Scottish Office building at St Andrew's House organised by the Duddington Camp Committee and the Lochinvar Homeless Association.

At the same time 180 residents of Lochinvar Camp petitioned the Corporation about 'the conditions of housing being forced upon us', demanded that 'immediate action be taken' and a deputation of the Lochinvar Homeless Association be received. It was explained that this situation had come about because some tenants – that was the term used – were objecting to the conditions in the huts to which they had been moved during a process of re-arrangement.[36] Over the next two years organisations from the three main Edinburgh camps joined forces with local Labour MPs, Edinburgh and District Trades Council, building trades unions and local Communists to press Edinburgh Corporation over housing issues. The Conservatives had taken control of the Corporation again in May 1951 and this seems to have galvanised the local labour movement into action with the camp residents. In December that year two Edinburgh Labour MPs, the city's Co-operative Party and Trades Council pressed for a Secretary of State inquiry into why the Corporation had failed to meet its housing allocation despite a marked increase in its building workforce. They addressed a meeting of the Amalgamated Homeless Association which brought together the committees of the local camps, and urged them to 'put a little more ginger' into the demands put by deputations and demonstrations to the Corporation. Nevertheless, in what was clearly a move against the Communist Party, they 'warned the people without a house of their own against attaching themselves to one of the many organisations making capital out of the camp dwellers and the homeless'.[37]

Edinburgh Communists such as Donald Renton were involved however in the agitations that were organised early the following year. The committees of the Lochinvar, Duddington and Craigentinny Camp Associations – who had parted from the Edinburgh Homeless Association because of its 'non-political' stance – organised a housing conference in the city. This agreed on a petition for a public inquiry into the Corporation's 'extraordinary failure' to meet its housing allocation, for better incentives for building workers, an extension to requisitioning and opposition to council house sales. However when a demonstration later arrived at a Corporation Housing Committee meeting a deputation was refused entry until it was confirmed that no Communists were included.[38]

Attempts by camp residents to use political lobbying to improve their conditions were not confined to the Edinburgh area. Paul Burnham shows that the Amersham camps (which had several Labour and Communist activists among their number) campaigned with eventual success in 1949 for the Rural District Council to take over a camp and make substantial improvements to it. They had drawn on Communist MP Phil Piratin for support. Similar campaigns for improvements by them at other camps in the area were less successful although lobbying continued until the late 1950s. As we have seen squatters at Burnwood in Lanarkshire associated themselves with their Conservative MP to press their case for improvements, and this was the case in Sheffield too. The camp at Norton had been the one to which squatters had been moved after their original occupation had been in huts unfit for habitation; this had happened after council workmen had refused to demolish those huts until alternative accommodation had been organised. Although, again as we have seen, the squatters were originally pleased with their conditions, by 1950 problems with damp had prompted them to petition the council for improvements. Once again a local Conservative MP raised their case in the House of Commons and tried to meet the Mayor of Sheffield over the issue. Sheffield Labour councillors, like their colleagues in Lanarkshire, dismissed the MPs' actions as political opportunism. Doubtless this charge was accurate given that the issue enabled the MPs to criticise a Labour government or local authority over their respective housing records.

Similarly a Liberal prospective parliamentary candidate in Bristol attacked the 'appalling conditions' in the huts in one camp there in 1950, following talks with the residents.[39] Nonetheless these examples show that the camp dwellers were willing to organise and to use the political process to improve their circumstances.

Lobbying local authorities over the conditions was frequent too as was shown earlier in the chapter. What repeatedly emerged was the reluctance of councils to spend money on huts that would never be suitable for family accommodation so that the only hope of improvement was rehousing. In some cases squatters and councils put this case jointly to the Ministry. Camp residents at Shirehampton sent a telegram to the Ministry of Health in February 1947 protesting at the 'serious menace to health' presented by the damp in their huts. This squat came under Bristol Corporation, who took up the problem, although it was to be nearly three years before Bristol had confirmation from the Ministry that its housing allocation would be sufficient to rehouse the squatters. This was also the case when squatters' deputations to Lichfield RDC led to meetings between the residents, the council and the Ministry of Health about conditions at their camp. It was agreed that the council's housing allocation would be increased to enable the squatters to be rehoused. At Warmley in south Gloucestershire squatters sent a deputation to the RDC early in 1947, complaining about 'appalling conditions', 'intense cold and excessive damp'; they secured a 50 per cent reduction in their service charges. Residents continued to protest to the local authority and the ministry for another three years and both bodies agreed that their huts were 'totally unfit to live in'; lobbying such as this helped to ensure that housing allocations took account of the need to rehouse the squatters.[40]

Therefore the picture presented by the *New Statesman* article of apathy and despair in the Edinburgh camps was not an accurate one, even if the description of the conditions there certainly was. There are examples from several parts of Britain after 1946 of organisation among the squatters, and lobbying for better conditions and the acceleration of the housing programme. Political activists could still be closely associated with these actions too. The concerns of the squatters in many areas though were not only with the condition of their huts but their situation with the council housing waiting list. The final chapter will examine this and other issues that the camp residents continued to face.

NOTES

1   Paul Addison, *Now the War is Over: A Social History of Britain 1945-51* (London, BBC, 1985, p. 56); *Scotsman*, 23 August 1950; Becky Taylor, 'A Powerful Message from the Powerless: The E15 Mothers and Squatting in Post-War Britain', *History Workshop Online*, 27 October 2014 (www.historyworkshop.org viewed October 2014); Andrew Friend, 'The Post-War Squatters', in Nick Wates and Christian Wolmar (Eds) *Squatting: The Real Story* (1980, p. 119).

2   NA: HLG 7 /1/1023, War-time camps and hostels: occupation by unauthorised persons, Ministry of Health Note to Principal Housing Officers, August 1946.

3   NCRO: LHA/H/7/8, Correspondence concerning squatters in disused army huts at Greencroft 1946: Senior Regional Architect Newcastle on Tyne Region Ministry of Health: Squatters' Camps, Notes for Guidance of Regional Architects, 26 April 1947.

4   NA: HLG 7 /1/1023, War-time camps and hostels: occupation by unauthorised persons, Ministry of Works to Sir John Wrigley at the Ministry of Health, 22 August 1946.

5   NA: HLG 7 /1/1023, War-time camps and hostels: occupation by unauthorised persons, Sir John Wrigley, Report to Aneurin Bevan, 30 August 1946; draft of reply to Lady Davidson by Clement Attlee, 26 August 1946.

6   OLHC: OXOHA: LT900, BBC Radio Oxford, *Squatters' Delight* 1994.

7   Jim Tatters, interview with John Suggett and Don Watson, 2013. Jim Tatters later moved to a colliery job in Nottinghamshire because of the superior accommodation on offer there. *Sunderland Echo*, 7, 8 August 1946; *Lennox Herald*, 24 August 1946.

8   *Northern Daily Mail*, 16 August 1946; *Evening Times*, 16 August 1946; Dave Simpson, *No Homes for Heroes: Post War Squatters in Washington* (Sunderland, Gilpin Press, 2006, p. 99); *Sheffield Star*, 27 August 1946.

9   NA: CAB 130/13, Squatters in Military Camps: Minutes of Cabinet Committee on Squatting, 20 August 1946; Alex J Robertson: *The Bleak Midwinter, 1947* (Manchester, Manchester University Press, 1987).

10   Dave Simpson, *No Homes for Heroes*, p. 71; *Sunday Sun* 16 February, 16 March 1947; TWAS: CB.SS/A/2/23, Minutes of South Shields Town Council, 2 April 1947.

11   *Sunday Sun*, 16 March 1947.

12   *The Times*, 8, 23 August 1950.

13   *Stirling Sentinel*, 12, 19 November 1946; *Forres, Elgin and Nairn Gazette*, 14, 21 April 1948; *Glasgow Herald*, 13 September 1946.

14   DCRO: UD/CS/221, Chester le Street Urban District Council Correspondence re squatters at Roman Avenue military camp 1946-1954, letter from Mr. J.R. Henderson, 7 December 1946; Clerk of Council to the Ministry of Health Housing Division Newcastle, 10 September 1946.

15   DCRO: UD/CS/221, Chester le Street Urban District Council Correspondence re squatters at Roman Avenue military camp 1946-1954: letter from Mr. E.R. Simpson, 15 December 1946 and signed by sixteen camp residents.

16   *Lennox Herald*, 7 September 1946.

17   *Blaydon Courier*, 5 January, 9 February 1951; *Essex Newsman*, 21, 28 January 1948. On using representation see for example HALS: 59M76/DDC88, Minutes of Hartley Wintney Rural District Council Hutments Committee (Hartley Wintney Rural District Council Hutments Committee Minute Book, vol. 3, 1949-1952).

18   HC Debates, 9 December 1947, vol. 445 cc934-76934.

19   HC Debates, 10 October 1946, vol. 427 cc471-472.

20   HC Debates, 9 December 1947, vol. 445 cc934-76934.

21   Stephen Merrett, *State Housing in Britain* (London, Routledge and Kegan Paul, 1979, p. 243).

22   The discussion here is necessarily terse. A detailed summary of the historical debates over Labour's foreign policy at this time is provided in Rhiannon Vickers, *The Labour Party and the World Vol.1: The Evolution of Labour's Foreign Policy 1900-51* (Manchester, Manchester University Press, 2003); see also John Saville, *The Politics of Continuity: British Foreign Policy and the Labour Government 1945-46* (London, Verso, 1993) and Alan P. Dobson, *US Wartime Aid to Britain 1940-1946* (London, Croom Helm, 1986).

23   Stephen Merrett, *State Housing in Britain*, pp. 239-44.

24   *Gateshead Post*, 3, 10, 17 September 1948. On CP membership see Andrew Thorpe, 'The Membership of the Communist Party of Great Britain 1920-1945', *Historical Journal*, Vol. 3 No. 43 (2000, pp. 777-800.)

25   HC Debates, 14 March 1950, vol. 472 cc901-3; HC Debates, 9 December 1953, vol. 521 c2031.

26   *Glasgow Herald*, 9, 26 December 1952; 4 June, 24 October 1953; HC Debates, 25 May 1954, vol. 528 cc191-3; HC Debates, 18 February 1958, vol. 582 cc127.

27   Violet Fraser, *Huts for Houses: A Forres Squatter's Childhood* (Moray, J & J Publishing, 2012, pp.187, 192); *Forres, Elgin and Nairn Gazette*, 16 April 1947, 8 May 1948; TWAS: CB.SSS/A/2/23, Minutes of South Shields Town Council, 3 July 1946; *Lennox Herald*, 13 July 1946; *Fife Herald and Journal*, 13 May, 5 June 1946; *Leven Mail*, 12 June 1946; *Western Daily Press*, 25 August 1948; Alan Holmans, 'Housing', in A.H. Halsey and Josephine Webb (Eds), *Twentieth Century British Social Trends* (London, HMSO, 2000, p. 483).

28   Nicholas Timmins, *The Five Giants: A Biography of the Welfare State* (London, Harper Collins, 2001, pp. 181-2); Stephen Merrett, *State Housing in Britain*; on the Glasgow campaign see Charlie Johnstone, 'Early Post-War Housing Struggles in Glasgow', *Journal of the Scottish Labour History Society*, no. 28 (1993, pp. 7-29).

29   NA: T227/817, Emergency Housing: Policy and Requisitioning 1951-1953, Secretary of State for Scotland Stuart to Chancellor of the Exchequer Butler, 3 February 1953; letter from the Scottish Office to the Treasury, 13 July 1953.

30   NA: T227/817, Emergency Housing: Policy and Requisitioning 1951-1953, Working Party on Requisitioned Properties for Use in Housing, draft of third interim report, 1952.

31   NA: T227/818, Emergency Housing: Policy and Requisitioning 1953-1957, report for Public Accounts Committee, March 1956.

32   NRS: DD6/167, Requisitioning   and   Families   Inadequately   Housed,

Department of Health for Scotland internal memorandum, 3 May 1951; NA: T227/817, Emergency Housing: Policy and Requisitioning 1951-1953, letter from Department of Health for Scotland to Ministry of Housing and Local Government, 27 May 1952.

33   CEA: SL/2/2/6, Minutes of the Corporation of Edinburgh Housing Committee, 27 June 1950; *Evening News*, 13 November, 13 December 1951.

34   *Yorkshire Evening Post*, 25 February 1948; *Derby Evening Telegraph*, 31 July 1950; CEA: SL2/2/7, Minutes of the Corporation of Edinburgh Housing Committee, 21, 29 January 1952.

35   Neil McCallum, 'In Transit', *New Statesman and Nation*, vol. XLIII, no. 1095 (1 March 1952, pp. 240-42).

36   CEA: SL2/2/6, Minutes of the Corporation of Edinburgh Housing Committee, 10 October 1950, 13 November 1951; *Evening News*, 13 November 1951.

37   *Evening News*, 3, 12 December 1951.

38   *Evening News*, 7, 10, 30 January 1952.

39   Paul Burnham, 'The Squatters of 1946: A Local Study in National Context', *Socialist History*, no. 25 (2004, pp.32-8); *Sheffield Telegraph*, 12, 18 March, 20 April; *Western Daily Press*, 22 February 1950.

40   *Western Daily Press*, 27 February 1947, 27 September 1950; *Tamworth Herald*, 1 January, 28 May, 18 June 1949; *Western Daily Press*, 12 February 1947, 1 January 1948, 29 March 1950.

Chapter Eight
SQUATTERS AND WAITING LISTS:
THE POLITICS OF ALLOCATION

Evictions

This chapter is concerned with the issues the squatters of 1946 could face when it came to acceptance for council housing. It is worth noting first though that towards the end of the 1940s evictions, for several reasons, began to be enforced in some of the occupied camps as well as private property. One reason which was cited was concern over public health. Early in 1949 the Department of Health for Scotland evicted 23 families from a former RAF camp near Inverness because the conditions in the huts, which had been occupied six months earlier, were 'a menace to public health'. A demolition crew began work leaving families sheltering in such abandoned Nissen huts as they could find. The crew were then faced with the 'boos and shouts' of the squatters who had nowhere else to go; as in Sheffield three years earlier the workmen refused to continue until alternative accommodation had been found for the families. Institutional arrangements were duly made.[1]

In other cases the reason was that the land on which the camp was built was now sought for other purposes. Less than a year after the Inverness evictions the squatters outside Portsmouth were also evicted and the families dispersed, despite a campaign on their behalf by supportive Labour activists. Three families with their eight children had been squatting in former RAF huts for three years but the Ministry of Works required the land to be de-requisitioned so that it could be sold for agricultural use. Chichester Rural District Council had obtained an injunction against the squatters for trespass and began to demolish the huts. Once again the workmen downed tools in response to the distress of the occupants who had nowhere else to go. The families occupied the last hut, with their possessions piled outside; the council stated that they had over a thousand people 'waiting patiently for their turn for a council house' and that it would be 'extremely unfair to let others jump the queue because they had been evicted from government buildings they had walked into without authority'. Local Labour councillors acting as unofficial advocates protested that it was 'nothing short of criminal' that evictions should take place even though council officials admitted that there were no emergency accommodation or welfare institution places available in the area.

The Portsmouth squatters appear to have been treated in a vindictive fashion. They were dispersed into temporary accommodation organised by churches and sympathisers whilst the RDC maintained that it 'had no intention of putting them into council houses'. When sympathisers took them in to their own council houses Chichester Rural District Council threatened them with proceedings for creating overcrowding. The Ministry of Works applied to the County Court to have a squatter gaoled for contempt of court in that he had disobeyed the injunction to leave the huts. Nevertheless the County Court judge rejected the application, observing that 'there is no contempt in this at all. He is at his wits' end to get housing.' Labour Party activists contacted all local MPs to have the issue raised in the House of Commons and met the Parliamentary Secretary to the Ministry of Health to prevent further action and to try to ensure 'that there is little likelihood of a similar mass eviction being repeated'.[2]

Around the same time squatters in Derbyshire were evicted following court orders: families occupying an empty British Transport Commission property in Chesterfield, which the BTC had eventually decided it needed, and fifteen families from the Empire Hotel in Buxton. This building had been requisitioned by the army, left empty, squatted since 1946 and three years later apparently still required by the forces. In both cases water and sanitation were not being supplied and the living conditions were being described as an increasing danger to public health. In Buxton the local Conservative MP along with the local authority had been trying for some time to have an empty camp provided as an alternative but the relevant ministries had not produced one. Eventually at the end of 1949 a mass eviction took place in dramatic circumstances with the police arriving to find the squatters behind nailed-up doors and barricades. As in Chesterfield the families were split and dispersed to various institutions; seven men were prosecuted and two of them were gaoled. The court was told that these two were political activists from Liverpool whose influence had changed the atmosphere at the squat from one of co-operation to 'one of hostility and resistance'.[3]

In Carlisle, where in 1946 as we have seen around sixty families in the first wave of squatting had occupied almost an entire street, the outcome was also eviction. The local labour movement had lobbied the Corporation to allow them to stay and to provide services. A local Labour MP has spoken on their behalf; also, having received deputations from the squatters, local branches of the National Union of Railwaymen and the Women's Co-operative Guild had written supporting their requests for power supplies. Nevertheless when the squatters' representatives met the Town Clerk he confirmed that when the properties were de-requisitioned the Corporation would demolish them and build flats; legal proceedings would be taken against the squatters to require them to leave. He stated that whereas each family's housing application would be considered on its merits 'it could not be emphasised too much that no-one would be given any degree of priority because they had squatted'. He later told the Ministry too that the Corporation would not allow squatters to 'secure distinct advantage by reason of their unlawful acts over literally hundreds of others whose names have been on the lists for years.' The squatters for their part assured him that 'they had no desire to jump the queue over others' and queried, just as the political left was doing elsewhere, whether the Corporation was using its powers of requisitioning to the full. They also suspected a political bias against them with a claim that 'certain elements in the Council have taken full advantage ... of the Communist slant that had been put on squatting activity'.[4]

A number of the families moved out and several were indeed rehoused as priority cases of need. Some thirty remaining cases appeared in the County Court and after three days of hearings the Corporation was granted possession orders for the properties. This was not before the judge had made his views about overcrowding in the city clear. The squatters' case had been pleaded by the women, 'some with babes in arms', because the men were at work, and they had described the 'impossibility' of renting rooms when there were children. Although the judge had no option but to grant the orders he stated that the 'defendants were good citizens of Carlisle and, as he had met them, nice people, but life had treated them harshly'.[5]

In the same year legal action was attempted against 'unauthorised squatters' by Amersham RDC in Berkshire. As elsewhere the council was keen to clear the camp but as soon as residents moved out, other squatters moved in without agreement by the authority. When they appeared in the County Court those in the dock were, as in Carlisle, women with children because the men were working. Unlike in Carlisle the judge found in their favour and instructed the council to 'assist them with their housing problems': this was duly done by improvements and renovations to their huts.[6]

These legal cases were not the end of the squatting response to housing problems at this time. In Glasgow for example, where the issues were persistently acute, the Govan Tenants' Association tried to launch a programme of what it called 'unofficial requisitioning'. This meant organising families to occupy large houses which had been left empty and up for sale for some time. Less than a month later the police responded with thirty arrests under the Trespass (Scotland) Act and when the cases came up in early 1954 they caused what was described as 'the worst demonstration ever to have occurred in a Glasgow court'. Police had to clear the Sheriff's Court after fighting broke out when an RAF veteran and squatter was gaoled. Eight weeks later the court had to be cleared again when the Secretary of the Tenants' Association, William Irvine, was gaoled for contempt of court following the original disturbance. The squatting wave of the 1940s had led to prosecutions and evictions in Glasgow under the Trespass Act, but the desperation of families seeking decent accommodation was such that they were still prepared to break the law to secure it. There were obviously still activists willing to help to organise them, and it was not until the rehousing programmes of the 1960s took effect that such actions died down.[7]

Boundaries

At the beginning of the camp squatting wave the Cabinet had taken the view that the squatters should be neither favoured nor penalised when it came to the council housing waiting lists. At the same time the Home Secretary had seemed to intimate that local authorities might regard the camp residents as less of a priority for council housing, compared to others on their lists, on the grounds that their accommodation needs had already been met.

It was explained in a previous chapter that at least by the end of the 1940s the Treasury was anxious to see the squatters rehoused and their hutments demolished, if only because the government was spending increasing sums on buildings that would never be fit for purpose at the expense of the general building programme. Where possible they were providing incentives to local authorities to include such rehousing in their building schemes. As we have seen though by no means all local authorities took a positive view of the camp squatters in their areas, and some resented what they saw as a symptom of the national housing problem and a consequence of lethargy by government departments, being passed to them to manage. One source of contention was the primary eligibility criterion for admission to the housing waiting list: residency or established connections within the local authority boundary.

It was also noted earlier how at the beginning of the squatting movement the Secretary of State for Scotland had been impatient with local authorities who protested at having to respond to squatters who had come from outside their areas. He had used an analogy with the Poor Law, under which elected representatives had been responsible for funding unemployment and other benefits within their local authority areas from the rates. At times of high unemployment and pressures on the rates they had sought to ensure that local people were the recipients of locally raised expenditure, rather than claimants from other areas. Nevertheless the politics of rationing meant that the Poor Law analogy was unfortunately an appropriate one, and appropriate across Britain. Councils having to manage high demand and limited, slow supply also received their allocations on the basis of the needs of their local residents. The needs of people who had recently come to the area or who were outside its boundaries were another matter.

Thus when Frome UDC in the Bristol area was discussing its allocation of new housing it decided that 'it was not prepared to accept any responsibility for rehousing squatters'. Nor did it accept the fact that 'the rehousing of people who live just outside the urban boundary and who wish to live in the urban district was their liability'. There could be more involved too. Wellingborough Rural Council in Northamptonshire agreed conversion and adaptations to squatted huts to meet ministerial concerns about public health. When members learned that many of the squatters had come from outside the area some of them wanted to 'help our own squatters first' because 'they are our own people from our own villages' and 'charity begins at home'. It seems likely that in some rural areas there was some suspicion or at least reserve about outsiders which would not have helped the squatters' case for rehousing and consideration for the waiting lists. There were other reasons too why their case for consideration could be damaged, and one of those was the stigma that could be attached to the act of squatting.[8]

Local responses and stigma

Although the press coverage of the camp squatting movement had not been hostile and the public attitude to the movement was judged to be sympathetic not all the reactions to squatters in the localities were positive. For example a woman squatting at a disused anti-aircraft site in Tynemouth complained that 'some people seem to think that because we are moving into places like these that we belong to the lower end of the social scale'. Tynemouth was a middle-class seaside town continually alert to potential threats to its tone, and so that was probably to be expected. In Gateshead, where the council had taken over a former anti-aircraft site at Lobley Hill for accommodation, 'Lobley Hill Householder' complained to the local paper that in so doing the council had 'officially countenanced squatting' and were threatening 'the prestige of a good estate' nearby. This was also reflected in the reactions of some local authorities. Central government was not in a position to dictate to local councils about how to deal with the occupied forces camps once the responsibility had been passed to them. A number resisted the idea of having anything to do with the camps and their inhabitants at all. Rawnmarsh Urban District Council in Yorkshire had refused to accept the 36 families occupying Air Ministry property as tenants and resented having to supply even basic services to them. There was support for one councillor's view that 'we are badgered by these people because they feel it is our duty to see to their every desire. They should not be there.' Even when one council did agree to renovate occupied huts to alleviate 'squalid' conditions this was in the face of councillors who 'didn't think we had a duty to people who are squatters'.[9]

In Scotland service camps did not became vacant in some cases until later than was usual in the rest of Britain and so occupations by the homeless still occurred after 1946. One example in 1948 provides a good example of how hostile responses by local authorities had consequences for the squatters in terms of public attitudes towards them. This was in the Elgin and Nairn area where Forres Town Council had been one of the many that had approached the army about taking over a camp but had been refused, and therefore members described the squatting situation as 'one of those messes carried out by some of our government departments'. Initially they turned down a Department of Health for Scotland proposal to take over a camp because it consisted, so it was said, of 'nothing more than sheds with no conveniences'. Further, the Provost claimed that the state of the occupied camp at Balnageith 'was a public scandal' and the Convenor of the Public Health Committee stated that the huts just outside the burgh boundary were in the worst public health state and were being squatted by 'some absolutely strange people' who were not connected to the area. He was reluctant for the council to take any responsibility for them. The residents of the Balnageith huts protested vigorously to the local press about the remarks made about them in the council meeting. They pointed out that all but one of the families were local people, they all had Elsan toilets, and most were not in broken down huts. They were 'weather-proof, warm and dry … and some of the brick huts were as good as houses'. They had far less over-crowding than when they had lived as families in one room in Forres, and in fact 'this is a palace as regards room space'. They believed that because of the remarks at the meeting 'the community are going to think we are a lot of cannibals here'. A married couple ('both ex-RAF and used to service huts') who were interviewed claimed that it was common knowledge that there were bigger health hazards in some of the houses in the town. The interviewees confirmed that the huts were near a water supply and some had a supply indoors; there were no vermin or pests. They were better off in terms of housing, they said, than many of the country people in the area. The squatters maintained that if the council could confirm that they were going to be allowed to stay then they would do more to improve the huts. Finally, they objected to 'people in responsible positions making certain statements which are unwarranted and based on hearsay'. At the end of April 1948 Moray Council Housing Committee agreed to take over huts when the Department of Health for Scotland agreed to meet the water, drainage and sewage costs. Nevertheless several councillors were still reluctant to take the responsibility and the Medical Officer of Health agreed that 'managing the camps was a distasteful job'.[10]

These official, negative attitudes, fully reported in the local newspapers, seem to have filtered down to the community at large and thus promoted stigma and discrimination against the camp squatters. Violet Fraser was a child in one of the camps in the area and has recalled how children like her from the huts could be taunted by other children who were taking a lead from their parents:

> We were called 'the squatters' and this became a dirty word for us. They did not seem to care that so many of us were local people with husbands and fathers who fought in the very recent war. These men had fought to free millions of people from monstrous prejudices, only to come up against it in their own home town … I never ever told my parents about how we were treated or the name calling that went on at school and in the town. The children in our huts stayed together as a group for protection from the town children … It seems to me that some people in the town took their lead from the Council … 'Squatter' was still a dirty word and even the local dairy wouldn't deliver milk to us.

She continues that Forres Town Council wanted permission to build a new housing scheme but were told they would only get permission if they rehoused the squatters. As we have seen this was the Treasury approach designed to deal with the deteriorating conditions in the huts coupled with the rising costs to the Ministry of Health of maintaining them. When the council finally did so 'they had the cheek to say that the squatters fitted in admirably … There was an anti-squatter brigade formed by the current tenants of Rosyvale, they got up a petition to try to stop us moving into the houses, but fortunately nothing came of it and we were allowed to move in.'[11]

In other areas of Scotland there is some evidence of this discrimination too. In his research Charlie Johnstone interviewed a woman who had spent a good part of her childhood in a camp before her family were rehoused to a peripheral estate near Glasgow. She had always preferred not to mention to people that her family had been squatters. This was a reaction to the stigma they had experienced and the treatment they had received from a variety of public agencies, something that in her case had brought long-term psychological consequences. Similarly, in Edinburgh a housing researcher came across a woman who had spent part of her childhood in one of the camps outside the city but refused to talk about it, still honouring her late mother's insistence that squatting should never be discussed outside the family.[12]

Stigma could also be attached to the camp squatters in other parts of Britain. At the camp near Norton Fitzwarren in Somerset one squatter has recalled that securing the support of the council and local establishment was not straightforward:

> We elicited the help of our Rural District Councillor who flatly refused to help us achieve our aims and scathingly referred to us as 'rogues and scoundrels'. It was made quite clear to him that should he try to visit again he would not be made welcome. There was no help either from the Rector of Norton who, in a public meeting, referred to us as nothing more than 'scum' from the Armed Forces. It was not lost on the squatters that neither of these gentlemen had served in the Armed Forces.

In another rural area, outside Oxford, Fred Armstrong remembered that the camp dwellers did not get a particularly positive response from the nearby villagers. They had to work to be accepted:

> Oh yes, the villagers would never let you forget you were a squatter. Yet some of our conditions were probably better than theirs, the old houses they had up there. But we got on great with them at Oakley, we used to go in 'The Sun', the local pub, the husband and wife who kept 'The Sun' were our Labour councillors, and stuck up for us. There were lots of fetes, and we used to muck in with them, we got on great with them in the end. I say in the end, we had to win them over, but in the end we were equals.[13]

There is some evidence that actual discrimination could be the result. The *New Statesman* article of 1952 on the camps outside Edinburgh, quoted in a previous chapter, had noted that the camp committees were trying to fight the stigma that was being associated with squatting. The committees reported that their residents were experiencing discrimination when they applied for jobs, and the example was given of a young woman rejected for nurse training in Edinburgh simply because she was living in the camp. The hospital matron had apparently made assumptions about her attitude to hygiene and cleanliness based solely on her having the camp as her address. The Mass Observation team that had interviewed squatting families in the camps outside London had picked up an example of just this issue six years earlier. One interviewee explained to the team why they were thinking of changing the address of the camp to 'The Drive, Gladstone Park': some of the tenants had applied for jobs but when they gave their address and were asked 'Are you the squatters?' that was the last they heard about the jobs.[14] This type of attitude did not bode well for the integration of camp squatters into the mainstream of the local authority housing programmes.

Waiting lists and housing programmes

Some groups of squatters feared that far from being given priority – something no group appears to have sought anyway – their local authority had excluded them from the housing waiting list altogether. There are examples of this fear being entirely justified. As was noted in a previous chapter the occupants of the camp at Chester le Street had lobbied both their UDC and the local Ministry of Health Housing Division about conditions in their huts:

> We have done all we can to make these huts clean and comfortable, but nothing we do seems to prevent the rain from coming in, or the things being covered in rust, so do you think it would be possible to let us have some waterproof sheeting for the roofs.

They quoted press reports that squatters were regarded as householders and were therefore ineligible for the pre-fabricated houses. They contended that if they actually *were* householders then the council had some responsibility for repairs, and if they were in condemned properties – unfit for human habitation according to the council – then they should be entitled to be on the housing list. It is clear from another letter signed by sixteen residents that their perceived absence from the housing list was a major concern. In this subsequent and poignant letter they also pleaded for a 'fair turn' when it came to rehousing:

Three of our womenfolk had inquired about this at the Council and they had been told that the names of squatters had been removed from the housing list.

We do not ask for priority or any unfair advantage. We only ask that our names be replaced on the housing list, in our right and proper turn. We stress the fact that we took possession of these huts to relieve overcrowding and not to get our names moved up the list ...

... We have inquired as to what turn we stand for a house, and we have been informed none whatsoever. Lots of people seem to think we want priority, but we don't all we wish is a fair turn. It seems so unfair that we should be condemned through coming into these huts when we really came in out of pure necessity, which we can well prove.

We are quite willing to send a deputation to your meeting to state our facts, if you would be agreeable, but no-one seems to want to hear our side of the story; we are condemned without a hearing. This letter is on behalf of all the squatters at Roman Avenue Camp.[15]

The previous chapter noted that the occupants of the Burnwood camp at Carluke in Lanarkshire had involved their local Conservative MP in their campaign for better conditions. The state of their huts was only part of the problem however: the MP told the press that most if not all of the tenants would be satisfied with their accommodation for the time being 'if they could be assured that they were on the council's waiting list for houses and that they would be considered when houses were being allocated in the district'. He claimed that correspondence from the county council showed that the camp tenants were excluded from the waiting list because they had chosen to live in the camp.[16] Other councils may not have excluded camp squatters altogether but placed them at such a low priority, regardless of need, that they may as well have been excluded. At the annual conference of the Royal Sanitary Association of Scotland in 1949 the Inspector for Renfrew Council described how his council prioritised housing applications. On a list of sixteen categories the highest priority was for people living in accommodation classed as unfit for habitation, the second was for those in overcrowded accommodation; the sixteenth, and last, was the category 'squatters in condemned property, service camps and hostels'. No rationale was offered for this policy, and possibly this council had adopted the Home Secretary's implied suggestion that the squatters were not a priority because their needs were being met. Alternatively Renfrew Council may have adopted an intransigent policy as matter of principle.[17]

Another and egregious example of an official marginalising of the squatters came from Glasgow City Corporation. As a Scottish Office adviser informed the Secretary of State for Scotland in 1952 after a meeting with its representatives, 'They also informed me that Glasgow Corporation will have nothing to do with squatters.' In the context of pressure to take back use of the Barlinnie Prison Officers' quarters by rehousing the squatters there he also explained that:

> The Department of Health for Scotland insists that squatters put their names on the waiting list of the appropriate local authority in order to ensure that they get a house in due course. This could not be done in the case of Glasgow families since Glasgow Corporation refused to accept squatters on to their waiting list.

This intransigence had obviously eased by the beginning of 1956, when the Corporation agreed to rehouse the remaining Barlinnie squatters. They had been there for nearly ten years and in steadily deteriorating conditions.[18]

Therefore it took nearly a decade before Glasgow Corporation would even admit squatters to their housing waiting lists, still less actually rehouse them. The memoranda quoted here do not explain the reasons for this policy, which as we have seen was in marked contrast to the attitudes adopted by other local authorities. Possibly the Corporation had agreed with the Home Secretary in 1946 that the squatters had had their needs met; possibly they had wished to deter further squatting activity, in the light of the occupation of empty hotels and large houses in Glasgow; possibly they had not wished to be seen to be complicit in contentious actions that upset their control over the housing issue. Certainly, whatever the reasons the consequences for the camp squatters around Glasgow must have been serious, both in terms of the increasingly dilapidated accommodation they were enduring and the social consequences described above.

Out of turn

Most local authorities were intent on emphasising that squatters would not receive any special consideration when it came to housing simply because they were squatters. The attitudes expressed at the conference of the Association of Durham Urban District Councils in 1946 have already been described. Similarly in the same county the housing chairman of Hetton Rural District Council was keen to squash 'the idea that had got about' that the council would provide alternative accommodation for squatters. In order to protect the interests of those queuing on the housing list they would evict squatters from private property and those occupying empty condemned property could not expect the priority given to residents of slum clearance areas. Elsewhere in County Durham Consett Urban District Council originally agreed that the squatters in the former Bevin Boys' hostel 'shall not be regarded as eligible for temporary houses', meaning the pre-fabs the council were erecting. This decision – presumably taken because the occupants' accommodation needs had been met – was revoked five years later on the strict understand that there was to be 'no queue-jumping'.[19]

In Scotland there were 3,200 families living in requisitioned properties by 1951 and the end of requisitioning meant that they were scheduled to be rehoused by the end of 1953. A number of local authorities were also managing ex-services camps on requisitioned land as 'clearing houses' into which they put people on waiting lists until their turns came, the camps at Edinburgh being an example. The whole expense was borne by the Exchequer and as we have seen it was anxious to 'reduce the number of families in the camps as quickly as possible'. The Department of Health for Scotland agreed that special allocations of houses to facilitate rehousing from requisitioned properties should be conditional on including residents from the 'clearing houses' so that the huts could be demolished. Nevertheless:

> This does not, of course, apply to camps which have been occupied by squatters. We cannot offer additional allocations for the rehousing of squatters – though we can indicate confidentially that any application for an increased allocation <u>on general grounds</u> by a local authority who propose to rehouse squatters in their area would be sympathetically considered.

In other words there were official minds at the Department of Health for Scotland who believed, five years after the camps were first occupied, that the government could not be seen to be responding positively to the pressure of the squatters by 'rewarding' them with rehousing. The rehousing of squatters would have to be camouflaged within the general housing programme, and there is an example of why this policy was adopted. At a local election meeting in Falkirk a month after this memorandum a right-wing councillor stated that after a council deputation had visited the Scottish Office they had been allocated 24 houses to rehouse squatters. He said that this was 'something that had never before been made public' and that he had wanted to object to it in the council but the Provost, he claimed, had refused to let him speak because 'a promise had been given to the Department of Health that nothing would be divulged'. Admittedly no new houses had been given to squatters but nevertheless 'there were many young couples living with their parents who would have been glad of the requisitioned houses that had been given to the squatters. There was a principle involved here.' Clearly the Scottish Office inclination to keep allocations to rehouse squatters confidential was a prescient move when it came to some local authorities. Nonetheless controversies – or at least adverse and public comment from councillors – could still occur on the subject of squatters and housing.[20]

Near Stockton, then in County Durham, the same objection emerged among elected members three years later. By 1954 conditions at a Greatham camp had deteriorated, and in addition the Rural District Council had cut off their electricity supply in order to investigate where the large quantity of power being used was actually going. The residents responded with a deputation to the authority and an invitation to their local MP to visit and see their conditions for himself. Having done so he pronounced them 'deplorable'; the council agreed and pointed out that both they and the Ministry wanted such huts to be cleared as soon as possible but they had no houses available as an alternative. When it looked possible that they might get an additional allocation 'for the express purpose of rehousing' the camp residents it was in the face of some councillor complaints. Once again, the argument ran that 'it was unfair to rehouse squatters before people on the list who have waited years for a house'. Similarly further south, a report to the local authority on Lincoln's housing progress mentioned that occupiers of hutments were being rehoused, leading to the committee chairman having to confirm that these were families whose names were on the housing list and denying 'any suggestion that squatters had been moved out of their turn'. In 1952 Dundee Corporation was struggling with the issue of the 743 families who were squatting in derelict tenements in the city. The Chief Sanitary Inspector proposed that the authority buy and renovate currently inferior properties so that the tenants could be rehoused and the squatters moved into the homes they had left. The problem, as councillors saw it, was that this would involve giving those 'legal tenants' a 'greater priority' and therefore this 'would upset the pointage system and cause heartburnings in other parts of the city'.[21]

These sensitivities about moving people out of their turn are understandable, particularly in the context of the traditional pressure that many local authorities had been under about their allocation policies.

Tenancy accusations

As we have seen in an earlier chapter individual local authorities' procedures for selecting and allocating tenancies had been a source of contention since the inter-war period. Those who found themselves waiting on the housing lists for years could develop a resentful and cynical attitude to their situation. As we have also seen, this was not helped by the lack of transparency in the allocation systems and the suspicion that decisions were made by a closed inner circle of councillors and officials. The post-war housing programme transformed a number of British local authorities into landlords, sometimes major landlords, in some cases for the first time. It required the introduction or overhaul of council house letting systems in a context of acute need outstripping supply. Applicants were generally allocated points according to their level of need and so rehousing was to be done in priority order. Nevertheless local suspicion about how all this actually worked in practice continued.

In Felling-on-Tyne for example the Communist Party branch secretary claimed that the reason rumours were circulating about the Urban District Council's housing allocation practice was because there was 'only vague information about the allocation policy'. He suggested that the Council publish a list in the newspaper of all prospective tenants so that it would be apparent that they were all priority cases. Two months later, in March 1947, the chairman of the Housing Lettings Committee attended public meetings 'that had well-nigh been demanded' to discuss local policy. He appealed to his audiences 'to help quash ugly rumours with regard to letting – that councillors accepted bribes and that councillors' families and friends were getting priority'. He explained that the council were following the Ministry's instruction to give priority to those from condemned houses and slum clearance areas, and the requirement to fill new council houses meant a priority for those with families, regardless of the circumstances of others. Nevertheless this controversy continued in the Felling area until at least the end of 1947.

In another part of the county the chairman of the Blaydon Urban District Council Housing Committee stated that he was aware of the rumours circulating about favouritism but claimed that 'contrary to our critics in the fish queues' each house was allocated very carefully. He organised a public meeting to explain the lettings policy and how the points system was allocating priorities; despite 'prolonged uproar' from sceptics at the meeting he maintained that the discontent was 'due to malcontents and mischief makers and those gullible enough to listen to them'. Similarly members of Stanley UDC, where the waiting list had almost doubled between 1948 and

1949, found it necessary to dispel rumours about their allocations policy and challenge 'anyone with real information' about abuse to come forward.[22]

Further south in Bedfordshire a councillor was criticised by his colleagues when he reported public dissatisfaction with the lettings system, 'having heard it said that if you went to the right pub, or the right shop, or the right chapel, or the right church on Sunday you would get a house ... he was not suggesting that it was all true but we have to deal with this'. Similarly in Scotland the Glasgow Corporation, as we have seen, had believed it important to state in the report *Glasgow's Housing Progress* that it used a points system based on need for tenancy allocations. This was part of its attempt to rebut critics of its housing record and policies. Here too councillors and housing officials stated that those with evidence of favouritism should come forward and the claims would be investigated. However there is some evidence from Glasgow as to why this rarely happened and the same would probably have applied elsewhere:

> People would hear of somebody who wisnae in as bad a position as them getting a hoose, and they were convinced that they were on the waiting list before them. But the greatest ploy of the housing authorities at that time was ... eh ... you tell us the name of the person. Well, you see, there was a loyalty among the working class and they didnae want to do this kind of thing ...[23]

Where local authorities were under such pressure to demonstrate that their housing procedures were above board they could have become particularly wary of local sensitivities about 'queue jumpers'. This may well have been an ingredient in some of the attitudes towards rehousing squatters, alongside any others derived from resentment at their original action.

Some official attitudes: 'Squatters being what they are ...'

There is evidence that in official circles there could be the same negative assumptions about the camp squatters as had been voiced at Forres Town Council. In 1949 the President of the Sanitary Inspectors' Association of Scotland stated that the service camps pressed into use for housing were more trouble than they were worth, because of squatters; they had occupied places that were unfit even for licensing and which sometimes had no proper sanitary accommodation. He warned of the potential social problems created by the squatters who, 'paying no rent they had no responsibility, no sense of citizenship and no interest in the welfare of others'. As a characterisation of the squatting movement of 1946 in Scotland and elsewhere this is, as has been demonstrated, little more than a travesty. Those who had occupied the ex-service camps had put a great deal of their own efforts into improving conditions, had been more than keen to pay rents and charges, and had shown a high degree of community organisation and cohesion. They wished to be tenants, not squatters, and often referred to themselves as such. As the ILP's Councillor Gibson had put it in Glasgow in 1946 they came across as 'nice, decent types of artisans'. It is not clear how far the Sanitary Inspectors – important figures when it came to liaising with the squatters – shared the perspective of their Association's President, who clearly saw the camp squatters as an underclass.[24]

The 'licences' referred to above applied when a camp had not been taken over by a local authority. In these cases the squatters were asked to make payments for services such as sanitation, refuse collection and power as 'licences' and not 'rents' to avoid establishing the legal relationship of landlord and tenant. In the early 1950s the Department of Health for Scotland, to whom such fees were paid north of the border, explained its approach towards payment arrears in an internal note:

> The Department of Health frequently takes action to recover outstanding payments and in extreme cases resorts to evictions for continued default. But where families contain large numbers of children or where the defaulter is an aged person, or where there are other good reasons, the Department does not enforce default ... squatters being what they are, short of evictions on a substantial scale which would not be politically practical, there must inevitably be a proportion – and in certain camps a high proportion – of uncollected payments.[25]

This is a more diplomatic expression of the sentiments of the President of the Sanitary Inspectors' Association but there is no indication in this correspondence of the scale of uncollected payments or the extent to which the people described were abusing the system.

This was in the same year that the Secretary of State for Scotland had informed the Chancellor of the Exchequer that local authorities were reluctant to rehouse squatter families 'out of turn'. As was noted in the previous chapter there was concern that were matters left to the local authorities the camps, increasingly expensive to maintain, would not be cleared for some time. A civil servant later said of the families concerned that:

... the majority are difficult types – squatters and so on – whom local authorities are reluctant to rehouse. A number appear to have no settled area of residence before entering the camps and it is difficult to fix housing responsibility in these cases to any particular authority. It may be necessary to consider before long the question of further special measures to deal with these families ...[26]

This of course was what lay behind the inclusion of additional housing allocations to clear the camps, although rarely identified as such. Again the assumption that the squatters were 'difficult types', and the question is begged of the extent to which this was justified. It is the case that some of the squatted camps contained residents who dodged payments or whose behaviour consistently disturbed their neighbours, and where the camp community was unable to resolve the issues informally. In Swindon for example the council had to pursue a railwayman and his wife, squatting in former Fire Service accommodation, for non-payment of charges, and exactly the same issue came up in Hampshire where a couple of families were accruing rent arrears to the extent that they had to be threatened with court proceedings. Similarly when members of Spilsby RDC in Lincolnshire dealt with the issue of council tenant rent arrears they did not argue with a colleague's opinion that many of those who owed rent had been squatters in the first place. The accuracy or otherwise of the statement was not challenged.[27]

Some squatted houses in Hamilton in Lanarkshire were taken over by the national housing association, the Second Scottish National Housing Company, in 1946. The secretary complained to the Department of Health about the state of cleanliness and order, the general neglect of communal areas like courts and closes which 'reflected most unfavourably on the tenants'. His report criticised what he termed the 'low standard of living and the irresponsible conduct of the tenants'. At the former Bevin Boys' hostel in Consett the secretary of the squatters' committee had to write to the UDC to complain about one of the tenants and ask the council to take action, but 'the party concerned had now moved out'. Similarly near Tewkesbury in Gloucestershire two camp residents formally complained to the council about the behaviour of one particular family and hinted that they might have to withhold their own rent payments unless something was done about them. The family concerned proved to be frequent rent evaders for almost two years and were also suspected of interfering with gas meters to obtain a free supply.[28]

As has been mentioned Amersham Council experienced problems with new 'unauthorised' squatters moving in when the original families moved out, and this persisted into the late 1950s. These later arrivals proved to include some 'rogue tenants' who amassed rent arrears and whose presence obstructed the clearance of the camp for house-building. Sometimes though it was circumstance that dictated why some camp occupiers had to resort to behaviour that caused disapproval. For example the residents of the occupied former RAF camp at Gainsborough in Lincolnshire caused controversy for months when they helped themselves to wood from huts and buildings on the site that were not in use. There were local protests about the consequent 'eyesore' and two men were prosecuted for stealing wood that still in effect belonged to the Air Ministry. They told the court that they had taken the wood because they had no access to coal and fuel, something the police confirmed in court. It is possible that they were unable to register with a coal merchant because they had no 'official' address, something more supportive councils elsewhere had been able to resolve for their camp occupiers.[29]

There is another related issue to consider and this is raised by Colin Ward. One of his works quotes, in passing, from a press report of the situation in a camp in Lancashire during the winter of 1947. This camp included the original occupiers from the movement of the previous year and also 'official squatters', people accommodated there as a matter of policy by the local council. Both groups were awaiting their turn on the housing waiting list but according to the journalist there was a qualitative difference between the attitudes of the two:

A commentary on the situation was made by one of the young welfare officers attached to the housing department. On her visit of inspection she found that the original squatters had set to work with a will, improvising partitions, running up curtains, distempering, painting and using initiative. The official squatters, on the other hand, sat about glumly without any initiative or lifting a hand to help themselves, and bemoaning their fate even though they might have been removed from the most appalling slum property. Until the overworked corporation workmen got around to them they would not attempt to improve affairs themselves.[30]

There is obviously a great deal of ideological leverage to be made here as the journalist is probably aware. As an anarchist Ward uses this article to contrast the benefits to people, as he sees it, of taking their own independent action as opposed to the inertia and dependency that are the likely results when people have action imposed upon them by some state apparatus. In any event the account suggests a potential contrast between the high levels of organisation and self-management evident from the press coverage of the camp movement and what may have been happening later. For example were the initiators and first waves of the camp squatters followed, officially or otherwise, by people with less commitment to what they were doing and how they were living, because they had not chosen to occupy these huts?

Mention has already been made that former service camps were a resource for local authorities in meeting their responsibilities under the 1948 National Assistance Act. Part Three of this legislation required councils to accommodate people who would otherwise be homeless, and one of the reasons Edinburgh Corporation, for example, had given to the Treasury for not clearing a camp was that it was needed for just this purpose. Accounts of the later squatting movements in Britain show that former squatted camps such as Hornchurch Airfield near London were still being used as Part Three accommodation by local authorities as late as 1969. This suggests that the persistence of the huts, by this time probably the worst and most inconveniently situated accommodation available to councils, was due to their use as emergency accommodation. As commentators pointed out, this can only have contributed to the social exclusion and ostracism of the families concerned.[31]

Notwithstanding these examples, were there enough grounds to justify the comments at the Scottish Sanitary Inspectors' conference, or the statement within the Scottish Office about rent payments? Any such justification would have to prove that the residents of the squatted camps and installations demonstrated higher rates of persistent rent arrears, anti-social behaviour and neglect of their accommodation than others in private rented, housing association or council properties at the time. An exercise of such nature is outside the scope of this discussion and the evidence to make it worthwhile is likely to be only scantily available. At the same time these last two chapters have shown there is evidence that, rather than succumbing to lethargy, there were squatters who continued to lobby and campaign for improved conditions and for equitable consideration on the waiting lists.

Summary

The occupations of the empty camps from 1946 were widespread. They were also, largely due to the slow progress of the housing programme, of a far longer duration than had been anticipated either by the authorities or the squatters themselves. It was inevitable that the ranks of the squatters included an element that did not share the standards and values of the others. The evidence is insufficient to suggest though that being a squatter as such meant a greater likelihood of being a bad or disruptive tenant. As time went on and conditions in the huts deteriorated it is possible that some resented paying for the conditions they were living in and behaved accordingly; it is likely that some too would have suffered from the tendency of observers to blame people for being the cause of their own sub-standard environments. Nevertheless, to repeat, the squatters included many who campaigned for improvements and assurances about rehousing.

It is clear that some local authorities discriminated against the squatters over places on their housing waiting lists. This was not just a case of ensuring that a queue based on needs and priorities was not disrupted. In some instances they were firmly at the end of the queue, or not allowed to be on it at all, simply because they had moved into the camps without authority. For some of the squatters this attitude had serious consequences for their quality of life. In 1946 the vehement critic of the squatters, Glasgow Labour MP Jean Mann, seems to have been almost gloating when she praised Glasgow Corporation for not adopting the local camps and continued that 'squatters may begin to wish, with the wind whistling around their ears, that they had remained on the waiting list'.[32] The apparent vindictiveness of this Corporation and others, and the aggressive attitude that some took towards their squatters, not only condemned them to harsh conditions for longer than necessary but could help to attach social stigma to them as well. As has been mentioned the results of this discrimination could be long-lasting, and some of the squatters of 1946 paid a heavy price for their initiative in seeking their own solution to overcrowding.

In fairness to the local councils their task was unenviable. As we have seen they had intractable problems of managing great housing need versus limited supply, and in a context sometimes where local folklore suspected favouritism in council tenancy allocations. As we have seen this could be a legacy of opaque council procedures in the past but even with a system based on published criteria of priority accusations of unfairness could persist. Therefore councillors would have been concerned to be seen to be acting fairly and this explains why they avoided any suggestion that squatters were receiving special treatment. There would have been an air of controversy about the squatters' action, as well as a potential challenge to the role of the local authority over housing and thus a need to assert control of the narrative by not being seen to be rewarding direct action. The pressures of demand over supply also meant that to be seen to be 'putting local people' first could be politically expedient. This could be a delicate matter when the Treasury made housing available specifically for rehousing squatters from huts that were increasingly dilapidated and expensive to maintain. The squatters were not looking for any priority, of course: they simply wanted to ensure that they had the same chance as others for council accommodation.

The case of squatting in Britain over these ten years after the Second World War raises a number of issues. The final chapter will bring these together in a concluding discussion.

NOTES

1   *Glasgow Herald*, 17, 18 February 1949.
2   *Portsmouth Evening News*, 29 April, 2, 3, 6, 19 May, 21 June, 16 September 1950; HC Debates, 15 May 1950, vol. 475 cl 22w.
3   HC Debates, 2 November 1949, vol. 469 cc 553-62; *Derby Evening Telegraph*,7, 29 December 1949; *Derbyshire Times and Chesterfield Herald*, 3, 10 March 1950.
4   CA: CA/C/6/555, Squatters in Carlisle Corporation Property 1946-1948, correspondence; Memorandum of interview representatives of the Rydal Street 'squatters' had with the Town Clerk, 21 September 1946; Town Clerk to North West District Ministry of Health, 9 November 1946.
5   *Carlisle Journal*, 3 March 1947.
6   Paul Burnham, 'The Squatters of 1946: A Local Study in National Context', *Socialist History*, no. 25 (2004, pp. 34-5).
7   *Aberdeen Evening Express*, 23 November, 16 December 1953; 13 January, 15 March 1954.
8   *Western Daily Press*, 4 October 1950; *Northampton Mercury*, 15 December 1950.
9   *Shields Evening News*, 16 August; *Gateshead Times*, 20 September 1946; *Sheffield Daily Telegraph*, 28 September 1950; meeting of Bingham RDC reported in the *Nottingham Evening Post*, 21 April 1950.
10 *Forres, Elgin and Nairn Gazette*, 13 March, 14, 21, 28 April 1948.
11 Violet Fraser, *Huts for Houses: A Forres Squatter's Childhood* (Moray, J & J Publishing, 2012, pp. 32, 41).
12 Charlie Johnstone, *The Tenants' Movement and Housing Struggles in Glasgow 1945 – 1990* (PhD University of Glasgow, 1992, p. 234); information given to the author by Mr DJ Johnson-Smith, PhD candidate, University of Edinburgh, 2014.
13 SHC: A\BVF/2/4, Extract from memoirs of an ex-serviceman looking for accommodation in Norton Fitzwarren 1946. OXOHA: LT900, BBC Radio Oxford, *Squatters' Delight*, 1994. Some confirmation of the point about conditions being little better in farm labourers' housing at the time is in a letter in the *Essex Newsman*, 28 January 1949.
14 Neil McCallum, 'In Transit', *New Statesman and Nation*, 1 March 1952, p. 241; SA: MO, A1/2/48/1/A – Squatting 1946, File Report 2431.
15 DCRO: UD/CS /221, Chester le Street Urban District Council Correspondence re squatters at Roman Avenue military camp 1946-1954, letter from Mr. J.R. Henderson, 7 December 1946; letter from Mr. E.R. Simpson, 15 December 1946, and signed by 16 camp residents.
16 *Glasgow Herald*, 4, 5 June 1953.

17   NLS: *Transactions of the Royal Sanitary Association of Scotland 1949* (Glasgow, Royal Sanitary Association of Scotland, 1949, p. 87).

18   NRS: HH57/1080, Barlinnie Prison: Squatters in Nos. 4 and 5 Quarters: notes by Scottish Office officials after a meeting with the Department of Health for Scotland, 29 May 1952; notes for a briefing for the Secretary of State for Scotland, 22 October 1952; Glasgow City Corporation Factor to the Director of Prison Services, 30 January 1956.

19   *Durham Chronicle*, 18 October 1946; DCRO: UD/Co 13, Minutes of Consett Urban District Council, 20 October 1947, 4 March 1952.

20   NRS: DD6/167, Requisitioning and Families Inadequately Housed: Department of Health for Scotland internal memorandum, 3 May 1951. The underline is in the original. *Falkirk Herald*, 28 April 1951.

21   *Northern Daily Mail*, 4, 30 June 1954; *Lincolnshire Echo*, 4 October 1950; *Dundee Courier*, 19 August 1952.

22   *Heslop's Local Advertiser*, 14 December 1946, 15 March, 13 December 1947; *Blaydon Courier*, 28 January, 4 February, 4 March 1949.

23   *Biggleswade Chronicle*, 15 February 1952; 'Mrs. R.' quoted in Charlie Johnstone, *The Tenants' Movement and Housing Struggles in Glasgow 1945 – 1990* (PhD University of Glasgow, 1992, p. 179).

24   *The Scotsman*, 25 June 1949.

25   NRS: HH57/1080, Barlinnie Prison: Squatters in Nos. 4 and 5 Quarters, Correspondence between Director of Scottish Prison Service and Department of Health for Scotland, 5 January 1953.

26   NA: T227/817, Emergency Housing: Policy and Requisitioning 1951-1953, Letter from the Scottish Office to the Treasury, 13 July 1953.

27   WHSC: G24/132/356: Swindon Borough Council Housing Committee Correspondence: Squatters 1946-1948; HALS: 59M76/DDC87: Minutes of Hartley Wintney Rural District Council Hutments Committee, 14 January 1948 (Hutments Committee Minute Book, vol. 2, 1948-1949); *Lincolnshire Echo*, 25 October 1950.

28   NRS: E879/43, Second Scottish National Housing Company, Letter from Secretary of SSNHC to Department of Health for Scotland, 19 November 1946; DCRO: UD/Co/3, Minutes of Consett Urban District Council, 3 September 1946; GA: TBR/B136, Removal of squatters at Southwick Park 1946, correspondence; Information to the Town Clerk to the Ministry of Health, 9 November 1948.

29   Paul Burnham, 'The Squatters of 1946: A Local Study in National Context', p. 33; *Lincolnshire Echo*, 25 April 1950.

30   'The Squatters in Winter', *News Chronicle*, 14 January 1947 and quoted in Colin Ward, *Housing: An Anarchist Approach* (London, Freedom Press, 1976, p. 28).

31   CEA: SL2/2/9: Minutes of the Corporation of Edinburgh Housing Committee, 27 November 1953; Ron Bailey, *The Squatters* (Harmondsworth, Penguin Books, 1973, pp. 7-8).

32   'Jean Mann Defends the Government', *Forward*, 21 September 1946.

Chapter Nine
CONCLUSION

Labour, housing and the squatters

Labour's housing policy, in Bevan's words, was 'to refuse the Tory claim to hand the whole building programme over to speculative builders to produce houses for those with the money to pay for them'. Instead Labour wanted 'to give preference to families in the greatest need who want houses at reasonable rents'. Some historians have criticised this approach. Paul Addison believes for example that with housing in 1946 '... what turned a shortage into a crisis was the popular belief that the state must provide'. Andrew Thorpe notes that by 1950 79 per cent of the new housing was owned by the local authorities and argues that therefore Labour 'was clearly adding further to their clientage up and down the country'. Both ignore the experience of the pre-war years and how it had affected Labour thinking. Thorpe also ignores the fact that the Conservative Party not only continued but expanded (albeit to inferior standards) Labour's council house building programme when they returned to office in1951. Were they too seeking to add to their 'clientage' or were they reflecting a consensus about how to meet housing need? Home ownership in the post-war period was beyond the economic reach of most of the British population.[1]

However if Labour's overall housing strategy in 1945 can be explained and defended against such criticism, this account of the squatting movement reveals other shortcomings which relate to Labour's limitations as a whole. Historian Alex J Robertson has noted 'certain apparent similarities' between how the Attlee governments handled the balance of payments issue and the fuel and power problem during 1946. He comments that 'there seems to be the same fatal inability to translate awareness of the problem and its political consequences into any kind of effective remedial action before a thoroughgoing crisis broke'.[2]

The same must surely be said about the housing crisis and the direct action that was taken in response to it. Housing may have been a lower order of crisis than the two discussed by Robertson, which damaged economy and society throughout the country. Nonetheless it was still severe, and Bevan's first biographer Michael Foot has recalled that:

> The housing shortage caused more anguish and frustration than any other of the nation's manifold post-war problems; all over the country the need was desperate and every MP and every local councillor was being besieged by the endless queue of the homeless.[3]

As we have seen Bevan would not entertain the idea of using surplus forces accommodation for housing because it would have meant a significant retreat from his vision of affordable quality housing for all; for him quality was the key. He would not have been alone in that but he refused at first to take emergency measures as a compromise until the homeless made the decision for him. Bevan is reported to have said that 'if he had urged anybody to take the camps over in the condition they were in there would have been howls from the Communist Party and from the squatters that they were being asked to go in to impossibly hard conditions'. There is some evidence to support this. Jean Mann's article in defence of the government's actions has been referred to; in that article she stated that in 1943 Secretary of State for Scotland Tom Johnson had proposed re-conditioning army huts for use after the war. This was strongly opposed at a meeting in Glasgow apparently where it was seen as offering sub-standard accommodation to ex-servicemen: 'The only people who should go in there are the sanitary inspectors', it was said. Similarly in Bristol a Conservative councillor, commenting on the squatting controversy in the city, recalled that his proposal in 1945 that the council take over camp accommodation had been 'treated with contempt' by Labour councillors. 'They derided me', he claimed, 'for even suggesting that people could live in Nissen huts.'[4]

Nevertheless people were ready to live in Nissen huts and to create communities there in defiance of official disapproval. The words of a senior civil servant were quoted previously but bear quoting again:

> ... until squatting began nobody in his right senses could believe that families would be content to live in dormitory huts of this nature. The squatting epidemic has shown that large numbers of people are in such desperate need of accommodation that they are only too glad to squat in empty and unpartitioned huts ...[5]

It was not just Conservative councillors who were suggesting the use of redundant forces accommodation. As we have seen a large number of local authorities across the country were enquiring too. Although conditions in some camps were undoubtedly poor – and became very grim as time went on – there were clearly a number at the top of the range that could have been used as auxiliary temporary accommodation. As the Treasury Working Party had put it in 1952, they 'compared favourably in terms of quality of construction, amenity and durability' with the wartime pre-fabs. Councils, aware of the potential, had been lobbying to take them over before weather, vandalism and neglect took the toll that they did. Early action may have prevented the camps from 'being in the condition they were in' and the use of the best of them for housing would have been welcomed by the homeless, as witnessed by the huts that they were willing to take over. It would have shown a co-ordinated government machine making the best use of the resources that were available and avoided much of the political criticism that squatting generated for the government. Bevan in this instance had his vision, though, and all concerned were expected to wait until it was realised, regardless of their circumstances and the fact that it was impossible to predict how long that realisation was going to take.

However it was the refusal to work co-operatively with the camp squatters that reveals so much. Peter McIntyre's group in Glasgow proposed that the camp committees in Scotland run their camps in co-operation with the government or the local authorities. Also, that if the skills of the tradesmen among the squatters were used, and the raw materials were supplied to them, then the cost to the government of refurbishing camps would be offset. This of course was turned down as unacceptable to the Ministry of Health. This is an example of 'labourism' (the principle of the British labour movement that social change is only achievable through existing institutional frameworks and activities) in a specific historical context. Labour at this point saw working-class people as the recipients of progressive government policies rather than active participants in them. This was recognised in some quarters and it became a source of criticism as the 1940s wore on. For example the annual conferences of the Trades Union Congress and the Labour Party heard complaints from representatives of the engineering, railway and mining trades unions that their managements were just as remote and the workers just as disempowered under nationalisation as they had been under private ownership.

Similarly, before 1948 many hospitals included 'workmen governors' on their management boards, there to represent the interests of local workers whose subscriptions from their wages ensured their hospital treatment. When the new National Health Service took over such subscriptions were unnecessary and therefore the workmen governors were removed. The effect was to leave hospital management as the preserve of senior clinicians and administrators and with no representation for staff or patients. In another field altogether the Arts Council of Great Britain was established in 1945 following a number of initiatives during the war that had toured exhibitions and performances to workplaces and non-traditional venues, and also encouraged participation in local music and drama. The policy of the new Arts Council on the other hand was one of 'few but roses': not helping to spread cultural opportunities but promoting a few outlets of artistic excellence. What links housing with these other examples is the reality of unequal partnership: the central state takes responsibility for policy and implementation without ground level engagement with the public and their participation in ideas for reconstruction after the war.[6] The squatters were not following this script.

Attlee was to say of his governments that their aim had not been a reformed capitalism but progress towards democratic socialism, and that 'our experience in the war had shown how much could be accomplished when public advantage was put before private vested interest. If this was right in war then it was also right in peace.' This has been queried of course by historians who have drawn attention, for example, to the fact that nationalisation was less to do with socialism and more to do with transferring the responsibility for loss-making industries from the private sector to the state, and releasing private capital for re-investment elsewhere. In the case of requisitioning unused private property to rent to those in dire need of accommodation it is clear that 'private vested interests' had little to fear from Labour. The wartime coalition governments had been compelled to introduce and then to extend requisitioning as a result of popular pressure as well as housing need, and Labour extended the programme again for the same reasons. Neither the coalition nor Labour addressed the administrative obstacles that hindered the effectiveness of requisitioning as it stood, even though these had been made clear. There was no mechanism either to ensure that local authorities took full advantage of such powers as they had. The example of the up-market hotels and apartment blocks in London and Glasgow is particularly telling. Ross McKibbin among others has noted how the idea of 'fair shares' had been a powerful rhetorical device during the war years.[7] It is not fanciful to suppose that ensuring these properties were used to meet acute housing need and not private interest would have had public support in 1946, and indeed the squatting movement as a whole deserves to be considered in discussions about the public appetite for change at this time.

Michael Foot's hagiography of Aneurin Bevan says of the response to squatting that 'an outbreak of direct action which could have spread like a prairie fire was kept in check' and that the government was able to reassert its authority because it insisted that houses were to go to the neediest first. Without that safeguard, according to Foot, 'a mass movement of lawless rage against the housing shortage could have swept through many cities, disrupting altogether any fair system of allocation.'[8] How far is this assessment justified?

What Foot is not taking into account is that the Communists organising the 'luxury squats' did so as part of a campaign over requisitioning as well as direct action for the homeless. They were targeting empty private property that had been requisitioned but was now to be returned to the housing market of the affluent. Their political aim was to galvanise the government into ensuring that local authorities found it straightforward to requisition such properties for use by families on their priority housing lists, and would be required and not just enabled to do so. This was 'lawless' but with the intention of strengthening the law and creating more resources for which 'fair systems of allocation' would be possible. If Labour had had a less timid approach to requisitioning, as the left generally had called for, the 'luxury squatting' would have been less likely to happen. Instead, to contradict Attlee's phrase, private vested interest was put before public advantage, and the law was used to complement the existing powers of the propertied in Scotland. As the analysts of popular movements in the United States have said of such incidents in general, 'political reverberations are likely when powerful groups have large stakes in the disputed institutions'.[9] The Communist retreat followed the recognition that they were unable to influence the government in the way that they had assumed was possible.

A squatting movement

The squatters in these immediate post-war years were referred to as a 'movement' at the time. The characteristics of this movement are worth examining. It was a product of the social dislocations produced by the war, such as population movements, new households, and raised expectations; added to which were the cumulative effects of housing shortages and the frustrations of being unable to begin or return to a normal family life. When the camp squatters acted collectively and in sufficient numbers the state was not strong enough to defend its property with reliability and thus the law could not be enforced. It would not have been politically expedient to do so either given that public sympathy lay with the squatters. Similarly although the Scottish law of trespass was originally deployed it fell out of use against the camp squatting movement.

Some of the camp squatting initiatives were undoubtedly the result of action by the homeless themselves without any leadership, encouragement or prompting by the politically active and their initiatives were outside the traditional political party or trade union structures. Nonetheless there are many examples where Communist Party activists led, encouraged or provided practical support to the squatters. Later authors who state that the Communists came late to the squatting movement have not examined the evidence available in local newspapers. Some active branches included veterans of pre-war housing struggles, and who were known locally to be such, and their engagement with those suffering acute housing need was a continuation of their activity. The Party did not have a monopoly over this role either. Others, not involved with the CP but who could definitely be said to be politically socialised, such as Peter McIntyre's group in Glasgow, and individual Labour or ILP activists elsewhere, took it on also. In some but apparently few cases these leaders, enablers or supporters were squatters themselves.

For socialist activists of different affiliations the direct action, like any such, would have been seen as a potential step in a long-term political struggle. Requisitioning powers, and the class and property relations at stake in them, were a case in point. The squatters had more limited objectives and therefore took their support where they could find it. A good example is the Burnwood camp outside Carluke in Lanarkshire: originally occupied with the support of the Communist Party the residents later sought out support from a Conservative MP. Others approached prospective parliamentary candidates of any party who were willing to take up their cause. Those who took part in the 'luxury' squats were not 'dupes', as both the Conservative press and *Tribune* claimed, but people willing to accept the option that had been created for them. Nor, as James Hinton has identified, was any leadership of the squatters an entirely one-way street. Some of the London squatters only acquiesced in ending the occupation after an argument, and a section of the Birmingham group disassociated themselves from the CP following negative publicity.[10]

Local authorities

A crucial development was the transfer of responsibility for the squatted camps to the local authorities. This was the point at which what could be presented as an outbreak of local actions that had compelled a response from central government became a series of issues that had to be pursued at the local level. There does not seem to have been any attention paid to the camps in the House of Commons after the discussion of the Under-

Secretary's report at the end of 1947. Individual MPs raised concerns about the huts in their constituencies into the 1950s but there was no national debate as such. Similarly there was little subsequent coverage in the national press and thus a subsequent assumption that the matter had evaporated. There had been some discussion in a few camps about the possibility of a national squatters' organisation to represent their interests and to lobby on their behalf. There does not seem to be any evidence that this was ever really pursued. One reason probably is that with the transfer of responsibility the issue became the local implementation of the housing programme and the resources for it. Therefore the squatters' concerns were directed at their local authorities. The squatted camps slipped from the government agenda – other than Treasury concerns about their cost – and it was at local levels that politics, in this case the politics of rationing, were conducted.

The responses by local authorities ranged from acceptance and incorporation, with authorities like Consett and Hartley Wintney co-opting squatter representatives on to the council committees that managed their camps, to the exclusion practised by Glasgow, Chester le Street and others. It is understandable that councils were unwilling to use scarce resources on hutments that were never going to be fit for purpose. Even so, many of the camp occupants were obviously ready to put a great deal of effort into their huts and again costs could have been offset by their labour if materials had been supplied. It is also understandable that local authorities were very sensitive about not being seen to house people 'out of turn'. Excluding the residents from housing waiting lists on the other hand was vindictive. The government may have considered that the squatters should be neither rewarded nor penalised for their action when it came to council housing lists, and indeed all the evidence suggests that the squatters themselves wanted fair treatment not special treatment. The government was not in a position to ensure that this happened though and leaving the matter for local authorities to manage meant, at least in some cases, unnecessarily extended periods in bad accommodation with little prospect of escape and with stigma and discrimination. This must have seemed like a punishment for initiative.

Political impact

Did the squatters of 1946, whose overriding concern was housing for their own families, have an influence on policy and politics, other than a temporary embarrassment for the government? Their action had changed government policy over the use of surplus service accommodation; they do seem to have motivated Bevan to set housing targets, accelerate some de-requisitioning of government-held property for housing, and to further encourage local authorities to use such requisitioning powers as the government was prepared to allow. Squatters drew dramatic attention to housing need, and the costs involved in maintaining the huts they commandeered prompted the Treasury to allocate additional funding and housing allocations to local authorities – even if, in some cases, the use of the funds to rehouse squatters had to be surreptitious and disguised within the overall housing programme.

It has been noted that the local elections of November 1946 were largely inconclusive as regards a verdict on squatting and the housing programme. A year later however Labour sustained losses of council seats around the country, and the verdict was that housing difficulties were part and parcel of the continuing shortages, rationing and restrictions that were wearying the electorate. When it came to the general elections of 1950 and 1951 the judgement was that Labour lost because it could no longer command sufficient votes from the middle classes. This was as true of Scotland as it was for England and Wales. The Conservative rhetoric of bureaucracy and bungling that was generated when the camp occupations began may have been relevant here. However the squatters of 1946 quoted in the press had not criticised the Labour government as such and there may be some reflection of this in the voting returns: the working-class vote in the cities, the votes among those at the sharpest end of the housing crisis, remained loyal to Labour.[11]

Finally, recognition must be paid to the squatters themselves. As James Hinton states, by taking the law into their own hands the squatters had to 'overcome some powerful cultural constraints'.[12] Perhaps this is especially true of those women, some with children, who occupied huts while their husbands were serving abroad. Unlike their elected government they had wide imaginative horizons when it came to assessing the solutions available for housing problems. Many who had occupied the worst huts continued to show resilience and fortitude in campaigning against bad conditions in their camps for some time afterwards. This movement of 1946 was one in which people in dire housing need came to believe that they could change their individual circumstances through acting collectively with others in the same position. In so doing they challenged not so much the authority of government as the assumption that it knew best.

NOTES

1   *Newcastle Journal*, 3 October 1946; Paul Addison, *Now the War is Over: A Social History of Britain 1945-51* (London, BBC/Jonathan Cape, 1985, p. 56); Andrew Thorpe, *A History of the British Labour Party* (London, Palgrave, 2001, p. 113); home ownership survey quoted in David Kynaston, *Austerity Britain 1945-1951* (London, Bloomsbury Publishing, 2007, p. 155).

2   Alex J Robertson, *The Bleak Midwinter, 1947* (Manchester, Manchester University Press, 1987, p. 151).

3   Michael Foot, *Aneurin Bevan: A Biography Vol. 2: 1945-1960* (London, Davis-Poynter, 1973, p. 62).

4   According to Ellen Wilkinson in a speech at Jarrow, *Newcastle Journal*, 13 September 1946; Jean Mann, 'Jean Mann Defends the Government' *Forward* (21 September 1946); *Western Mail*, 17 August 1946.

5   NA: HLG 7 /1/1023, War-time camps and hostels: occupation by unauthorised persons: Ministry of Works to Sir John Wrigley at the Ministry of Health, 22 August 1946.

6   David Rubinstein, 'Socialism and the Labour Party: the Labour Left and Domestic Policy 1945-1950', in David E. Martin and David Rubinstein (Eds), *Ideology and the Labour Movement: Essays Presented to John Saville* (London, Croom Helm, 1979, pp. 226-57). The Arts Council issue is explained in detail in Andy Croft, 'Betrayed Spring: The Labour Government and British Literary Culture', in Jim Fyrth (Ed.), *Labour's Promised Land?: Culture and Society in Labour Britain 1945-51* (London, Lawrence and Wishart, 1995, pp. 197-224).

7   C.R Attlee, *As It Happened* (London, Odhams Press, 1956, p. 190); James Hinton, *Labour and Socialism: A History of the British Labour Movement 1867-1974* (London, Harvester, 1983, p. 171); Ross McKibbin, *Classes and Cultures: England 1919-1951* (Oxford, Oxford University Press, 1998, p. 533).

8   Michael Foot, *Aneurin Bevan: A Biography Vol. 2: 1945-1960*, p. 83.

9   Frances Fox Piven and Richard A. Cloward, *Poor People's Movements: Why They Succeed, How They Fail* (New York, Pantheon Books, 1977, p. 24).

10 The 'dupes' charge is in *Tribune*, 20 September 1946; James Hinton, 'Self-Help and Socialism: The Squatters' Movement of 1946', *History Workshop*, Issue 25 (Spring 1988, p. 118-19).

11 David Rubinstein, 'Socialism and the Labour Party: the Labour Left and Domestic Policy 1945-1950', p. 243. For detailed discussions of the general elections see John Bonham, *The Middle-Class Vote* (London, Faber, 1954); D.E. Butler, *The British General Election of 1951* (London, Macmillan, 1952); S.B. Chrimes (Ed.), *The General Election in Glasgow, February 1951: Essays by Members of the Staff of the University of Glasgow* (Glasgow, Jackson and Son, 1951). See also David Butler, *British General Elections Since 1945* (Oxford, Blackwell, 1995).

12 James Hinton, 'Self-Help and Socialism: The Squatters' Movement of 1946', p. 118.

BIBLIOGRAPHY

Cumbria Archives

CA/C/6/555, Squatters in Carlisle Corporation Property 1946-1948

City of Edinburgh Archives

SL/2/2/1–SL/2/2/9, Minutes of the Corporation of Edinburgh Housing Committee 1946-1954

Durham County Record Office

UD/CS/221, Chester le Street Urban District Council: Correspondence re squatters at Roman Avenue military camp 1946-1954
UD/Co 13, Minutes of Consett Urban District Council 1946-1952

Gateshead Local Studies Library

High Infant Mortality in the Administrative County of Durham: Report of the County Medical Officer (1907)
Annual Reports of the Medical Officer of Health for the Chester le Street Rural District Council and Urban District Councils 1926-1946
Annual Reports of the Medical Officer of Health for the County of Durham 1926-1946
Heslop's Local Advertiser, 1945-1950

Gloucestershire Archives

TBR/B136, Removal of squatters at Southwick Park 1946.

Hampshire Archives and Local Studies

59M76/DDC86, Hartley Wintney Rural District Council: Squatters Committee Minute Book 1946-1948.
59M76/DDC87, Hartley Wintney Rural District Council: Hutments Committee Minute Book 1948-1949,
59M76/DDC88, Hartley Wintney Rural District Council Hutments Committee Minute Book 1949-1952.

Labour History Archive and Study Centre

CP/CENT/EC/01/04, Minutes of the Executive Committee of the Communist Party of Great Britain September and October 1946.
CP/IND/POLL/66/06, Harry Pollitt: Speech in support of the squatters in Cranbourn Street, London 12 September 1946.
CP/LOC/SCOT/01/02, Report of the Scottish Committee of the Communist Party of Great Britain January 1945-June 1946 and Resolutions of the Scottish Congress 21-22 September 1946.
CP/LOC/SCOT/01/03, Scottish Committee of the Communist Party of Great Britain: Scottish Bulletin 31 August 1946.

The Mitchell Library

C1/3/114 – C1/3/125, Minutes of the Corporation of Glasgow Housing Committee 1946-1955.
Corporation of Glasgow, *Glasgow's Housing Progress* (1946).

The National Archives

CAB/195/3/46, Cabinet Secretary's Notebook, 6 July 1945.
CAB/128/5, Cabinet Minutes, 14 March 1946.
CAB/128/6, Conclusions of the Meeting of the Cabinet, 14 August 1946.
CAB/128/6, Conclusions of the Meeting of the Cabinet, 9 September 1946.
CAB/129/12, Squatters in Army Camps.
CAB/129/13, Squatters in Army Camps.
CAB/130/13, Squatters in Military Camps.
CAB/195/4, Notes from the Cabinet Meeting, 9 September 1946.
CAB/195/4, Notes from the Cabinet Meeting, 17 September 1946.
HLG7/1023, War-time camps and hostels: occupation by unauthorised persons 1946-47.
HLG7/1024, War-time camps and hostels: occupation by unauthorised persons 1946-47.
HLG7/1025, War-time camps and hostels: occupation by unauthorised persons 1946-47.
HLG7/585, Requisitioning for Families Inadequately Housed: Circular 2845, 1943-1949.
HLG/101/539, Requisitioning of Unoccupied Houses 1946-1951.
HLG 7/597, Squatters: General Correspondence 1946-1948.
MUN 5/49/300/31, Commission of Enquiry into Industrial Unrest for Division 7 Wales and Monmouthshire 1917.
MUN 5/49/300/32, Commission of Enquiry into Industrial Unrest for

Division 8 Scotland 1917.
MUN 5/49/300/34, Commission of Enquiry into Industrial Unrest Summary of Reports 1917.
PREM 8/227, Prime Minister's Office: Squatters in Army Camps 1946.
T227/816, Emergency Housing: Policy and Requisitioning 1942-1951.
T227/817, Emergency Housing: Policy and Requisitioning 1951-1953.
T227/818, Emergency Housing: Policy and Requisitioning 1953-1957.

The National Library of Scotland

Forward.
Party Organiser.
Communist Party of Great Britain, *Report of the Central Committee to the Fifteenth Party Congress* (1938).
Transactions of the Royal Sanitary Association of Scotland 1945-1949.

The National Records of Scotland

HH57/1080, Barlinnie Prison: Squatters in Nos. 4 and 5 Quarters.
E879/43, Second Scottish National Housing Company: Squatters.
DD 6/167, Requisitioning and Families Inadequately Housed.

Northumberland County Record Office

LHA/H/7/8, Correspondence concerning squatters in disused army huts at Greencroft 1946.
LHA/H/7/8, Newcastle on Tyne Region Ministry of Health: Squatters' Camps: Notes for Guidance of Regional Architects, 26 April 1947.
NRO 0880/71, Minutes of Blyth Town Council 1945-1946.

Oxfordshire History Centre

 OXOHA: LT900, BBC Radio Oxford: *Squatters' Delight* (audio recording, 1994).

Somerset Heritage Centre

A\BVF/2/4, Extract from memoirs of an ex-serviceman looking for accommodation in Norton Fitzwarren 1946 – South West Heritage Trust.

Sussex Archives

The Mass Observation Archive File Report 2431, Squatters 1946.

Tyne and Wear Archives

CB.SS/A/2/23, Minutes of South Shields Town Council 1946-1947.
UD.NB/20/49, Newburn Urban District Council: Squatters at Hill Head Camp, West Denton.
UD.NB/1/25, Minutes of Newburn Urban District Council 1946,
UD.WH/A/1/40, Minutes of Whickham Urban District Council 1946.

Wiltshire and Swindon History Centre

G24/132/356, Swindon Borough Council Housing Committee Correspondence – Squatters 1946-1948.

Oral History

Jim Tatters, interview with John Suggett, 2012.
Jim Tatters, interview with John Suggett and Don Watson, 2013.

Theses

Johnstone, Charles, *The Tenants' Movement and Housing Struggles in Glasgow 1945-1990*, (PhD University of Glasgow, 1992).
Ryder, Robert, *Council house building in County Durham 1900-1939: the local implementation of national policy*, (M.Phil. University of Durham, 1979; available at Durham E-Theses Online: www.etheses@dur.ac.uk)

Websites

Arborfield Local History Society: www.arborfieldstory.org.uk
Amersham Local History Society: www.amersham.org.uk
British Newspaper Library: www.britishnewspaperarchive.com_
British Pathe News: www.britishpathe.com
Chalfont St Giles History Society: www.chalfontstgiles.org.uk
The Glasgow Story: www.the glasgowstory.com
Hansard 1803-2005: www.hansard.millbanksystems.com
Vale of Leven Project: www.valeofleven.org.uk

Books and Articles

Addison, Paul, *Now the War is Over: A Social History of Britain 1945-1951* (London, BBC/Jonathan Cape, 1985).
Allport, Alan, *Demobbed: Coming Home After the Second World War* (New Haven, Yale University Press, 2009).
Attfield, John and Williams, Stephen (Eds), *1939: The Communist Party and the War* (London, Lawrence and Wishart, 1984).

Attlee, C.R., *As It Happened* (London, Odhams Press, 1956).

Bailey, Ron, *The Squatters* (Harmondsworth, Penguin Books, 1973).

Baxell, Richard, *Unlikely Warriors: The British in the Spanish Civil War and the Struggle Against Fascism* (London, Aurum Press, 2012).

Bellamy, Joyce and Saville, John (Eds), *Dictionary of Labour Biography Vol. VII* (London, Macmillan, 1984).

Blackwell, Jackie (Ed.), *Who Was Harry Cowley?* (Brighton and Hove, QueenSpark Books, 2006).

Bonham, John, *The Middle- Class Vote* (London, Faber, 1954).

Bramley, Ted, *The Battle for Homes* (London, Farleigh Press, 1945, p. 64).

Bramley, Ted, *Bramley's Speech at the Old Bailey: The Trial of the London Communists Arrested for Action on Behalf of London's Homeless, September 1946* (London, London District Communist Party, 1946).

Branson, Noreen, and Heinemann, Margot, *Britain in the Nineteen Thirties* (London, Granada Publishing, 1973).

Branson, Noreen, *Britain in the Nineteen Twenties* (London, Weidenfeld and Nicolson,1976).

Branson, Noreen, *History of the Communist Party of Great Britain 1927-1941* (London, Lawrence and Wishart, 1985).

Branson, Noreen (Ed.), 'London Squatters 1946', *Our History* no. 80 (August 1989).

Branson, Noreen, *History of the Communist Party of Great Britain 1941-1951* (London, Lawrence and Wishart, 1997).

Bruley, Sue, *Women in Britain since 1900* (London, Palgrave, 1999).

Burnham, Paul, 'The Squatters of 1946: A Local Study in National Context', *Socialist History* no. 25 (2004, pp. 20-46)

Burn Russell, Dr James, *Life in one room: or, some serious considerations for the citizens of Glasgow* (Glasgow, James Maclehose and Sons, 1888).

Butler, D.E, *The British General Election of 1951* (London, Macmillan, 1952).

Butler, David, *British General Elections since 1945* (Oxford, Blackwell, 1995).

Butt, John, 'Working-Class Housing in Glasgow 1900-1939' in MacDougall, Ian (Ed.), *Essays in Scottish Labour History: A Tribute to W.H. Marwick* (Edinburgh, John Donald, 1978, pp. 143-70).

Campbell, John, *Nye Bevan: A Biography* (London, Hodder and Stoughton, 1994).

Chrimes, S.B. (Ed.), *The General Election in Glasgow, February 1951: Essays by Members of the Staff of the University of Glasgow* (Glasgow, Jackson and Son, 1951).

Cole, G.D.H. and Cole, M.I., *The Condition of Britain* (London, Gollancz Left Book Club, 1937).

Collison, Peter, *The Cutteslowe Walls: A Study in Social Class* (London, Faber and Faber, 1963).

Commissioner for the Special Areas, *First Report* (London, HMSO, 1935).

Commissioner for the Special Areas, *Second Report* (London, HMSO. 1936).

Commissioner for the Special Areas, *Third Report* (London, HMSO, 1936).

Commissioner for the Special Areas, *Fourth Report* (London, HMSO, 1937).

Croft, Andy, 'Betrayed Spring: The Labour Government and British Literary Culture' in Fyrth, Jim (Ed.), *Labour's Promised Land? Culture and Society in Labour Britain 1945-51* (London, Lawrence and Wishart, 1995, pp. 197-224).

Croly, Chris, 'When Home was the Torry Battery', *Leopard: The Magazine for North East Scotland,* (June/July 2006, pp. 12-15).

Croucher, Richard, *Engineers at War 1939-1945* (London, Lawrence and Wishart, 1982).

Croucher, Richard, *We Refuse to Starve in Silence: A History of the National Unemployed Workers' Movement 1920-1946* (London, Lawrence and Wishart, 1987).

Damar, Sean, *Glasgow: Going for a Song* (London, Lawrence and Wishart, 1990).

Daunton, M.J., *Coal Metropolis: Cardiff 1870-1914* (Leicester, Leicester University Press, 1977).

Dobson, Alan P., *US Wartime Aid to Britain 1940-1946* (London, Croom Helm, 1986).

Duncan, Robert and McIvor, Arthur (Eds), *Militant Workers – Labour and Class Conflict on the Clyde 1900-1950: Essays* in *Honour of Harry McShane* (Edinburgh, John Donald, 1992).

Dyos, H.J., *Exploring the Past: Essays in Urban History* (Cambridge: Cambridge University Press, 1982).

Eatwell, Roger, *The 1945-1951 Labour Governments* (London, Batsford Academic Press, 1979).

Engels, Frederich, *The Condition of the Working Class in England* (Oxford, Oxford University Press, 1999).

Fiddimore, David, *The Forgotten War* (London, Pan Macmillan, 2008).

Fielding, Steven, Thompson, Peter, and Tiratsoo, Nick, *England Arise!: The Labour Party and popular politics in 1940s Britain* (Manchester, Manchester University Press, 1995).

Fishman, Nina, *Arthur Horner: A Political Biography Vol I 1894-1944* (London, Lawrence and Wishart, 2010).

Foot, Michael, *Aneurin Bevan: A Biography Vol.1: 1897-1945* (London, Davis-Poynter, 1962).

Foot, Michael, *Aneurin Bevan: A Biography Vol. 2: 1945-1960* (London, Davis-Poynter, 1973).

Fox Piven, Frances and Cloward, Richard A., *Poor People's Movements: Why They Succeed, How They Fail* (New York, Pantheon Books, 1977).

Fraser, Hamish, 'Municipal Socialism', in Morris, R.J. and Roger, Richard (Eds), *The Victorian City: A Reader in British Urban History 1820-1914* (London, Longman, 1993, pp. 258-81).

Fraser, Violet, *Huts for Houses: A Forres Squatter's Childhood* (Moray, J & J Publishing, 2012).

Friend, Andrew, 'The Post-War Squatters' in Wates, Nick, and Wolmar Christian (Eds), *Squatting: The Real Story* (London, Bay Leaf Publications, 1980, pp. 110-19).

Grayson, John, and Walker, Maggie, *Opening the Window: Revealing the Hidden History of Tenants' Organisations* ((London, Tenant Participation Advisory Service and Northern College, 1996).

Hanley, Lynsey, *Estates: An Intimate History* (London, Granta Press, 2012).

Harland, Jim, *Blyth Memories* (Newcastle on Tyne, Summerhill Books 2013).

Henderson, Stan: *Comrades on the Kwai* (London, Socialist History Society, 1990).

Hill, Diana Murray, 'Who are the Squatters?', in Madge, Charles (Ed.), *Pilot Papers: Social Essays and Documents* vol.1 no.4 (November 1946, pp. 11-28).

Hinton, James, *Labour and Socialism: A History of the British Labour Movement 1867-1974* (London, Harvester Press,1983).

Hinton, James, 'Self-Help and Socialism: The Squatters' Movement of 1946', *History Workshop*, Issue 25 (Spring 1988, pp. 100-126).

Hinton, James, '1945 and the Apathy School', *History Workshop Journal*, Issue 43 (Spring 1997, pp. 266-73).

Hobsbawm, Eric, *Industry and Empire: An Economic History of Britain since 1750* (London, Weidenfeld and Nicolson, 1969).

Holmans, A.E, *Housing Policy in Britain: a History* (London, Croom Helm, 1987).

Holmans, Alan, 'Housing' in Halsey, A.H. and Webb, Josephine (Eds), *Twentieth Century British Social Trends* (2000, pp. 469-511).

Hunt, Tristram, *Building Jerusalem: The Rise and Fall of the Victorian City* (New York, Metropolitan Books, 2005).

Johnson, P.B, *Land Fit for Heroes: The Planning of British Reconstruction 1916-39* (Chicago, University of Chicago Press, 1968).

Johnstone, Charlie, 'Early Post-War Housing Struggles in Glasgow', *Journal of the Scottish Labour History Society*, no. 28 (1993, pp. 7-29).

Johnstone, Charlie, 'Housing and Class Struggles in Post-War Glasgow' in Lavalette, Michael and Mooney, Gerry (Eds.), *Class Struggle and Social Welfare* (London, Routledge, 2000, pp. 139-55).

Kynaston, David, *Austerity Britain 1945-1951* (London, Bloomsbury Publishing, 2007).

Laybourn, Keith, 'Recent Writing on the History of the ILP' in Jones, David, Jowitt, Tony and Laybourn, Keith (Eds), *The Centennial History of the Independent Labour Party* (Halifax, Ryburn Academic Publishing, 1992, pp. 317-37).

Mackenney, Linda, 'Introduction' to McLeish, Robert, *The Gorbals Story* (Edinburgh, 7:84 Publications, 1985, pp. 5-18).

Mann, Jean, 'Jean Mann Defends the Government', *Forward* (21 September 1946).

Marr, Andrew, *A History of Modern Britain* (London, Fontana, 2007).

Marsh, Kevin and Griffiths, Robert, *Granite and Honey: the Story of Phil Piratin, Communist M.P.* (London, Manifesto Press, 2012).

Maynell, Colin A., 'Nineteenth-century Slums in Leamington Spa and the Introduction of Public Health Reforms', *Warwickshire History*, vol xvi no.2 (Winter 2014/15, pp. 86-98).

McCallum, Neil, 'In Transit', *New Statesman and Nation* (1 March 1952, pp. 240-42).

McGrory, David, *Coventry's Blitz*, (Stroud, Amberley Publishing, 2015).

McIlroy, John, Campbell, Alan and Gildart, Keith (Eds), *Industrial Politics and the 1926 Mining Lockout: The Struggle for Dignity* (Cardiff, University of Wales Press, 2009).

McKibbin, Ross, *Classes and Cultures: England 1919-1951* (Oxford, Oxford University Press, 1998).

McKinlay, Alan, and Morris, R.J. (Eds), *The ILP on Clydeside, 1893-1932: from foundation to disintegration* (Manchester, Manchester University Press, 1991).

McLaurin, Susan, *The Housewives' Champion: Dr G.C.M. M'Gonigle, Medical Officer of Health for Stockton-on-Tees 1924-1939* (Stockton, Printability Publishing, 1997).

McShane, Harry, and Smith, Joan, *No Mean Fighter* (London, Pluto Press, 1978).

Mates, Lewis, *The Great Labour Unrest: Rank and file movements and political change in the Durham coalfield* (Manchester, Manchester University Press, 2016).

Melling, Joseph, 'Clydeside rent struggles and the making of Labour politics in Scotland 1900-39' in Roger, Richard (Ed.), *Scottish Housing in the*

Twentieth Century (Leicester, Leicester University Press, 1989, pp. 54-89).

Merrett, Stephen, *State Housing in Britain* (London, Routledge and Kegan Paul, 1979).

Merrett, Stephen and Gray, Fred, *Owner Occupation in Britain* (London, Routledge and Kegan Paul, 1982).

M'Gonigle, G.C.M. and J. Kirkby, J, *Poverty and Public Health* (London, Gollancz Left Book Club, 1936).

Miliband, Ralph: *Parliamentary Socialism: A Study in the Politics of Labour* (London, Merlin Press, 2009).

Ministry of Labour, *Reports of Industrial Conditions in Certain Depressed Areas: Durham and Tyneside* (London, Ministry of Labour, 1934).

Ministry of Labour, *Reports of Industrial Conditions in Certain Depressed Areas: Scotland* (London, Ministry of Labour, 1934).

Morgan, Kenneth O., *Labour in Power 1945-1951* (Oxford, Oxford University Press, 1989).

Morgan, Kenneth O., *The People's Peace: British History 1945-1989* (Oxford, Oxford University Press, 1990).

Morgan, Kevin, *Against Fascism and War: Ruptures and Continuities in British Communist Politics 1935-41* (Manchester, Manchester University Press, 1989).

Morgan, Kevin, *Harry Pollitt* (Manchester, Manchester University Press, 1994).

Orwell, George, *The Road to Wigan Pier* (London, Gollancz Left Book Club, 1937).

Palfreeman, Linda, *Salud! British Volunteers in the Republican Medical Services during the Spanish Civil War 1936-1939* (Brighton, Sussex Academic Press, 2012).

Pfautz, Harold (Ed.), *Charles Booth on the City: Physical Pattern and Social Structure* (Chicago, University of Chicago Press, 1967).

Piratin, Phil, *Our Flag Stays Red* (London, Lawrence and Wishart, 1978).

Pollitt, Harry, *The Squatters: Pollitt's speech at the London demonstration 12 September 1946* (London, London District Communist Party, 1946).

Ravetz, Alison, 'Housing the People' in Fyrth, Jim (Ed.), *Labour's Promised Land? - Culture and Society in Labour Britain 1945-51* (London, Lawrence and Wishart, 1995, pp. 159-60).

Robertson, Alex J, *The Bleak Midwinter, 1947* (Manchester, Manchester University Press, 1987).

Rodger, Richard (Ed.), *Scottish Housing in the Twentieth Century* (Leicester,

Leicester University Press, 1989).

Rubinstein, David, 'Socialism and the Labour Party: the Labour Left and Domestic Policy 1945-1950', in Martin, David E and Rubinstein, David (Eds), *Ideology and the Labour Movement: Essays Presented to John Saville* (London, Croom Helm, 1979, pp. 256-8).

Saunders, Bob, 'The Glasgow Squatters, 1946', *Scottish Marxist* no.7 (October 1974, pp. 25-28).

Saville, John, *The Politics of Continuity: British Foreign Policy and the Labour Government 1945-46* (London, Verso, 1993).

Short, John R, *Housing in Britain: The Post War Experience* (London, Methuen, 1982).

Simpson, Dave, *No Homes for Heroes: Post War Squatters in Washington* (Sunderland, Gilpin Press, 2006).

Smith, Joan, 'Taking the leadership of the labour movement: the ILP in Glasgow, 1906-1914', in McKinlay, Alan and Morris, R.J. (Eds), *The ILP on Clydeside, 1893-1932: from foundation to disintegration* (Manchester, Manchester University Press, 1991, pp. 56-83).

Spector, Jack, 'Occupation of Daws Hill Camp, High Wycombe', *Our History*, no.10 (November 1985, pp. 8-9).

Stedman Jones, Gareth, *Outcast London: A Study in the Relations Between Classes in Victorian Society* (London, Peregrine Books, 1984).

Stevenson, John, and Cook, Chris, *Britain in the Depression: Society and Politics 1929-39* (London, Longman, 1994).

Taylor, Becky, 'A Powerful Message from the Powerless: The E15 Mothers and Squatting in Post-War Britain', *History Workshop Online*, 27 October 2014.

Thomas-Symonds, Nicklaus, *Nye: The Political Life of Aneurin Bevan* (London, I.B. Tauris, 2015).

Thompson, Willie, *The Long Death of British Labourism: Interpreting a Political Culture* (London, Pluto Press, 1993).

Thorpe, Andrew, *Britain in the 1930s: The Deceptive Decade* (Oxford, Blackwell, 1992).

Thorpe, Andrew, 'The Membership of the Communist Party of Great Britain 1920-1945', *Historical Journal*, Vol. 3 No. 43 (2000, pp. 777-800).

Thorpe, Andrew, *A History of the British Labour Party* (London, Palgrave, 2001).

Tiratsoo, Nick (Ed.), *The Attlee Years* (London, Pinter Publishers, 1991).

Timmins, Nicholas, *The Five Giants: A Biography of the Welfare State* (London, Harper Collins, 2001).

Vickers, Rhiannon, *The Labour Party and the World Vol.1: The Evolution of Labour's Foreign Policy 1900-51* (Manchester, Manchester University Press,

2003).

Ward, Colin, 'Brighton Vigilantes', *War Commentary* (28 July 1945).

Ward, Colin, *Anarchism in Action* (London, Freedom Press, 1973).

Ward, Colin, *Housing: An Anarchist Approach* (London, Freedom Press, 1976).

Watson, Don, '*We Don't Intend Paying It*: The Sunderland Rent Strike 1939', *North East History*, no. 38 (2007, pp. 103-19).

Watson, Don, *No Justice Without A Struggle: The National Unemployed Workers' Movement in the North East of England 1920-1940* (London, Merlin Press, 2014).

Watson, Don, 'Poles Apart: the Campaign against Polish Resettlement in Scotland after the Second World War', *Scottish Labour History*, vol. 49 (2014, pp. 107-24).

Webber, Howard, 'A Domestic Rebellion: The Squatters' Movement of 1946,' *Ex Historia*, King's College, London (August 2012, pp. 125-47).

Webster, Charles, 'Healthy or Hungry Thirties?', *History Workshop*, Issue 13 (Spring 1982, pp. 110-30).

Williams, Chris, *Democratic Rhondda: Politics and Society 1885-1951* (Cardiff, Cardiff University Press, 1996).

Worley, Matthew, *Labour Inside the Gate: A History of the British Labour Party between the Wars* (London, IB Tauris, 2005).

INDEX

Also from The Merlin Press

NO JUSTICE WITHOUT A STRUGGLE
The National Unemployed Workers Movement in the North East of England 1920-1940
Don Watson

Unemployment in the 1930s conjures up images of the Jarrow March - but there was far more to unemployed protest than that.

This is a full regional history of the National Unemployed Workers' Movement. It portrays the impact of mass unemployment, poverty and oppressive benefits systems, and analyses the reactions of the trade unions, and the Communist and Labour parties. It also discusses questions of gender, opposition to fascism and local electoral politics.

The book uses oral history and draws on state, police, and trade union records, Communist and NUWM archives together with comprehensive newspaper coverage. With contemporary photos.

'an inspiring tribute to movement that marched for jobs Meticulously researched, with excellent notes and references, this book's a great read and it's a worthy memorial to those whose commitment to the class struggle is a legacy we can only strive to match.' *Morning Star*

Paperback   ISBN 978-0-85036-618-1

ENEMY WITHIN
The Rise and Fall of the British Communist Party
Francis Beckett

This survey considers the political problems faced by the CPGB. It attributes its successes to policies which allowed the CP to work critically with the Labour Left and its failures to the impact of Moscow: the 'Third Period' and the abrupt Soviet-Nazi pact.

'… the best political book I have found for a long time.' *Daily Telegraph.*
Second edition, with additional chapter, 12 pages of photos

Paperback   ISBN 978-0-85036-477-4

www.merlinpress.co.uk